FILM THEORY

CW01496830

In *Film Theory: Rational Reconstructions*, W.
about how film theory gets written in the first place:

- How does it select its objects of study and its methods of inquiry?
- How does it make discoveries and explain filmic phenomena?
- How does it formulate and solve theoretical problems?

He asks these questions of film theory through a rational reconstruction and a classical commentary. Both frameworks clarify and reformulate vague and inexact expressions, redefine obscure concepts, and examine the underlying logic of film theory arguments. This not only subjects film theory to rigorous examination; it also teaches students how to write theory, by enabling them to question and critically interrogate the logic of previous film theory arguments.

The book consists of nine chapters that closely examine a series of canonical film books and essays in great detail, by Peter Wollen, Laura Mulvey, Thomas Elsaesser, Stephen Heath, and Slavoj Žižek, among others.

Warren Buckland is Reader in Film Studies at Oxford Brookes University, UK. He is the author of several books, including *The Cognitive Semiotics of Film* (2000), *Directed by Steven Spielberg* (2006), *Puzzle Films* (ed., 2009) and *Film Theory and Contemporary Hollywood Movies* (ed. 2009). He is also the editor of the quarterly journal the *New Review of Film and Television Studies* (Routledge).

Praise for this book:

'With an impressive breadth of scholarship, and minute attention to implicit and explicit arguments, Buckland traces the basic problems that various theories have sought to resolve while expertly scouting the emergence and use of concepts. ... No other book has so effectively synthesized nor offered such close readings of the theoretical material discussed here. Moreover, Buckland's talent for clear and systematic exposition makes his study accessible and pleasurable without in any way depriving it of its acumen. All students of film theory will be reading this for years.'

Martin Lefebvre, *Concordia University, Canada*

'Warren Buckland provides both a reconstruction of and a commentary on some of the most relevant contributions to film, in an attempt to bring to the foreground the *whys* and the *hows* that move these discourses.'

Francesco Casetti, *Yale University, USA*

'Essentially a reconstruction of the intellectual contexts within which key concepts of film theory were developed, Buckland subjects these concepts to rigorous logical and historical analysis, revealing their origins in theoretical debates of the time, and evaluating their significance for the present. This is an invaluable contribution to the ongoing renewal of the field of film theory.'

Marc Furstenau, *Carleton University, Canada*

FILM THEORY

Rational Reconstructions

Warren Buckland

To Sean
with best wishes,
from Warren

Routledge
Taylor & Francis Group
LONDON AND NEW YORK

First published 2012
by Routledge
2 Park Square, Milton Park, Abingdon, Oxon OX14 4RN

Simultaneously published in the USA and Canada
by Routledge
711 Third Avenue, New York, NY 10017

Routledge is an imprint of the Taylor & Francis Group, an informa business

© 2012 Warren Buckland

The right of Warren Buckland to be identified as author of this work has been
asserted by him in accordance with sections 77 and 78 of the Copyright, Designs
and Patents Act 1988.

All rights reserved. No part of this book may be reprinted or reproduced or utilized
in any form or by any electronic, mechanical, or other means, now known or
hereafter invented, including photocopying and recording, or in any information
storage or retrieval system, without permission in writing from the publishers.

Trademark notice: Product or corporate names may be trademarks or registered
trademarks, and are used only for identification and explanation without intent to
infringe.

British Library Cataloguing in Publication Data
A catalogue record for this book is available from the British Library

Library of Congress Cataloging in Publication Data
Buckland, Warren.
Film theory : rational reconstructions / Warren Buckland.
p. cm.
Includes bibliographical references and index.
1. Motion pictures – Philosophy. 2. Film criticism. I. Title.
PN1995.B7975 2012
791.4301 – dc23
2011039110

ISBN: 978-0-415-59097-6 (hbk)
ISBN: 978-0-415-59098-3 (pbk)
ISBN: 978-0-203-14366-7 (ebk)

Typeset in Perpetua
by Taylor & Francis Books

Printed and bound in Great Britain by
TJ International Ltd, Padstow, Cornwall

THIS BOOK IS DEDICATED TO MY MOTHER

CONTENTS

LIST OF FIGURES

ACKNOWLEDGEMENTS

This book began as occasional small-scale papers that set out to examine key film theory arguments in minute detail. I was motivated by the sense of frustration at not quite grasping the meaning, significance, and agenda behind key essays and books that constitute the core of film theory. Many of my students shared this frustration, since they were coming to the texts cold, with little prior knowledge of what these texts were addressing or why they used particular approaches over others. I soon realized that simply reading these texts (let alone summaries of them) was not enough; they had to be dissected and their theoretical problems needed to be exposed using an explicit method or procedure that breaks down these texts into their conceptual and logical components. Despite the numerous divisions to which I have subjected these texts using an explicit method (outlined in the Introduction), I still feel there is space to make finer distinctions and create additional subdivisions, since I have not reached the foundation or source of each text, if indeed there is a 'foundation' to discover.

I wish to thank various people who patiently followed this project over several years: those who commissioned papers from me (not really knowing what they would receive when I said I would write a 'rational reconstruction'), authors who read my rational reconstruction of their own work, and colleagues who read and gave feedback on earlier drafts: Edward Branigan, Thomas Elsaesser, Ruggero Eugeni, Alison McMahan, Toby Miller, Barry Salt, Jan Simons, Wanda Strauven, Eleftheria Thanouli, Yannis Tzioumakis, and Michael Wedel.

Oxford Brookes University awarded me a sabbatical in the Autumn of 2010 to work on Chapters 6, 8, and the Introduction. Parts of the Introduction were presented at 'Practicing Theory', the 2011 ASCA International Workshop and Conference. Earlier versions of chapters have appeared in the following publications, although all have been rewritten and updated for this book: Chapter 2, *Literary and Linguistic Computing*; Chapter 3, *Mind the Screen*, edited by Jaap Kooijman, Patricia Pisters, and Wanda Strauven; Chapter 4, *A Companion to Film Theory*, edited by Toby Miller and Robert Stam; Chapter 5, *Semiotica*; Chapter 7, *The Cinema of Attractions Reloaded*, edited by Wanda Strauven; Chapter 9, the *New Review of Film and Television Studies*.

INTRODUCTION

Rationally reconstructing film theory

In the last thirty years, film theory concepts have been reworded and rephrased with varying degrees of success, and clarified or confused in equal measure. In this book I do not aim to add to this genre; I do not present yet another summary or rewording of received ideas in film theory. Summaries simply replicate the expressed concepts of a theory in slightly different terms. They posit film theory as a set of doctrines, a body of inert knowledge to be taught, learned, and repeated. Instead, my aim is more fundamental – not to repeat, but to encounter film theory from a perspective that may render it unrecognizable. I ask a series of questions about how film theory gets written in the first place:

How does it select its objects of study and its methods of inquiry?
How does it make discoveries and explain filmic phenomena?

And, most crucially,

How does it formulate and solve theoretical problems?

I ask these questions of film theory through two operational frameworks: a rational reconstruction of film theory, combined with a 'classical' commentary.

Commentaries

> Every subject matter has its catchphrases to enable us to stop thinking before we have got a solution to our problems. ... [I]t is easy to stop thinking about the logical status of fictional discourse if we repeat slogans like 'the suspension of disbelief' or expressions like 'mimesis'. Such notions contain our problem but not its solution.
>
> (Searle 1979, 60–61)

In Gérard Genette's terms, a commentary is a metatext, a second-degree text that is 'derived from another pre-existent text'. It is a 'descriptive or intellectual text' that 'speaks about' the pre-existent text (1997, 5). One aim of commentaries is to speak accurately and comprehensively about difficult and obscure passages in ancient Greek or Latin texts. Commentaries therefore make explicit the implicit assumptions and premises behind a text by defining and contextualizing its terminology (which involves taking the text's meaning literally). They can help us go beyond the slogans and catchphrases of a discipline, which we usually take for granted, and instead rethink the fundamental problems that lie behind those clichéd expressions. Commentaries also rewrite and clarify inexact formulations, and they shun abstract generalities, by developing a micro-analysis of a text – sticking close to the text's surface, which has the advantage of maintaining its individuality.

In using these reading strategies, I intend to make explicit the implicit assumptions behind the film theory books and essays scrutinized in the following chapters; to clarify their inexact formulations ('inexact formulations' is the most frequently cited problem found in some corners of film theory); and avoid writing broad, sweeping, general summaries. Instead, I shall develop a micro-analysis by focusing on the specific words, phrases, and sentences authors use to formulate their theories.

I will also use another technique from ancient commentaries – the *schema isagogicum*, or introductory schema, consisting of a set of preliminary questions to be asked before studying an author. It commonly consisted of up to seven steps: clarifying the theme (aim, purpose) of the work; specifying its place in the author's corpus; its utility; an explanation of the title; the work's authenticity; discussion of its division into chapters and sections; and spelling out to what part of philosophy it belongs (Mansfeld 1994, 10–13). I will use some of these categories informally in the opening section of each of the following chapters.

This micro-reading practice has migrated from classical studies into critical theory. In a celebrated example, Joyce's *Finnegans Wake* has generated several book-length commentaries (Tindall 1969; Hart 1974; McHugh 1980; Gordon 1987). Roland Barthes's *S/Z* is a form of commentary on Balzac's short story 'Sarrasine'. Barthes says he aims through a 'step-by-step commentary' to study Balzac's text 'down to the last detail', reading in '*slow motion*', not simply to replicate the text nor analyse it using theoretical categories, but to produce something in between replication (image) and analysis (1974, 12–13). In a review of *S/Z* Raymond Jean wrote: 'one finishes this book with the feeling that the Ancients were quite right to consider the *commentary* as the most "active" form of criticism. For it is indeed a commentary that Barthes intends to offer us here' (quoted in Holsinger 2005, 178).

Carlo Ginzburg reminisces about his experiences of close reading as a student at the Scuola Normale Superiore in Pisa in the 1950s. In an interview in *The New York Times* he recalls a seminar in which he was asked 'to spend an entire week analyzing only 10 lines of a book written by a leading 19th-century historian'. He goes on to say:

> It was the slowness that fascinated me. Every phrase, every word had to be dissected for their possible implications. I came to understand that texts can have hidden, invisible meanings. It was not an easy lesson. In my speech, my writing, my judgments about people, I tend to be very quick. I learned the importance of reading and rereading one page, even a single passage, for days, weeks.
>
> (Ginzburg, quoted in Ray 2008, xviii)

Other scholars have provided commentaries on difficult and obscure passages in contemporary philosophy and critical theory. Baker and Hacker's four volumes of what they call an 'analytical commentary' on Wittgenstein's *Philosophical Investigations* is probably the most exhaustive example (see, for example, Baker and Hacker 2004). Not surprisingly, Jacques Lacan has also received extended commentaries and explications of his work. The first and most famous in English is Anthony Wilden's *The Language of the Self* (1968), written like a standard classical commentary – a philological analysis in the form of 65 pages of endnotes that aim to contextualize and untangle the meaning of difficult words and passages in Lacan's essay 'The Function of Language in Psychoanalysis'. In addition, Muller and Richardson, in *Lacan and Language* (1982), attempt to be comprehensive in offering three types of commentary on all the essays translated in *Ecrits: A Selection* (Lacan 1977). Each chapter of Muller and Richardson follows the same format: a general introduction or overview to each essay; a map of the essay under discussion (in the form of a precise outline of the entire text); plus comprehensive endnotes, in the manner of a philological classical commentary. In their introduction, Muller and Richardson justify their strategy by pointing out that there exists 'a hermetic obscurity in Lacan's writings that is all the more infuriating for being so deliberate. That is why they seem so much like a rebus: the reader feels that something significant is being said if only he could find out what it is. It is the modest purpose of these pages to follow the sequence of these essays – to work with the puzzle and try to comprehend this use of language – in order to gain some sense of what that something might be' (1982, 3). In place of an ancient Greek or Latin text, in Lacan we are instead confronted with 'a hermetic obscurity'. Much of film theory is also afflicted with the same obscurity, which therefore necessitates a commentary on it. In film studies, only one book-length commentary of a single text has been written, by William Rothman and Marian Keane (2000), a page-by-page, and on occasions line-by-line, commentary on Stanley Cavell's difficult and (until recently) neglected book *The World Viewed* (1971/1979). Rothman and Keane present a standard exegesis-commentary of the words on the page in consecutive order: '[we] attend to the utterly specific words of *The World Viewed*' (2000, 28). But they also develop a self-reflective stance, in which they follow their thoughts while reading: 'one must follow one's own thoughts as they are prompted by the words on the page' (28). They end up writing a lucid and comprehensive (almost 300-page) commentary on Cavell's book.

Rational reconstruction

> Rational reconstruction as a rational 'again'-construction ('re-' as 'again') is interested in making an object 'more equal to itself', e.g., by extracting essential elements and reformulating and restructuring them. Its task is revealing formal or representational problems and managing them by realizing immanent possibilities to improve precision and consistency of the object of reconstruction.
>
> (Davia 1998)

> For the Vienna Circle, rational reconstruction was a central component of its extremely ambitious wider cultural and political agenda. The particular goal was to define knowledge precisely, but for the purpose of *using* it to rid humanity of the ghosts holding us in thrall to the ancient superstitions of traditional society as well as the unreflective conformities of modern societies.
>
> (Carus 2007, 15–16)

I frame my commentaries within a rational reconstruction of theories. A rational reconstruction is a form of inquiry that extracts from a theory its key concepts and their relations, and reformulates them in both logical and empirical terms. It is therefore a form of translation that clarifies and refines the definition of concepts by making explicit underlying logical relations and implicit (unexamined) background assumptions; by spelling out valid and invalid inferences; and, most importantly, by imposing the requirement that they conform to the principle of verifiability (which does not define the meaning of concepts in a statement in terms of abstract properties, but in terms of their links to immediate experience).[1] Because of their abstractness, many concepts and their relations are indistinct, obscure, and inconsistent, and their referents vague. Conceptual clarity is lost in inconclusive, ambiguous, meandering discussions that try to conceal paradoxes and contradictions. More generally, concepts are weighed down by the ghosts of ancient superstitions (metaphysical speculations and Romantic notions of pre-rational intuition). Concepts need to be anchored in experience in order to define them as meaningful; abstract empty concepts that go beyond experience are defined as meaningless.

The logical positivists of the Vienna Circle in its early years (1926–32) developed a stringent form of rational reconstruction. In *The Logical Structure of the World* (commonly known as the *Aufbau*, first published in 1928), Rudolf Carnap combined the logicism of Frege, Russell and Whitehead with Hume's radical empiricism.[2] This combined approach was Carnap's method of clarifying concepts, by reducing them to immediate experience and reconstructing them in the axioms of formal logic:

> The main problem concerns the possibility of the rational reconstruction of the concepts of all fields of knowledge on the basis of concepts that refer to the immediately given. By rational reconstruction is here meant the searching out of new definitions for old concepts. ... The new definitions should be superior to the old in clarity and exactness, and, above all, should fit into a systematic structure of concepts.
>
> (2003, v)

For Carnap, empirical knowledge can be systematically formalized and reduced to a single unified standard – universal logical axioms – in order to make it completely clear, transparent, and consistent.

The *Aufbau*'s method of rational reconstruction strictly followed the analysis of statements in line with the principle of verifiability. Yet, the problems this principle creates are manifold. First, its main problem is one of incompleteness – verification can never be finalized because of its inability to cover all possibilities (for it is limited to a finite number of observations). Second, it posits a level of *direct* observation or *immediate* experience, unhampered by theory. Third, in speaking of immediate experience, the positivists adhered to Hume's understanding of experience as subjective impressions.[3] And fourth, although verifiability rules out metaphysics and theology as meaningless, it also rules out statements made in general conceptual theories.[4] Mario Bunge identifies several: information theory, game theory, systems theory (cybernetics), automata theory, and general field theory. 'These theories', he writes, 'are concerned with the gross structure and behaviour of systems of almost any kind, regardless of their physical and chemical constitution: they are stuff free. ... they either "apply" in a given case or they don't' (1973, 33–34). They are general theories which are not empirically based; they do not emerge from observation and are not, therefore, reducible to verifiability or falsifiability. Their function is to guide and regulate the formation of specific theories:

> Far from providing a detailed 'picture' of real systems and specific forecasts, those theories are *generic frameworks* helping one to think of whole classes of entities in a variety of domains, from hardware engineering through management and politics. By the same token they solve no particular problems without further ado – but on the other hand they help discover and pose new problems and they clarify basic ideas.
>
> (1973, 34)

These general conceptual frameworks are 'empirically untestable *in toto*, in the sense that they make no specific predictions that might be checked against facts' (1973, 33). Bunge gives examples of general frameworks and theoretical concepts from automata theory and general field theory. I shall give an example from film theory. General conceptual frameworks (e.g. semiotics or narratology) are not in themselves empirically testable; they have a regulative and enabling role in the formation of specific theories (e.g. film semiotics, film narratology). They apply these general frameworks to a particular concrete domain. This involves fitting the particular domain into the general framework. A semiotics of film conceptualizes film according to the premises of a general semiotics. If film does not fit, this does not invalidate general semiotics; it only invalidates a semiotics of film, based on the non-applicability of the semiotic framework to the domain of film.[5] The history of film semiotics has witnessed a gradual fitting of film into a general semiotic framework – from the minimal application of Metz's early essays (discussed in Chapter 4) to the extreme of Umberto Eco's triple articulation model of the filmic image, taking to its furthest limit the semiotic notion that images are made up of arbitrary conventions (1976a). As a specific domain, film semiotics does have factual content; it is indirectly linked to experience, and has been modified in light of its contact with data.[6]

This diversion into general conceptual frameworks emphasizes that verifiability and falsifiability are not universally applicable; they are not the common standard by which to evaluate all theories. The uncompromising standards of other aspects of the *Aufbau* became apparent to Carnap soon after its publication in 1928. He began to relax his utopian aim to unify all knowledge via its reduction to a single logical framework that strictly adhered to verification. His principle of tolerance states that 'we do not want to impose restrictions but to state conventions. ... Everyone can construct his logic, i.e., his language form, however he wants' (quoted in Carus 2007, 256).

In addition to verifiability, Carnap constructs the logic of his rational reconstruction by dividing concepts into various kinds, ordering them, reducing them to their basic components, and defining the logical relations between these basic components (Carnap 2003, 5–7). I take on board Carnap's later principle of tolerance, which states that it is not necessary to reconstruct statements using a single universal axiomatic logic. I do not aim to systematically formalize film theory to universal logical statements that refer to the immediately given. In place of axiomatic logic and the immediately given, I use a different reconstructive strategy – one based on the work of Rudolf Botha (1981; outlined below), which nonetheless retains the same agenda as Carnap's rational reconstruction: to be precise, rigorous, and systematic when analysing abstract, ambiguous, inconsistent concepts. Like Carnap, Botha divides concepts into various kinds, orders them, reduces them to their basic components, and defines (to some extent) their logical relations.

But what, if anything, do we use to replace verification? A rational reconstruction does not involve analysing concepts in a vacuum, treating them as inert doctrines. Instead it entails examining the rationale for a concept – to identify, that is, the way the concept is used to address an actual problematic state of affairs, and how a problem was formed to address that state of affairs. Theory, then, is not simply a generic conceptual framework, or a set of doctrines, nor is it simply a series of empirical generalizations. Instead, it is a series of answers to a set of problems. It is this examination of theory as problem-driven that serves as a suitable replacement for verification.

Problem formation

> I propose that the rationality and progressiveness of a theory are most closely linked – not with its confirmation or its falsification – but rather with its *problem solving effectiveness*.
>
> (Laudan 1977, 5)

I aim to clarify and refine the definitions of film theory concepts by making explicit each theory's underlying logical relations, implicit background assumptions, and inferences. Integral to this aim is the need to focus on theories as responses to problems, which requires a reconstruction of the original state of affairs from which the problems arose, because problems emerge out of particular theoretical frameworks. Following Larry Laudan I privilege the conceptual problem-solving effectiveness of theories, rather than focus exclusively on their empirical verification or falsification. Any serious discussion of a theory must therefore analyse the problem the theory is addressing, for it is the problem that initiates inquiry and by which the theory should be held accountable. Stanley Wong links rational reconstructions to the problem-solving effectiveness of a theory: 'First, we reconstruct hypothetically the problem-situation in the context of which the theory was proposed. Second, we explain why the theorist (or someone else) might think that the theory is a satisfactory solution to the problem' (2006, 11). From this perspective, theories are solutions to problems; a problem – or, more accurately, a problematic state of affairs – is a gap in knowledge that creates uncertainty, and requires research to overcome it. This gap can be generated by the emergence of new (problematic) data, by conceptual paradoxes, or by criticizing known solutions from a new theoretical perspective.

When rationally reconstructing a particular film theory text, we ask: for what problem is this essay/book an attempted solution? Problems are not always formulated explicitly as a question; sometimes the question has to be reconstructed (rather than simply quoted) from the text. No problem is posed in isolation. Each is generated from a series of background assumptions – antecedent knowledge and presuppositions. The presuppositions constitute the given premises that define the problem as a problem. A question is deemed well-formed, for example, only within the context of its back-ground assumptions. The opening pages of each chapter will outline (under the heading 'problem-situation') the background from with the theoretical problem arose.

The conduct of inquiry

The main chapters of this book rationally reconstruct the structure of, and assump-tions underlying, canonical film theories. In general terms, this book tests theories both conceptually and empirically, although privileging the former. In specific terms, I use Rudolf Botha's (1981) philosophical study into the conduct of inquiry to analyse and test the way authors formulate conceptual and empirical problems and how they tackle them.[7] In terms of my reconstruction strategies, my primary aim is to gradually unfold the key concepts and problems of each theory. I begin (after outlining the problem-situation) by rearranging the parts of film theories according to the four central activities Botha identifies in the formulation of theoretical problems:

(a) analysing the problematic state of affairs;
(b) describing the problematic state of affairs;
(c) constructing problems; and
(d) evaluating data and problems.

(Botha 1981, 54)

This list is based on the distinction between a 'problematic state of affairs' and 'problems'. Whereas the former refers to aspects of reality not understood by a theorist (for the existing theories cannot adequately account for them), a problem formulates what the theorist needs to look for in order to resolve the problematic state of affairs.

Carrying out (a), analysis, consists of: (a.i) identifying exactly what is problematic – which involves isolating each component of the problematic state of affairs and determining how they are interrelated; and (a.ii) identifying and making explicit the implicit/unquestioned background assumptions informing inquiry, such as the nature conferred upon the object of analysis. This step also involves drawing out the consequences of these unexamined background assumptions. In general terms, analysis involves selection and abstraction of the object under discussion: '[the theorist] *abstracts* only one or a few of all the problematic aspects of an object of study for concentrated investigation. ... The object is considered to be problematic in only one respect or, at the most, in a few respects, while the object in fact has many problematic aspects' (Botha, 27). Different theorists from the same school of thought may therefore single out for analysis different problematic aspects of the same object of study.

In carrying out (b), description, the problematic state of affairs must be accurately recorded and formally described. For Botha, description involves three processes:

(b.i)   collecting data;
(b.ii)   systematizing data; and
(b.iii) symbolizing the results.

(Botha 1981, 66)

In collecting data, the theorist records relevant information. The type of data deemed relevant to the problem needs to be spelled out clearly. Systematizing data involves the activities of *classifying, correlating, ordering*, and *measuring*. These activities enable the theorist to identify common properties amongst data, put similar data into classes, determine the relations between the classes, and specify what procedures were followed in measuring the data.[8] Finally, symbolizing simply involves representing data in a concise and accurate manner.

In carrying out (c), the construction of problems, the theorist brings the problematic state of affairs under the domain of concepts, organized into propositions. Botha goes on to identify four types of concept involved in the construction of problems (in the following list I have changed the linguistic terms to film studies terms):

(c.i)   phenomenological concepts, or factual data as they appear to consciousness; they are bound by immediate, given experience, and are intuitively known;
(c.ii)   filmic concepts, propositions about the nature of individual films;
(c.iii) cinematic concepts, propositions about the general nature of film, or the cinema 'as such'; and
(c.iv)   meta-theoretical concepts, which concern the aims and nature of theoretical inquiry.

(Botha 1981, 85)

Phenomenological concepts are distinct from the other type of concepts in that they refer to factual and sense data, while the other types (theoretical concepts) refer to an underlying unobservable reality. The ultimate objective of theoretical concepts is to construct a model of the unobservable underlying reality. For Botha, a model is not a mere summary of directly recorded data, but a description offering 'an image, repre-sentation or replica of something which cannot be observed in any direct manner' (1981, 129). The function of a model is to mediate between a theory and its object of study. The relation between theory and its object is therefore indirect.

Theoretical concepts construct hypotheses and models, and are founded on the hierarchy between underlying (latent, unobservable) reality and surface (manifest, observable) reality. A theory therefore consists of 'hypothetical systems of concepts which represent an underlying ... reality' (Botha, 20). A theory is a system of inter-related hypotheses, or tentative concepts, about the unobservable nature of reality (a reality assumed to be a regular, economical, cohesive structure underlying a chaotic, heterogeneous observable phenomena). Formulating hypotheses is dependent upon heuristic strategies: 'A heuristic strategy represents any means which may be system-atically used to create more favourable circumstances for the construction of hypotheses' (Botha, 109). Botha lists three common heuristic strategies:

- *problem decomposition*, in which large problems are broken down into smaller, more elementary problems;
- *analogies*, in which the analyst looks for previously solved problems in similar areas of research; and
- *abstraction/idealization*, in which a problem is simplified to make it manageable.

These heuristic strategies are important to the construction of theoretical concepts (and are key in the rational reconstruction of theories).

Finally, in carrying out (d), evaluating data and problems, Botha recognizes that the data or examples discussed and analysed in a piece of research need to satisfy certain criteria in order to be accepted as valid, reliable, and genuinely problematic. He also recognizes that only problems satisfying the criteria of well-formedness and significance are relevant problems worth pursuing.

(d.i) Data or examples constitute the evidence for the problems under analysis. Examples should not be regarded as obviously correct or appropriate types of evi-dence. Too many film studies publications simply present a theory and then illustrate the theory with 'positive instances', film examples that invariably prove the theory correct. Botha (70–74) introduces three criteria for evaluating data: *genuineness, correctness*, and *comprehensiveness*. In terms of *genuineness*, Botha refers to whether the data/examples under analysis reveal properties of the object of study. For *correctness*, has the data been correctly/mistakenly described? In particular, have its problematic aspects been correctly/mistakenly identified and described? The distinction between genuineness and correctness is made in order to identify genuine examples that are incorrectly described – a theorist may mistakenly describe an Agfacolor film of the 1940s as a Technicolor film, or a point-of-view sequence as not a point-of-view sequence. The point-of-view sequence is a genuine example of point of view, but has been described incorrectly. (At other times, of course, the example may not be gen-uine, in which case even a correct description of it is not relevant to the problem under analysis.) Many film theorists at some point will collect data from films, or certain aspects of films, to illustrate or apply their theories. The issue here is one of *comprehensiveness*: some will use the minimum number of examples to illustrate the problem being addressed, while others will privilege a large number of films. This concept also covers the issue of whether the examples are representative of the objects under study, and also factors that influenced the choosing of particular examples (physical context, perceptual context, observational expectations). Are the examples typical of the data under analysis? An empiricist would emphasize the significance of a large corpus, whereas a rationalist would place more emphasis on the quality of the data, in which quality is measured according to its bearing on the problem under analysis. If this rationalist stance is taken too far, the examples end up being chosen merely to illustrate the theory. (As we shall see in Chapter 8, Slavoj Žižek deliberately takes this position.) And were the data collected under the right conditions? Watching an Agfacolor film on a second generation VHS tape on television may lead to the analyst mis-describing the colours. In such cases, it is necessary to offer an operational definition, which spells out the procedures the analyst used to obtain and measure the data.

(d.ii) *Well-formed problems*. Just as Popper argued that a hypothesis is scientific if it is falsifiable (if it is testable), so a problem is well-formed if it is in principle solvable. In addition, the ability to generate several new lines of research is a mark that a problem is well-formed, for it encourages researchers to set up a series of new theories, methods of inquiry, and guidelines to solve it. A well-formed problem is also based on correct assumptions and on clearly formulated rather than obscure concepts. Botha gives the example of an ill-formed problem in linguistics: 'How should a grammar of English specify the fact that gerundive nominals are logically more transparent than derived nominals?' (53). This is ill-formed because the expression 'logically more transparent' is obscure and incomprehensible; it is also unclear exactly what is being singled out as problematic.

(d.iii) A *significant problem* is one whose solution expands our existing knowledge, insights, and understanding. This can be achieved via the solution's general reach (it applies to a large number of cases); its transformative power (it generates new knowledge by transforming our pre-existing conceptions); and novelty value (the new knowledge it generates is sufficiently distinct to warrant attention).

The box on p. 11 outlines the four central activities Botha identifies in the formulation of theoretical problems. Each chapter of this book will follow this same structure, although if a subcategory does not apply ('measuring data', 'cinematic concepts', and so on) then it will not appear as a chapter subheading.

I plan for the rational reconstructions and commentaries to supplement one another. The commentary is bottom up, focusing on how an actual theorist in one particular text formulates and tackles a specific theoretical problem. The rational reconstruction acts from the top down, imposing on film theories a grid of principles, which represents how theories, or theoretical problems, are constructed and tackled. The four categories of problem formation do not represent what actually happens in the formulation of theoretical problems; it is not meant to be a psychologically real grid, but a study that distinguishes the logical aspects of problem formation.

Rationally Reconstructing Film Theory Problems (based on Botha 1981)

Problem-situation

Analysing the problematic state of affairs
Identifying what is problematic
Background assumptions

Describing the problematic state of affairs
Collecting data
Systematizing data (*classifying, correlating, ordering, measuring*)
Symbolizing the results

Constructing problems
Phenomenological concepts
Filmic concepts
Cinematic concepts
Meta-theoretical concepts

Evaluating data and problems
Genuineness, correctness, and comprehensiveness
Well-formedness
Significance

Both the rational reconstruction and the commentary aim to understand and begin to explain a theory, to spell out its underlying design and logic, rather than simply agree or disagree, praise or blame. Wong writes that 'the method of rational reconstruction [separates out] the question of understanding a theory from the question of agreeing with it. As a consequence we can appreciate why the theorist considered his theory as an appropriate response to the logic of the problem-situation as he saw it' (2006, 10). Evaluating a theory only comes after a long and complex reading and rational reconstruction of it.

Deep-level theorizing about film theory

[W]e must examine not merely the questions the theorist asks ... but the basis from which those questions spring and the consequences they imply. We must see every theory as broadly as possible, that is, we must see it systematically.

(Andrew 1976, 10)

Film Theory: Rational Reconstructions is influenced by several key books in film studies. Dudley Andrew's *The Major Film Theories* (1976) is a forerunner to the type of close scrutiny of film theory presented here. Andrew's book stands out from other summaries of film theory in that he reorganizes each theory identically, around the same structure: Aristotle's discussion of the four causes of natural phenomena (material, efficient, formal, and final causes). Andrew adapts Aristotle to film theory by identifying how each theory raises questions about: the raw material of film; the methods and techniques that shape the raw material; the resulting forms of film; and the purpose and value of cinema. Andrew acknowledges that '[n]o doubt this approach does injustice to some theorists, because it imposes a kind of logical schema on their remarks which may fit them clumsily, but it provides the constant perspective which will allow us to attain an overview of film theories' (1976, 8). The present book imposes a logical schema on seminal film theory texts published from the late 1960s to the present. But the advantages far outweigh the disadvantages, for it provides a consistent, rigorous perspective on the theories.

Noël Carroll's *Philosophical Problems of Classical Film Theory* (1988a) is another influence on the present book. From the perspective of analytic philosophy, Carroll critically interrogates and gains new insights into three classical film theorists – Rudolf Arnheim, André Bazin, and V. F. Perkins. Each chapter offers a detailed (50-page plus) commentary on each theorist's work, again organized around an identical structure: an exposition of each theory followed by a critical analysis. Carroll demonstrates a deep underlying logic structuring and organizing the work of these theorists.

I share with Malcolm Turvey's *Doubting Vision* (2008) the use of analytic philosophy to clarify concepts in film theory. Turvey employs the work of Gilbert Ryle and Wittgenstein to examine the use (or misuse) of perceptual concepts in the work of what he calls the revelationist tradition – Jean Epstein, Dziga Vertov, Béla Balázs, and Siegfried Kracauer. For this tradition, 'cinema's most significant feature is its capacity to reveal truths about reality invisible to the naked human eye' (Turvey 2008, 10). This argument is premised on the assumptions that human vision is limited, or flawed, and that cinema is a form of technology that can overcome and escape these limitations. Yet, the revelationist tradition commits a category mistake by confusing different types of phenomena. Turvey argues that both Balázs and Kracauer, when discussing the close-up, confuse what is invisible – that is, impossible for the unaided eye to see (e.g. ultraviolet light) – with visible things we do not normally pay attention to until presented in a close-up, such as (to use Kracauer's example) Mae Marsh's clasped hand in *Intolerance* (1916). The objects shown in close-ups are still visible objects; they simply go unnoticed until shown in close-up. A close-up can reveal a detail previously unseen, such as a hand, but it cannot reveal the invisible, such as ultraviolet light. Turvey concludes that Balázs and Kracauer mistakenly categorize one logical type (things visible but unseen) with another logical type (invisible things), based on the assumption that vision is flawed.

Finally, this book is also influenced by Francesco Casetti's *Theories of Cinema* (1999). Casetti's book focuses on broad trends within film theory after 1945, rather than the work of individuals. He uses Thomas Kuhn's term 'paradigm' to name the framework – or common reference point – within which a community of scholars conducts its research. Scholars are bound together by their theories – by a shared set of theoretical and methodological presuppositions. Casetti identifies three components of theory: 'There is a nucleus of basic ideas that frames the research; there is a network of concepts that establishes the order and the modality of the exposition; and there are several concrete observations that make verification possible' (1999, 12). At any one point in the history of a paradigm, one of these three aspects of a theory will predominate. Casetti employs this threefold distinction to map the main paradigms of research in film studies.

The first paradigm is 'ontological theory'. This paradigm emphasizes the first aspect of theory – the nucleus of basic ideas, which are employed to ask broad questions such as: what is cinema as such? This is primarily a metaphysical study of film's essence, an attempt to define what the cinema is. The criterion for the resulting knowledge is its ability to get at the 'truth' of cinema. Casetti names the second paradigm 'methodological theory', which is notable for its reflexivity. This paradigm focuses much more than ontological theory on research design, on studying an aspect of the cinema using specific criteria from a particular standpoint. For example, a methodological theory systematically employs concepts from one perspective (e.g. narratology) to analyse aspects of film pertinent to that perspective (e.g. narrative structure), rather than study the cinema 'as such' from an all-encompassing omniscient position. The criterion for the resulting knowledge is 'correctness' of the research, which is measured in relation to the perspective that films are made to fit into. Casetti names the third paradigm 'field theory'. The field theorist intervenes in the interpretation of problems and questions raised by particular films, rather than simply conducting a detached analysis of film from a specific theoretical perspective. Casetti characterizes this paradigm as the theory's phenomenal dimension, its direct and intense engagement with particular films. Yet the field theorist does not lose sight of the general: this paradigm implies 'that generality is seen as a goal that can be reached only by starting from the singular, from the unique, even from the idiosyncratic' (1999, 180). The field theorist in fact links up the individual film to global questions of culture and politics. The criterion for the resulting knowledge is its ability to elucidate the questions and problems associated with a particular film, or small group of films.

In addition to discussing the internal structure of theories, Casetti also discusses their social, institutional, and historical contexts. He characterizes the ontological theorists as pioneering intellectuals who go beyond the reviewing of films in order to discover cinema's essence, which they discuss primarily in aesthetic terms. They disseminate their thinking via essays in key journals, which sometimes constitutes their career base. The classical film theorists fit into this institutional setting. Bazin, for example, wrote groundbreaking essays on the ontology and aesthetics of the cinema for *Cahiers du cinéma*, where he worked as editor. Methodological theorists, by contrast, are based in universities and are professionally trained in the disciplines that they apply to cinema. They are usually professors or researchers, and they publish their work in specialized academic journals. Field theorists engage cinema in general political and cultural debates. They are not just academic specialists in the sense of methodological theorists but have broken free from its narrow confines to become

13

public intellectuals. They disseminate their work via the mass media as well as academic journals.

Present-mindedness

In the following chapters I try to avoid 'present-mindedness', which is a failure to understand concepts historically. Sam Wineburg outlines the problems involved with present-mindedness: 'We discard or just ignore the vast regions of the past that either contradict our current needs or fail to align easily with them. ... We are not called upon to stretch our understanding to learn from the past. Instead, we contort the past to fit the predetermined meaning we have already assigned to it' (2001, 6). To understand any theory, a critic needs to comprehend it from the inside, in its own historical context, understand the questions to which the theory is an answer, rather than judge theories only in terms of whether they meet present needs, or conform to current values and norms.[9]

Present-mindedness ignores the fact that a text had meaning for a particular group or community at a particular time. So, to avoid present-mindedness, I will *not* try to determine the significance of these film theory texts to film studies today; instead, my rational reconstruction is embedded in the past, when the essay was first written and read. I aim to understand the essay on its own terms, not in terms of the values held today. This involves identifying the agenda of each theory of film, and then trying to deter-mine *if each theory satisfied its own agenda* – that is, if it formulated for its readership a significant problematic state of affairs, and whether it addressed it adequately.

Chapter contents

Chapter 1

In 'The Auteur Theory' (1969, 74–115) Peter Wollen develops an auteur-structuralism that goes far beyond the standard thematic reading of auteurs, by employing structural methods to analyse an auteur's deep, underlying themes. Wollen tries to reconcile rational knowledge (as articulated in structuralism) with the traditional auteurist's Romantic notion of a subjective, pre-rational authentic intuition – one that spontaneously expresses and creates interior human meanings ignored by ration-alism. To reconcile these two opposing views of knowledge, Wollen posits the existence of a hypothetical object as the focus of his analysis – a specific, thematic structure underlying all the films of the same auteur but not found in the films of other auteurs.

Chapter 2

Whereas Wollen goes far beyond the standard thematic reading of auteurs, in 'The Statistical Style Analysis of Motion Pictures' (1974) Barry Salt goes far beyond the standard stylistic reading of auteurs by employing statistical concepts to identify and quantify the stylistic constants of film directors. Salt's essay is based on empirical generalizations of data collected from different parameters of the shots of several films (shot scale, shot length, camera height, camera movement, plus the number of reverse angles). Salt's results accurately reveal actual physical properties of shots, which can be directly verified. Nonetheless, we will encounter a dispute concerning whether epithets such as 'fluidity of camera movement' can be attributed to a film based solely on the number of moving shots it contains.

Chapter 3

In 'Tales of Sound and Fury: Observations on the Family Melodrama' (1972/1987), Thomas Elsaesser also addresses a problematic state of affairs generated from an auteurist perspective (the colour scheme of Sirk's films, including *Written on the Wind*). The essay's problematic state of affairs goes far beyond its auteurist data, by combining it with a psychoanalytic study of the genre of melodrama. The object of analysis in this essay is the 'melodramatic imagination', a term Elsaesser uses to draw parallels between the film melodrama and the history of the European novel and drama, in which individual heroes internalize class conflicts and turn them into personal struggle, which are then manifest in the films' excessive *mise en scène*.

Chapter 4

Christian Metz's film semiotics represents the transition from classical to contemporary film theory (or, in Casetti's terms, from ontological to methodological theories). Film semiotics replaces the study of film's essence with an analysis of its specificity, defined in terms of its underlying system of codes. This chapter will examine how Metz formulated hypotheses describing that underlying reality, in 'Cinema: Language or Language System?' (1974a: 31–91; first published 1964), and his book *Language and Cinema* (1974b; first published in 1971).

Chapter 5

Heath's essay 'On Screen, In Frame: Film and Ideology' (1976) outlines the agenda of contemporary film theory – the main problems contemporary film theory addressed in the 1970s. Heath examines the problem of how cinema in capitalist society perpetuates ideology. Building on the semiotics of Metz, in conjunction with Althusser and Lacan, Heath argues that film is a 'specific signifying practice' that creates the illusion of a coherent subject position for the spectator to occupy. He also briefly examines the way political avant-garde film tries to dissolve ideology and its effects by disrupting the creation of coherent subject positions.

Chapter 6

In 'Visual Pleasure and Narrative Cinema' (1975), Laura Mulvey proposes and examines a new object of study in film theory, the unconscious ideological-patriarchal nature of the cinematic apparatus. Mulvey makes this task manageable by breaking it down into smaller concepts – the cinema's construction of a male gaze, gendered (masculine) subject positions, and patriarchal narrative forms. In the early 1970s, the existing theories (the images-of-woman approach) could not adequately account for the patriarchal representation of women in film. Mulvey creates a problematic state of affairs by criticizing these existing theories from a new theoretical perspective: a series of underlying abstract concepts from psychoanalysis – especially Freud's concepts of castration, voyeurism, and fetishism.

Chapter 7

Tom Gunning's essay 'The Cinema of Attraction(s)' (1986/1990) had a significant impact on early cinema scholarship. Gunning examines the hypotheses that early cinema (around 1895–1906) was dominated by the attraction, and that it inspired the avant-garde movements of the early twentieth century (including French Impressionism and Surrealism). For Gunning, the link between early cinema and these avant-garde movements is the concept of the 'attraction', supplemented with the contemporary film theorist's concept of the spectator position. The attraction does not set up a voyeuristic subject position, but is knowingly exhibitionist, aiming to confront and astonish the spectator.

Chapter 8

Slavoj Žižek's 'The Universal: Suture Revisited' (Part One of his book *The Fright of Real Tears* [2001]) reopens the debate around Lacan's concept of suture in light of the 'Post-Theory' critique of Lacanian psychoanalysis (Bordwell & Carroll [eds] 1996). Žižek's main logical move is to expand the domain of suture by linking it up to the political concept of hegemony, and the philosophical concepts of the universal, the particular, and the individual. He also moves the discussion away from the Imaginary look (which has previously dominated discussions of suture and vision in the cinema) and towards Lacan's conception of the Symbolic Gaze.

Chapter 9

In 'What is a Camera?' (Chapter 3 of his book *Projecting a Camera* [2006]), Edward Branigan uses Wittgenstein's thesis of the language-game to describe the multiple, contradictory, literal and metaphorical meanings of the seemingly self-evident notion of 'the camera' in the work of different film theorists. He identifies eight 'types' of camera, distinguished according to semantic meaning, mental processes, and narrativity. Branigan's chapter presents a sustained analysis of film theory concepts from the perspective of Wittgenstein's later philosophy, a perspective that can resolve one of the major issues that cumulatively builds as the chapters of this book progress: the clash between different theoretical perspectives, and the evaluation of one theory from the perspective of an incompatible theory (an issue I address directly in the Conclusion).

The chapters can be loosely organized into four groups: Chapters 1–3 respond to and develop the traditional approach to auteurism of the 1950s; Chapters 4–5 represent the various facets of film semiotics, which constitutes the core of contemporary film theory; Chapters 6–8 juxtapose the agenda of contemporary film theory with broader perspectives – feminism, early film history, and a philosophically-psychoanalytically inflected politics. Finally Chapter 9, based on Wittgenstein's later philosophy, brings us back to the analytic methods of this introduction.

Most of the theories analysed in this book belong to Casetti's 'methodological theories' category. Žižek, however, belongs in part to 'field theories' – a celebrated public intellectual who engages with the questions and problems raised in idiosyncratic films (or the exception) in order to characterize film in terms of general (the universal) and global (political and cultural) issues. To some extent, Peter Wollen and Laura Mulvey were also field theorists, in their role as intellectual/political activist (respectively) and as political film-makers (working together) in the 1960s and 1970s. However, Wollen's chapter on auteur theory (and, more generally, the book it was published in) marks his transition to the methodological theories category (his *Signs and Meaning in the Cinema* became one of the key books in establishing film studies in the university in Britain and the United States), while Mulvey's 'Visual Pleasure and Narrative Cinema' galvanized the methodological theory carried out from a feminist perspective in the 1970s and 1980s.

Unobservable concepts

All of these film theory concepts are united in being unobservable and abstract: an 'underlying thematic structure', 'subject positions', the 'male gaze', the 'attraction', 'suture', and so on. Elsaesser begins with observables (colour schemes in the films of Douglas Sirk) and moves on to abstract unobservables (the melodramatic imagination). Salt's work deals primarily in observable concepts, although from these he makes unobservable inferences concerning the general history of film style, or the stylistic patterns across a director's entire oeuvre. All of the concepts analysed in this book set out to indirectly explain observable surface phenomena – that is, to explain these phenomena in terms of the unobservable abstract properties that underlie them: 'if we want to explain experience we must *rise above it* by analyzing it in nonexperiential terms' (Bunge 1998, 453). These film-theoretical concepts share this trait with other theoretical concepts such as 'atoms', 'sub-atomic particles', 'electric field', Newton's conception of 'position' and 'velocity', Darwin's theory of 'natural selection', and so on. These terms refer to abstract entities; their meanings cannot be reduced to observations and experience.

Although I aim to analyse these theories into their basic concepts and to clarify exactly what they designate, we need to keep in mind that all theories are composed of limiting concepts, or ideal types; they do not designate empirical singular referents located in space and time, but use heuristic strategies to make the task of theorizing manageable. Bunge reminds us that 'no theory portrays literally a real thing, event, or process. . . . theories are constructions with materials (concepts, hypotheses, and logical relations) that are essentially different from their referents' (1998, 439–40). Theories are simplified, partial, mediated, approximate representations. This book aims to rationally reconstruct the approximate representations posited by film theory since the 1960s.

Violent encounters

Due to a lack of space and time, I have been unable to rationally reconstruct some important developments in film theory: not only the classical film theory of Arnheim, Bazin and Kracauer, but also Bakhtin and film (e.g. Robert Stam 1989), cognitive film theory (e.g. Bordwell 1985; Murray Smith 1995; Ed S. Tan 1996), Sean Cubitt (particularly his analysis of the history of cinema in terms of pixel, cut, and vector [2004]), and Gilles Deleuze's two books on cinema (1986; 1989). Deleuze requires a book-length rational reconstruction in order to unpack the problem-situation behind his work, to clarify the problematic states of affairs he is addressing, and to make explicit the logical relations between his concepts. Turvey in fact has carried out work in this area, examining from an analytic perspective Deleuze's concept of the time-image (2008, 93–98). More broadly, Manuel Delanda has carried out a reconstruction of Deleuze's ontology in an attempt to present this work to philosophers from the analytic tradition: 'I offer here not a direct interpretation of Deleuze texts but a *reconstruction* of his philosophy, using entirely different theoretical resources and lines of argument' (2002, 4; emphasis in the original). Although Delanda does not discuss Deleuze's cinema books, he hopes that 'once we understand Deleuze's world we will be in a better position to understand what could cinema, language or subjectivity be in that world' (2002, 8). He ends his introduction by mentioning that he is using analytic philosophy to examine a continental theory. This involves performing (to put it in Deleuzian terms) a certain 'violent encounter' with Deleuze's texts to make them speak to an analytic audience. At times *Film Theory: Rational Reconstructions* shares this encounter, since most of the theories it rationally reconstructs from its analytic per-spective derive from continental philosophy (with the exception of Salt in Chapter 2 and Branigan in Chapter 9). This has created the greatest anxiety when writing this book, but also the greatest excitement, for one gains a completely new and deeper insight into film theories that constitute the core of the discipline – but theories which too many scholars dismiss because the theories come up against some con-ceptual or empirical difficulty. But, for me, this difficulty is the starting point for examining a theory in more detail. 'One thing that one can do with a theory when it confronts empirical or conceptual difficulties', writes Lawrence Sklar, 'is to engage in a process of constantly recasting it in a wide variety of reformulations. By rearranging the theory's structural parts in numerous ways, and constantly reorganizing the theory in terms of a variety of possible alternative fundamental principles, one can hope to gain new insight into the internal structure of a theory' (Sklar 2000, 107).

Notes

1 More specifically, the verifiability principle adheres to Kant's analytic/synthetic distinction, and states that synthetic statements are meaningful only if verifiable in relation to direct observation, or immediate physical experience (while analytic statements are true a priori). Carnap (2003) included subjective impressions, physical objects, psychological states, and cultural objects as the main objects of experience. The early logical positivists tried to give a complete, exhaustive definition of concepts in terms of observables. In later developments, the logical positivists accepted unobservable aspects of reality if they could be linked to direct observations via what

Carnap called 'correspondence rules', P. W. Bridgman called 'operational procedures' (1927) and, more radically, what W. V. O. Quine called the 'web of belief' (see note 6, below). Such unobservables are therefore only partly defined in (or indirectly linked to) observational terms.

2 While illustrated primarily through the natural sciences, the method of logicism has been applied to the rational reconstruction of 'softer' subjects, such as economics (Stegmüller, Balzer and Spohn 1982; Wong 2006), psychoanalysis (Blanco 1998) and even, in one instance, to Roman Jakobson's poetic theory of language (Balzer and Göttner 1983).

3 P. W. Bridgman differed from this classical empiricist position by speaking of the immediate experience of *objects*, thereby avoiding subjectivism.

4 Furthermore, Popper's famous falsifiable principle argued that verifiability is problematic because no observation can definitively verify statements, but can only refute them. Verifiability also assumes the data are infallible. In addition, since the work of Pierre Duhem, philosophers have denied that an isolated statement by itself can be verified or falsified. They argue that theories are underdetermined by the data – that the same data can be described by different theories. Following Larry Laudan (1977), I shall emphasize empirical (and conceptual) *problems* more than empirical data and verifiability.

5 This process of fitting the particular domain into the general framework is one key activity of what Francesco Casetti calls 'methodological theories' (discussed below).

6 In proposing that theories are only indirectly empirical, I am following W. V. O. Quine's critique and revision of Carnap in his famous essay 'Two Dogmas of Empiricism' (1961, 20–46). Quine rejects both dogmas – the analytic/synthetic distinction (see note 1), plus the verification theory's reductionism (in which a statement's meaning is reduced to immediate sense experience). He replaced both with the 'web of belief' (influenced by Pierre Duhem), a holistic notion in which theoretical statements are not isolated but conceived as interrelated in a system. Some statements come into contact with empirical data, which then instigates a slight change or shift throughout the system. This means that all statements are open to revision (none are analytic), and statements that come into conflict with empirical data can be adjusted, or 'saved', by adjusting other statements in the system.

7 Botha (20) identifies nine aspects of inquiry (I have taken out the word 'linguistics' from this list): (1) choosing aims for inquiry; (2) formulating well-formed problems; (3) making discoveries; (4) giving theoretical descriptions of an underlying reality; (5) giving explanations of problematic data; (6) making predictions about unknown realities; (7) justifying hypotheses and theories; (8) criticizing hypotheses; and (9) reacting to criticism of hypotheses and theories. In this book I focus primarily on formulating well-formed problems, although this does overlap with several of the other aspects (giving descriptions and explanations, justifying theories, and so on).

8 Measuring is a key component of concept clarification in P. W. Bridgman's operationalism (1927). Bridgman links concepts, not only to objects but also to measurement – to the operations we perform to measure the concept. The concept (length, temperature, simultaneity, and so on) does not exist in an abstract realm, but is defined according to how it is measured by a particular empirical procedure. Like verification, defining a concept operationally is stringent, although it does set up an interesting challenge to try and specify how film theory concepts can be measured. I will refer to operationalism as and when necessary, and outline it in Chapter 2, when discussing Barry Salt's statistical style analysis, and in Chapter 9, when discussing Edward Branigan's film theory.

9 Developing a balanced view of any discourse from the past involves seeking 'to achieve the conflicting dual states: ... steering a course between the arch sin of judgements reached through a state of present-mindedness, and legitimately employing the interpretive advantages of an aerial view of conceptual developments' (Keith Smith 1998, 6).

1

AN IMPROBABLE ALLIANCE

Peter Wollen's 'The Auteur Theory'

[T]he 'politique des auteurs': the theory, which underlies all *Cahiers* criticism, that the director of a film is its author, that he gives it any distinctive quality it has and that his personal themes and style can be traced throughout his career, so that the corpus of his work can be discussed as a whole.

(Lee Russell 1964, 82)

[B]y a process of comparison with other films, it is possible to decipher, not a coherent message or world-view, but a structure which underlies the film and shapes it, gives it a certain pattern of energy cathexis. It is this structure which *auteur* analysis disengages from the film.

(Peter Wollen 1972 'Postscript', 167)

The problem-situation

Peter Wollen's *Signs and Meaning in the Cinema* (1969; 1970; 1972; 1998)[1] is a canonical text in the history of film theory. Even Wollen's critics note that *Signs and Meaning* 'must be, after *Film Form* [Eisenstein] and *What is Cinema?* [Bazin], the most widely read work of film theory among present-day film students' (Eckert 1973, 47). Its stature has increased exponentially since Eckert made this statement in 1973.

In the book's opening sentence, Wollen indicates that he will address the 'outstanding problems' (7) of film aesthetics by incorporating new theories into film studies. Wollen is notable for 'being there first': he presented the first sophisticated, theoretical exposition in English of Eisenstein (Chapter 1) and of Film Semiology (Chapter 3); plus he presented a structuralist reconfiguration of impressionistic, Romantic-laden Auteur Criticism (Chapter 2). In this chapter I will carry out a commentary on and rational reconstruction of Wollen's auteur-structuralist theory, its metaphors (such as 'decipherment' and 'catalyst'), and trace its roots back to Claude Lévi-Strauss's structural anthropology – particularly its classification of themes into binary oppositions. Lévi-Strauss argues that his structural method 'not only has the advantage of bringing some kind of order to what was previously chaos; it also enables us to perceive some basic logical processes which are at the root of mythical thought' (1963, 224). I will ask whether Wollen's theory brings order to the 'chaotic' auteur criticism, and determine if it helps us perceive some basic logical processes at the root of a director's corpus of films.

Auteur criticism, Wollen reminds us, is based on the background assumption that Hollywood films are not all alike, for 'masterpieces' can be found in the films of a small group of talented Hollywood directors 'whose work had previously been dismissed and consigned to oblivion' (74). Auteur criticism is evaluative criticism that transformed the critical climate towards popular American cinema, for it promoted the serious study of Hollywood films: it analysed Hollywood films with the same care and attention that critics used to praise European art films.

John Caughie (1981, 127) identifies a tension between Wollen's original 1969 chapter on auteurism and his 1972 postscript to *Signs and Meaning*. Whereas the 1969 chapter describes John Ford as a 'great artist' (102) and uses the term 'masterpiece' in relation to the films of great auteurs (77), in the postscript Ford (along with all auteurs) is reduced to a name in quotation marks – a semantic label naming a structure, an implied author, not the flesh and blood director. What we witness in the 1969 chapter is a hybrid text – one looking back to the auteurism of *Cahiers du cinéma* and Andrew Sarris, and one breaking out of its traditional aesthetics to forge a new theory based on structuralism. (We see a similar hybridity in Thomas Elsaesser's auteur essays written at the same time; see Chapter 3.) Bill Nichols said that Wollen 'wants his structuralism but he wants his proven method (*auteur* criticism) even more' (1976b, 616). The 1972 postscript reverses this priority: it presents a maturation of auteur structuralism, an explicit reformulation of its structural premises, together with its consequences. We can, in fact, identify three phases of auteurism in Wollen's work. First, the pre-structuralist auteurism of his *New Left Review* essays (1964–67; many reprinted in Wollen 1998); second, the initial structuralist phase (1969); and, third, the completion of that phase (the 1972 postscript).

Wollen's title raises its own problems. The original *Cahiers* position was called the *politiques des auteurs*; a policy. Sarris translated this (quite literally, as editor of *Cahiers du cinéma in English*) into the 'auteur theory', conferring upon it the status of a deductive series of propositions, rather than a series of inductive generalizations about a director's films. Wollen has decided to adopt Sarris's nomenclature, perhaps in the hope of moving auteurism away from the inductive to the properly theoretical (deductive).

Analysing the problematic state of affairs

Identifying what is problematic

The popular perception of Hollywood cinema as a mass of impersonal films lacking artistry constitutes the problematic data for Peter Wollen's chapter on the auteur theory. The auteur critic's attempt to 'save' a handful of Hollywood directors from oblivion designates the problematic state of affairs that Wollen addresses. This 'saving' process assumes that seeing a film with a recognized name attached confers added value upon that film.[2] This was not a new problematic in film studies when Wollen wrote his chapter in the late 1960s. But the way he address it is innovative – a risky, improbable alliance between auteurism and structuralism. The structuralism was innovative because it introduced a new (underlying) level of reality to study, together with rigorous and sophisticated methods to analyse that new reality.

Background assumptions

Combining auteurism with structuralism creates a clash between two modes of causality and two philosophical systems. For the traditional auteur critics, the director is a specific, purely subjective psychological cause, whose free will, desires, beliefs, and intentions consciously structure a film. Traditional auteurism is therefore based on the Romantic notion of a subjective, pre-rational authentic intuition, on spontaneous creativity, and individual expression, where film is seen to express what the director experiences. The distinctive properties that define an auteurist's films are thought to be located in a purely personal or subjective vision, ineffable 'sensibility' or obscure 'interior' meaning.[3]

Structuralists replaced individual expression, personal psychology and subjective vision with the Enlightenment's emphasis on rational knowledge – an impersonal system of underlying codes and structures. They replaced individual free will with general causes that determine the meaning of individual utterances, artworks, or films. When speaking or when making a film, the individual simply actualizes one possible combination of codes from the underlying system. His or her consciousness does not spontaneously create, for consciousness is determined and controlled by underlying structures: 'the apparent arbitrariness of the mind, its supposedly spontaneous flow of inspiration, and its seemingly uncontrolled inventiveness imply the existence of laws operating at a deeper level' (Lévi-Strauss 1970, 10). The primary aim of structuralism (and its close ally, semiotics, as we shall see in Chapter 4) is to study this underlying system. In terms of recounting a myth, Lévi-Strauss indicated that the individual may not even realize the significance of the stories they tell, for the meaning of a story or a sentence exists prior to its utterance, in the underlying system of codes from which it is generated.

What are the implications of structuralism for auteurism? For Geoffrey Nowell-Smith, 'when what one is looking for is a set of objective structures, the role of the author as subjectivity becomes almost peripheral' (1970, 133). Bill Nichols agrees: 'for Lévi-Strauss myths have no subject-author, no origin, no center, no specific causative links with the society that produces them. These all present difficulties when structuralism is linked to *auteur* study' (1976a, 462). It is within this structuralist framework that the director is no longer conceived as a creative, free-acting individual (the director making decisions on the set), but becomes a semantic label. The structuralist method of analysis entails deciphering – that is, abstracting or disengaging – from the experience of an auteur's films an underlying, elementary latent structure that confers upon the films their shape and identity. This is based on the background assumption that an auteur's films are unified, that they all manifest the same latent structure.

In summary, Wollen's version of the auteur theory posits the existence of a hypothetical object, a *specific, objective thematic structure* underlying all the films of the same auteur but not found in the films of other auteurs. Each of these italicized terms raises its own problems, some of which we shall encounter in the following pages.

In his critique of Wollen, Brian Henderson identified additional problematic states of affairs that auteur structuralism must address: 'The fundamental questions – whether films are like myths, whether modes of myth study are applicable to film study, and whether the auteur theory is compatible with Lévi-Straussian structuralism – are avoided by Wollen, elided by a skillful rhetoric which seems to answer them' (1973, 28). Towards the end of this chapter we shall determine if Henderson's 'fundamental questions' are in fact insignificant problems.

Describing the problematic state of affairs

Collecting data

In terms of data collection, the auteur theory functions as 'an operation of decipherment; it reveals authors where none had been seen before' (Wollen, 77). The theory collects data from American-born directors (Hawks, Ford, Ray), as well as from the Hollywood films of European directors (Hitchcock, Lang, Renoir), who were regarded as losing their identity when they entered Hollywood. (Compare this to the critical reception of directors today who move from the independent sector to Hollywood.) Auteur critics therefore discovered 'masterpieces' in the work of American-born directors as well as in the Hollywood work of European directors. Films we now take for granted as auteur 'masterpieces' – Ford's *The Searchers* (1956); Hitchcock's *Rear Window* (1954) and *Vertigo* (1958); Lang's *The Woman in the Window* (1944) and *The Big Heat* (1953) – were, in the 1950s, classified as anonymous genre movies. Similarly, in a reverse move, auteur theory downplayed the European work of former American directors (such as Joseph Losey).

However, Wollen plays it safe by focusing his chapter on two well-known directors already confirmed as auteurs by the *Cahiers* critics and by Sarris – Howard Hawks and John Ford. One advantage of using these directors is that they each have a comprehensive corpus the auteur critic can work with. Wollen collects data from the films that constitute the core of Ford's corpus – his Westerns (*My Darling Clementine* [1946], *The Searchers, Rio Bravo* [1959], *The Man Who Shot Liberty Valence* [1962], *Cheyenne Autumn* [1964]) – and notes that Hawks worked in almost every genre in Hollywood (81). Wollen's working hypothesis is that the films of these two well-known directors will yield fruitful results in his auteur-structuralism. This problematic state of affairs not only involves looking for distinctive traits across a series of films made within the impersonal Hollywood studio system; a second – opposite – problem emerges from the sheer diversity of Hawks's films: can the auteur critic identify the same distinctive properties in all of a director's films?

The type of data relevant to the auteur critic therefore needs to be clearly spelled out: not the general properties found in all classical Hollywood studio films (i.e. cinematic concepts); not the common features found in all films of the same genre

23

(generic traits); nor is the auteur critic looking for the distinctive properties of an individual film (what Metz called a 'singular textual system'; see Chapter 4). Instead, the auteur critic seeks to identify throughout the same director's corpus (whatever genre they are) a pattern of thematic preoccupations and similarities in visual style. One of the most important aspects of an auteur analysis therefore involves analysing individual films within the context of a director's entire output. In Wollen's terms, 'the analysis of the whole *corpus* ... permits the moment of synthesis when the critic returns to the individual film' (104).

Wollen first collected data from Hawks's and Ford's films in his *New Left Review* essays 'Howard Hawks' (1964) and 'John Ford' (1965), written under the pseudonym Lee Russell.[4] Both are written in the vein of Andrew Sarris, that is, they are pre-structuralist and discuss themes informally. The Hawks essay focuses almost exclusively on Hawks's action adventures, devoting only a few lines to the comedies. The Ford essay contains passages later excised from the Ford section of the auteur chapter of *Signs and Meaning*: a discussion of the influence of Andrew Jackson's populism on Ford; the role of the military (and the theme of defeat); plus a short stylistic analysis of Ford's films. Russell concludes by noting that:

> Alongside the themes of tradition and defeat are those of 'belongingness', of the search for a home, of community, of Irishness, of honour, etc. Often these elements are not consistently related; they are merely the arbitrary facets of what is nonetheless recognizably Ford's world.
>
> (1965, 73)

After discovering structuralism, Wollen revised his opinion on the recognizable Ford world – it was no longer full of inconsistent, arbitrary thematic elements. Instead, it consisted of a rigorous set of binary oppositions that gradually evolved as Ford's career progressed. (See 'filmic concepts', below.)

In his auteur chapter Wollen did not, therefore, 'try out' the auteur theory on unknown directors; he did not attempt to reveal authors where none had existed before, but limited himself to the established auteurs Hawks and Ford. Nor did he examine in any detail the peripheral films of these directors – such as Ford's *Donovan's Reef* (1963) (which Wollen only mentions briefly [102]) or Hawks's *The Land of the Pharaohs* (1955) (he simply points out in passing that this film does not share the same thematic preoccupations as Hawks's other films [81]).[5]

*Systematizing data (*classifying, correlating, ordering, measuring*)*

The strength and purpose of auteur theory lies in the way it systematizes its data, as Andrew Sarris recognized: 'the *auteur* habit of collecting random films in directorial bundles will serve posterity with at least a tentative classification' (1962, 8). We shall therefore examine this activity in some detail. Auteur theory systematizes its data primarily through classification and ordering.

Classifying objects

Classifying 'comprises the grouping together of objects, phenomena, events, etc. with one or more common properties' (Botha 1981, 75). Auteur critics classify a group of films according to the properties (or invariant traits) that only they have in common. Wollen uses three mutually exclusive oppositions to classify a director's films:

- theme/style (*mise en scène*)
- auteur/*metteur en scène*
- a posteriori/a priori.

He identifies the two main schools of auteur criticism: 'those who insisted on revealing a core of meanings, of thematic motifs, and those who stressed style and *mise en scène*' (78). Both attempt to identify the common properties that make an auteur's films distinct from all other films. But Wollen sees the stylistic approach by itself as superficial; for him, auteurs are distinguishable on a semantic level: by the thematic deep structures at the centre of their films. Style is not rigorously coded in the same way as the deep thematic level. In this, he is influenced by the structural methods of Lévi-Strauss: 'Myths, as Lévi-Strauss has pointed out, exist independently of style, the syntax of the sentence or musical sound, euphony or cacophony' (105).[6] For Wollen, an auteur's films share the same deep underlying structure, in contrast to the mere *metteur en scène*, who only controls the style of their films (78).

Finally, Wollen distinguishes directors according to the epistemological distinction a posteriori/a priori. The meaning of a *metteur en scène*'s films is a priori, that is, pre-exists the process of filming; it is located in the script. The auteur film exists a posteriori, for meaning is realized in the process of filming and is recognized retrospectively. The director adds meaning to the script: 'Incidents and episodes in the original screenplay or novel can act as catalysts; they are the agents which are introduced into the mind (conscious or unconscious) of the auteur and react there with the motifs and themes characteristic of his work. The director does not subordinate himself to another author; his source is only a pretext, which provides catalysts, scenes which fuse with his own preoccupations to produce a radically new work' (113). (The metaphor of the catalyst is explored below.)

Wollen maps the terms on the left of each opposition (theme/auteur/a posteriori) on to each other, as well as the terms on the right (style/*metteur en scène*/a priori). In regards to Ford and Hawks, Wollen performs a thematic analysis, identifying them as auteurs whose meaning is generated a posteriori. Thematic criticism is anything but arbitrary and unrestrained. Indeed, it is often criticized for reducing remarkably different texts to the same small set of indirect, general abstract meanings relating to human problems.[7] At the same time, the thematic critic would argue that the general abstract humanist meanings they attribute to texts are relevant because they encompass a wide range of experience and affect all forms of human communication. This is one of the strongest arguments for thematic criticism, since it begins to explain why films are made (beyond the profit motive) and why millions of spectators have the competence to comprehend and enjoy them, often across significant differences of religious, cultural, and political values.

Ordering

It is through the ordering of data that Lévi-Strauss's study of basic logical processes at the root of mythical thought come into play. Structuralism orders themes into their invariant basic components, and works out the logical relations between those features, which are ultimately reducible to binary oppositions. What this means is that each basic component receives its meaning via an opposition to another term – raw/cooked, male/female, East/West, consonant/vowel. Binary oppositions are a form of absolute ordering: they divide up thematic units into two mutually exclusive terms.

For Lévi-Strauss, mythical thought is rigorously organized into binary oppositions. He recognized the value of the binary opposition through Roman Jakobson's work on the ultimate constituents of language – the small number of distinctive features organized into opposing terms (vowel/consonant, grave/acute, and so on).[8] These distinctive features combine in different permutations to form the phonemes of a language; phonemes combine to form morphemes, which combine to form words, and so on.[9] Jakobson therefore identified language's ultimate, smallest set of units (distinctive features), their organization (binary oppositions), and their combinations (phonemes). Identifying from a structuralist perspective the ultimate constituents of any language similarly involves isolating its small number of basic units, organizing them into binary oppositions, and identifying their different combinations. Such a study does not presuppose that film is like natural language (or, indeed, myth).

Wollen attempts to bring order to the chaotic auteur studies by following this three-step process: he isolates a director's ultimate themes, reduces them to binary oppositions, and identifies their different combinations. One assumption in Wollen's structural auteurism is that auteurs create their own specific universe – their own system of beliefs, thinking and behaviour – by combining several binary themes in distinct ways. Ultimately, it is this system of binary oppositions, expressing a certain set of beliefs and way of thinking, that becomes the object of analysis for auteur structuralists. Under the subheading 'filmic concepts', below, we shall see the binary oppositions Wollen identifies in Hawks and Ford.

Constructing problems

Phenomenological concepts

Wollen's structuralist methodology is explicitly formulated against a phenomenological experience of films:

> [T]here is often a hostility towards any kind of explanation which involves a degree of distancing from the 'lived experience' of watching the film itself. Yet clearly any kind of serious critical work – I would say scientific, though I

know this drives some people into transports of rage – must involve a distance, a gap between the film and the criticism, the text and the meta-text. It is as though the meteorologists were reproached for getting away from the 'lived experience' of walking in the rain or sun-bathing.

(1972, 169)

'Lived experience' is therefore distinct from the reflexive activity of criticism and theory. Similarly, George Kubler says that, to study the rail network, it is not sufficient to follow the experiences or itinerary of a single traveler (1962, 6). Structuralist theory necessarily transcends everyday lived experience, since a structure is, by nature, non-phenomenal – it is not pre-given and cannot be perceived directly. Structuralism studies the underlying system of codes that determine the pre-given surface phenomena. Wollen emphasizes that reading a film from an auteur perspective involves a high degree of critical distancing, for the individual film one experiences must be read within the context of the director's other films – a context not simply based on the experience of those films, but on an abstraction: the underlying structure of themes the critic extrapolates or disengages from those films. Wollen uses the term 'decipherment' to name this activity of abstracting from films their underlying structure.

Filmic concepts

We have seen that auteur critics look for distinctive properties, not in individual films or in the cinema generally, nor the common and specific traits of genre films; instead they identify latent structural properties in a corpus of films attributable to the same director. This auteur structure is more complex and specific than cinematic concepts, but not as specific as individual films (singular textual systems).

Wollen takes Ford and Hawks as case studies to illustrate his theory. He argues that Hawks's adventure dramas contain the following motifs and themes:

- an exclusive group (a band of eccentrics); must pass a test to win admittance;
- the group members are bound together by rituals – including singing;
- the group's security is the first commandment;
- Hawks's heroes pride themselves on their professionalism;
- tension is manifest in the group when one of the team lets the others down;
- for Hawks's heroes, death is a routine occurrence;
- his heroes try to mask their nihilism with 'fun';
- there is an undercurrent of homosexuality in Hawks's films;
- women are only admitted to this all male group after a long process of induction;
- there is a clear identification between women and the animal world; and
- there is little or no married life in Hawks's adventure dramas.

These last three bullet points outline the role women play in Hawks's adventure dramas. (Elizabeth Cowie has re-examined Wollen's analysis of women in Hawks's

27

films, which we discuss in Chapter 6.) In Ford's films, by contrast, women are not a threat; instead they conform to their allotted roles of wives and mothers (88–90).

Wollen concludes that 'Hawks would be a lesser director … if his adventure dramas were the sum total of his work' (90–91). Following Robin Wood (1968, 68), Wollen sees Hawks's films as falling into two mutually exclusive categories, which are the inverse of each other: the adventure dramas and the crazy comedies. Hawks's claim as an author 'lies in the presence, together with the dramas, of their inverse, the crazy comedies', which represent 'the agonized exposure of the underlying tensions of the heroic dramas' (91). This tension is manifest in two themes:

- regression to childhood; and
- sex reversal and role reversal.

In these comedies, the women are the stronger characters, who frequently end up humiliating the male hero: 'The heroes become victims; society, instead of being excluded and despised, breaks in with irruptions of monstrous farce' (91). A binary opposition therefore exists between Hawks's adventure dramas and comedies. Because of this opposition, Wollen argues, Hawks's corpus of films becomes rich.

After discussing Hawks in some detail, primarily from a traditional thematic perspective, Wollen shifts his attention to Ford's heroes, whom he analyses in structuralist terms by focusing on binary oppositions:

> The most relevant are garden versus wilderness, ploughshare versus sabre, settler versus nomad, European versus Indian, civilised versus savage, book versus gun, married versus unmarried, East versus West.
>
> (94)

Wollen points out that each binary opposition can in turn be subdivided into other binary oppositions:

> These antinomies can often be broken down further. The East, for instance, can be defined either as Boston or Washington and, in *The Last Hurrah*, Boston itself is broken down into the antipodes of Irish immigrants versus Plymouth Club, themselves bundles of such differential elements as Celtic versus Anglo-Saxon, poor versus rich, Catholic versus Protestant, Democrat versus Republican, and so on.
>
> (94)

In the terms of formal logic, this process involves a successive 'division by dichotomy'. Each successive subdivision operates at a different level of generality, and uses different criteria to divide up the terms. In Wollen's example, the division by dichotomy begins with general terms, using the criterion of geographical location (East versus West), gradually moves towards more specific terms based on class and ethnic origins (Irish immigrants versus Plymouth Club), before becoming (in this example) more general again, with a division based on religion (Catholic versus Protestant) and American politics (Democrat versus Republican).

'Wilderness versus garden' is, according to Wollen, the 'master antinomy in Ford's films' (96) – and, in fact, one of the master antinomies of American culture, structuring its founding myth. A second related antinomy is between nomad (living in the wilderness) and settler (in the cultivated garden) (97). Both pairs feed into the quest for the Promised Land, a major theme in Ford's films. In terms of heroes who rule in his new land, Wollen divides them into another binary opposition: rational legal authority versus charismatic authority. Wollen therefore identifies three binary oppositions dominant in Ford:

- wilderness/garden
- nomad/settler
- rational legal authority/charismatic authority.

He gives three examples, focusing on the heroes in *The Searchers, The Man Who Shot Liberty Valence,* and *My Darling Clementine.*

The Searchers

Wilderness (nomad) versus garden (settler):

> Ethan Edwards [John Wayne] ... remains a nomad throughout the film. At the start, he rides in from the desert to enter the log-house; at the end, with perfect symmetry, he leaves the house again to return to the desert, to vagrancy. In many respects, he is similar to Scar; he is a wanderer, a savage, outside the law: he scalps his enemy. But, like the homesteaders, of course, he is a European, the mortal foe of the Indian. Thus Edwards is ambiguous; the antinomies invade the personality of the protagonist himself.
>
> (96)

This combination of binary oppositions embedded in Ethan Edwards makes him a complex, contradictory character.

Rational legal authority/charismatic authority: 'In *The Searchers,* ... the two kinds of authority remain separated' (101). That is, Edwards remains the charismatic authority figure who exists outside the law. In sum, Edwards embodies the values of the nomad, wilderness, and charismatic authority.

The Man Who Shot Liberty Valence

Wilderness versus garden: 'the image of the cactus rose ... encapsulates the antinomy between desert and garden which pervades the whole film' (96). In particular, Tom Doniphon (John Wayne) builds a log cabin and garden – but a garden full of cacti, not yet a real garden. However, before it can reach that stage, Doniphon burns it down when he realizes he will be unable to settle down. He never makes the full transition out of the wilderness.

Rational legal authority/charismatic authority:

> Ransom Stoddart [James Stewart] represents rational legal authority, Tom Doniphon represents charismatic authority. Doniphon abandons his charisma and cedes it, under what amount to false pretences, to Stoddart. In this way charismatic and rational-legal authority are combined in the person of Stoddart and stability is assured.
>
> (101)

By killing Liberty Valance in cold blood, Tom Doniphon is unable to make the transition to legal-rational authority. That place is taken by the lawyer Stoddart, who embodies it along with charismatic authority, for it is believed that he killed Valance in self-defence. Doniphon embodies the same three binary values as Edwards in *The Searchers*: nomad, wilderness, charismatic authority, while Stoddard embodies the two opposite terms – settler, garden – and dissolves the third opposition by embodying both terms: charismatic authority and rational legal authority.

My Darling Clementine

Wilderness versus garden: Wyatt Earp (Henry Fonda) visits the barber, 'who civilizes the unkempt' (96). The barber sprays Earp's hair with honeysuckle, an artificial perfume. The barbershop scene marks Earp's transition 'from wandering cowboy, nomadic, savage, bent on personal revenge, unmarried, to married man, settled, civilized, the sheriff who administers the law' (96). For Wollen, Earp's progress 'is an uncomplicated passage from nature to culture, from the wilderness left in the past to the garden anticipated in the future' (96).

Rational legal authority/charismatic authority. These two types of authority 'are combined naturally in Wyatt Earp' (101). According to Wollen, therefore, Earp begins like Edwards and Doniphon by embodying nomad/wilderness/charismatic authority, but transforms into the three opposite terms as the film progresses. Bill Nichols disputes Wollen's reading of *My Darling Clementine*, and offers an alternative structural analysis (discussed below).

As *My Darling Clementine* shows, Ford's system is not static; neither is each Western the same: 'different pairs are foregrounded in different movies' (94), or the opposite terms in the same pairs are foregrounded in different movies. In his later films, such as *Cheyenne Autumn*, Ford's attitude towards his themes underwent a reversal: 'in *Cheyenne Autumn* it is the Europeans who are savage, the victims. [Indians] who are heroes' (96).

In a controversial move, Wollen uses his structural method to carry out the auteur critic's traditional activity of evaluating directors. He finds Ford's films to be more complex than Hawks's because of 'the richness of the shifting relations between antinomies in Ford's work' (102). In Hawks, by contrast, one does not encounter a development and transformation of thematic structure; instead, the basic themes remain the same throughout his career. For Wollen, 'shifting relations' therefore names a valuable characteristic of the auteur film.

Meta-theoretical concepts

Between the Hawks and Ford analyses, Wollen pauses to reflect on his structural method (91–94). He suddenly changes to a specialized linguistic vocabulary:

> Hawks first attracted attention because he was regarded naïvely as an action director. Later, the thematic content which I have outlined was detected and revealed. Beyond the stylemes, semantemes were found to exist; the films were anchored in an objective stratum of meaning, a pleromatic stratum, as the Danish linguist Hjelmslev would have put it.
>
> (91–93)

Amongst the specialized vocabulary we can recognize two familiar words (style and semantics), which have simply been rendered, through the addition of the suffix-eme, to name units of communication. Stylemes are therefore units of style, and semantemes are units of meaning. Hjelmslev sometimes used the term 'pleromatic stratum' as a more general term to designate the semantic level. In terms of Wollen's analysis of Hawks, semanteme/pleromatic simply name the thematic level. These terms belong to an established tradition in structural linguistics, which aims to be explicit and rigorous in its study of units and levels of language. The problem, then, is not with the terms themselves (for they are in line with Wollen's drive towards turning auteurism into an explicit rigorous method), but with their sudden appearance in the chapter.

Wollen explores the structural method further before turning his attention to Ford's Westerns. The aim of the structural method in film studies is 'the definition of a core of repeated motifs' in a director's films, analogous to the structural study of myth and folklore in the work of Axel Olrik, Propp, and Lévi-Strauss (93). Wollen reminds us that it was Renoir who said that a director spends his whole life making one film (104). Wollen uses Renoir's comment to align auteur theory with a fundamental tenet of Lévi-Strauss's structural study of myth: to conceive each film as a variant or incomplete version of a director's 'archi-film', just as the anthropologist collects and studies variants of the same myth: 'Underlying the different, individual tales was an archi-tale, of which they were all variants' (Wollen, 93). This translates into a search for the same elementary structural patterns (binary oppositions) within the corpus of an auteur's films (which is the case with the John Ford Westerns mentioned above). In his 1972 postscript (168), Wollen stresses that this 'archi-film' does not pre-exist analysis; instead, it is constructed a posteriori, just as there is no one true version of a myth, but several incomplete variants – and it is from those variants that the anthropologist constructs a synthesis, the archi-tale. We can see Wollen's formulation as an example of structural causality, in which the structure is not an empirically present pre-existing object, but is an absent cause only noticeable in its effects in individual texts. In analogous terms, the archi-film can therefore only be inferred a posteriori from its effects in individual films. (To think of this archi-film as pre-existent is to fall back into an expressive theory of causality to which structuralism is opposed.)

In the last ten pages of his chapter on the auteur theory (which are usually excised when the essay is anthologized[10]), Wollen again reflects on his methods by charting the distinction between composition and performance in music, painting, and theatre. Whereas composition is coded or digital communication, consisting of discrete units, performance is graded on a continuous, analogue scale. He uses this distinction to return to the difference between an auteur and a *metteur en scène*. Whereas a *metteur en scène* is merely 'in command of a performance of a pre-existing text' (112), the auteur fuses the pre-existing text, which acts as a catalyst, with his or her own preoccupations. Caughie, suspicious of this chemical metaphor, nonetheless spells out its implications: the auteur 'individualizes the text, characterizes it and even gives it its value' (1981, 127).

Wollen's catalyst metaphor, like his auteur theory more generally, went through a transformation. In 1969, he discussed the script as catalyst (113, quoted above). Here 'catalyst' is simply used as a metaphor or substitute term for 'stimulus' – the script stimulates the auteur's mind, creating a reaction. More specifically, the auteur's thematic preoccupations mix with the script to create the individualized film. To some extent, this meaning of catalyst resembles Sarris's notion of interior meaning – 'the tension between a director's personality and his material' (see note 3). In contrast to the auteur and his/her interior meaning, *metteurs en scène* do not have any thematic preoccupations, merely stylistic preferences, and therefore they do not individualize the films they make.

In his 1972 postscript, Wollen wrote: 'it is possible to think of the film *auteur* as an unconscious catalyst' (1972, 168). This redefinition of the catalyst, away from the script and towards the director's unconscious thematic preoccupations, was formulated to position the auteur theory completely within structuralism, downplaying the conscious, active role of the director, to the extent that the directors on the set were seen as separate from 'the structures named after them' (168). It is this redefinition of the catalyst that led to Wollen's often-quoted distinction between Hawks (the director on the set) and 'Hawks' in quotation marks (the elementary thematic structure named after the director).

Finally, in 2002, in an essay devoted to Jean Rouch, Wollen defined the camera as a catalyst: 'Rouch erased the false line between documentary and drama, between camera as recording instrument and camera as catalyst for performance' (2002, 101). Here, Wollen simply replaces the auteur with the camera as transformative force.

The term 'catalyst' is used in chemistry to name an energy or force that decomposes existing elements or compounds (reactants) and facilitates the formation of new compounds (the product) without changing in itself; a catalyst simply speeds up the process of decomposition and composition. When mixed, reactants transform into products. A catalyst simply facilitates the transformation of reactants into products; the catalyst is an energy or force that assists in a chemical reaction.

Because a catalyst is not a part of the reaction's outcome, but simply enables the reaction to occur more quickly, we cannot think of the script or the director's thematic preoccupations as catalysts, since both are reactants that combine to form the product (the film). However, Wollen's 1972 postscript clarification – that the director's thematic preoccupations are unconscious – leaves open the possibility that his or her *conscious* activity is the catalyst. Dudley Andrew captures this sense of the term: 'Wollen's structuralism', Andrew writes, 'made room for the individual as "catalyst," that is, as an element, innocuous in itself, having the potential to initiate a complex reaction when dropped into the proper mix of other elements' (1993, 78).[11] For Andrew, the traditional romantic notion of the director as a specific, purely subjective psychological cause – whose free will, desires, beliefs, and intentions consciously structure a film – still has a limited place in Wollen's structuralist framework: the director as conscious agent actively mixes together in a chemical reaction the reactants (script and his/her thematic preoccupations) to determine the final composition of the product: the film. This can be represented schematically in the following form:

Auteur

- reactants: script elements and director's unconscious thematic preoccupations
- catalyst: director's conscious, purposeful activity (stylistic preferences)
- product: film.

Metteurs en scène do not add any unconscious thematic preoccupations to the mix. They simply facilitate the combining of script and film elements, without leaving any trace of themselves (in terms of thematic preoccupations) on the film:

Metteur en scène

- reactants: script elements
- catalyst: director's conscious, purposeful activity (stylistic preferences)
- product: film.

Evaluating data and problems

Genuineness, correctness, and comprehensiveness

Wollen introduced into auteur theory the two-tier reality of structuralism (surface phenomena/underlying structure) and took the underlying structure to be auteurism's new object of study. By relocating auteur theory's focus to the underlying level, Wollen attempted to solve the theory's problematic state of affairs – to identify a director's consistent signature. Wollen's solution was questioned in terms of his theoretical premises, the results of his analyses, and his evaluations of Hawks and Ford as auteurs. The genuineness and correctness of his analyses are closely tied up with his theory, which will therefore be addressed in the following sections (well-formedness and significance). In terms of the comprehensiveness of his analyses, we can discern the indispensable role the examples play in the overall structure of the chapter. Although the chapter is not subdivided by headings, we can divide it into the following sections:

- short history of auteur theory (74–78)
- criteria used to classify a film as auteurist (78–80)
- detailed case studies of Hawks (traditional thematic readings) (80–91)
- outline of structuralist methodology (91–94)
- return to case studies – structural analysis of heroes in Ford's Westerns (94–102)
- return to structuralist methodology – discussion of composition/performance (102–15).

Although Wollen quotes Nowell-Smith's summary of the structuralist method on page 80, he does not explicitly use it until page 94. The first analysis of Hawks (80–91) consists of traditional thematic readings. The essay has a dialectical structure: traditional thematic readings of Hawks followed by structuralist methodology, leading to structuralist readings of themes in Ford, followed by additional reflection on the structuralist methodology, this time focusing on its inverse – performance, the dimension of texts left out of structuralism. The analyses are therefore integral to the chapter; Hawks and Ford are not mere illustrations of the theory, since we gain valuable insights from Wollen's thematic readings, and the films (especially Ford's Westerns) play a decisive role in the formulation of the theory.

Well-formedness

Wollen's problematic state of affairs is carried over from traditional auteur theory: to change perception of Hollywood cinema as a mass of impersonal films by highlighting the artistry of a handful of directors. Wollen's solution to this problem is more complex than previous auteur theories addressing the same problem. He attempted to bring order into auteur theory by positing the existence of a hypothetical object, a *specific, objective thematic structure* underlying all the films of the same auteur. Nowell-Smith noted that: 'The structural approach, which has evolved, by a kind of necessary accident, out of the applications of the *auteur* theory … resolves many of the difficulties of the theory as originally put forward' (1967, 10). A few years later he clarified what those difficulties were: auteur-structuralism attempted 'to find a materialist (or if you prefer objective) basis for the concept of authorship' that would enable it 'to escape the Scylla and Charybdis of pro-*auteur* subjectivism and anti-*auteur* empiricism' (Nowell-Smith 1973, 96).

   Does structuralism bring order to subjective auteur theory and avoid anti-*auteur* empiricism via a materialist objectivity? Arguing from a traditional auteur position, Robin Wood declared: 'any sense we may receive of "scientific" objectivity is manifestly illusory; Wollen's account of Hawks reveals as strong a personal bias as one will find in the most admittedly "subjective" criticism, the more dangerous for being concealed beneath an appearance of detached analytic method' (1976, 202). Wood presupposes Wollen's analysis is complete and definitive, rather than the first stage in a fundamental reorientation of auteur theory. I would argue that Wollen's auteur chapter has the same status as Lévi-Strauss's programmatic essay 'The Structural Study of Myth' (1963, 206–31), which introduces and illustrates the structural method. This is in contrast to Lévi-Strauss's two-thousand-page, four-volume *Mythologiques* – his structural analyses of hundreds of myths. No such comparable work was been carried out by auteur structuralists, meaning that the theory has not been developed, refined, and practised in any depth. The existence of a hypothetical auteur structure remains unproven, but not falsified.

Significance

Whether Wollen's auteur structuralism expands our understanding of film can be judged from the considerable debate and reaction his chapter generated, a debate that overshadowed the other two chapters of *Signs and Meaning* (on Eisenstein and Film Semiology). These debates highlighted several issues that questioned the significance of the contribution of auteur structuralism to film studies, including:

(1) no place given to an auteur's film style;
(2) the problematic nature of binary oppositions (a. the level at which they operate – surface or deep?; and b. their downplaying of other logical relations); and
(3) the viability of using of Lévi-Strauss's anthropological methodology in the analysis of film.

Question (1) No place given to an auteur's film style

In relation to issue (1), at least four critics raised objections to a purely thematic-based auteur theory. Back in 1967, in his book on Visconti, Nowell-Smith mentioned the danger of ignoring style in the structural approach to auteurism: 'The structural approach ... brings with it, however, problems of its own [such as the neglect of] the importance of the non-thematic subject-matter and of sub-stylistic features of the visual treatment' (1967, 10–12). In his review of Wollen's book in *New Left Review*, Sam Rohdie also mentioned that film style should be incorporated into a deep thematic study, otherwise one ignores film's specificity: 'There is nothing in Wollen's argument specific to the medium of the movies or the way in which Ford and Hawks handle that medium. ... If structuralism is *the* key to cinematic understanding it needs to be used on various levels specific to the medium' (1969, 68–69). Raymond Durgnat echoed this sentiment: 'You can't perform a Lévi-Straussian analysis of Ford *qua* Ford until you can perform a structural analysis on his images' (1982, 305). Finally, Ron Abramson also developed this criticism that theme cannot be abstracted from style, for we only perceive theme through style: 'it is from the visual style that the pattern of motifs is abstracted' (1976, 563). The alternative, Abramson points out, is to think of the motifs as pre-existing in the script, which is what Wollen denies in his definition of the auteur (in contrast to the *metteur en scène*, where meaning is pre-existent in the script).

Yet Wollen clearly acknowledges that a structural analysis limited to underlying themes risks reductionism: reducing myths, fairy tales, and American movies down to the same utterly basic elements. He therefore recognizes that films need to be studied 'not only in their universality (what they all have in common), but also in their singularity (what differentiates them from each other)' (93). The moment of synthesis, including the incorporation of style into a thematic analysis, needs to be implemented to avoid reductionism. The final ten pages of the chapter address this in some detail. But such an aim was never carried out, for auteurism was quickly displaced by semiotics, psychoanalysis, and feminism in the 1970s (see Chapters 4, 5 and 6).

Question (2a) At what level do binary oppositions operate?

For Lévi-Strauss, the binary opposition is a form of cultural classification humans impose on their environment in order to control and understand it. The binary opposition functions in myth as a form of thinking that solves problems. In terms of problem-solving, 'mythical thought always progresses from the awareness of opposi-tions toward their resolution' (Lévi-Strauss 1963, 224), in which a mediator comes between the opposing terms to resolve their conflict.[12]

The key to these binary oppositions is that they are not on the myth's surface, but are deep and implicit, and require (in some cases) considerable analytical work to make them apparent. This is the case, for example, in Lévi-Strauss's brief study of the Oedipus myth (1963, 214–17). His analysis revealed that the myth articulates two binary oppositions: the overrating/underrating of blood relations, and a deep opposi-tion concerning the denial/affirmation of the autochthonous origin of mankind. Although Lévi-Strauss does not say in his essay, it seems that Oedipus is the mediator who transcends both oppositions.

Nowell-Smith argued that a director's thematic structure is deep, in the often-quoted passage from his book on Visconti: 'the defining characteristics of an author's work are not always those that are most readily apparent. The purpose of criticism becomes therefore to uncover behind the superficial contrasts of subject and treat-ment a structural hard core of basic and often recondite motifs' (Nowell-Smith 1967, 10; slightly misquoted in Wollen, 80). As we have seen, Wollen uses the term 'decipher-ment' to name this critical activity to uncover the 'structural hard core of basic and often recondite motifs'. Wollen's analysis goes beyond what we already know about a film, and therefore has potential value by revealing something new.

Rohdie agrees that binary oppositions are deep unconscious themes; they are not 'content banalities' (basic surface categories), but abstract deep categories (1976, 474). In the second half of his essay, Rohdie analyses Mr Deeds Goes to Town (Frank Capra, 1936). He identifies two thematic oppositions dominating the film – town/country, and sophisticated/naïve (1976, 477). He argues that the film begins by valorizing 'town' and 'sophisticated', but reverses these values as it progresses, ending by pro-moting 'country' and 'naïve'. He also identifies a series of secondary oppositions (including: opera/band, moustache/clean-shaven, wit/fun, 'fake' sentiment/'real' sentiment) (1976, 477) – the analysis of which, however, is in danger of reducing the film down to content banalities. Rohdie feels that his analysis does not reveal anything new about the film. After all, he simply concludes after two pages of analysis that its message 'rests upon the unmasking of the TOWN and all it stands for in fakery, cynicism, inhumanity, by the COUNTRY' (1976, 479). Yet, such a message can easily be found on the film's surface. Rohdie did not dig very deep; he did not get around to considering whether the binary oppositions he identified articulate and resolve more fundamental problems the film is addressing on a deeper level.

What then is the appropriate level at which to conduct a structural analysis? While Rohdie remained on the surface level, Nowell-Smith raised the opposite problem: 'if a policy of reduction to utterly basic elements is pursued to its logical conclusion, the specificity of particular authors is lost, or if you prefer transcended, in the resulting generality' (1970, 133). Tension therefore exists between analysing deep themes that are too general and abstracted from the film's surface, and analysing themes on the surface (content banalities), simply repeating what can be seen. Perhaps an adequate structural analysis of film must combine two extreme perspectives: use a considerable amount of analytic work to identify deep fundamental themes; and examine in detail, using *mise en scène* analysis, how those themes are manifest in individual shots and scenes. Exactly how does Ford manifest garden/wilderness (a variation of nature/culture) in a particular scene? In what particular shots and scenes is Capra able to change the modality of town-sophisticated, transforming its values from positive to negative? Exactly *how* is the thematic opposition and its transformation worked out, articulated, and manifest in his *mise en scène*? Is the change incremental, taking place over many scenes on a micro-level (fragments of dialogue, gestures, incidents)? Or does it happen suddenly, in one major scene?

Nichols answers some of these questions in an alternative reading to Wollen's structural analysis of *My Darling Clementine* (Nichols 1976b, 616–18).[13] We shall focus on his analysis of the film's ending, when Earp says goodbye to Clementine.

> Earp is at frame left, his horse behind him, standing in the dirt road that runs to the far distant base of a mountain peak. A rail fence stands along the right side of the road, behind the stationary figure of Clementine Carter. Earp bids Clementine farewell; he rises above her (swings onto his saddle) and prepares to follow the road leading to a peak above them both. The two figures are not simply in front of the fence. As a two-dimensional representation the image also places the fence *between* them. (The fence here punctuates the continuum culture/nature, but Earp will move above and beyond it.) The figures stand on common ground but only one will move along it. Clementine is now rooted to the soil (not isolated from it in the town's geometry) while Earp is clearly above it. Earp, though, doesn't exactly straddle two worlds; he exists apart from and above each. Charisma and the law remain apart but through his intervention, the space between them can be mediated.
>
> (1976b, 618)

Yet, for all its attention to film style, Nichols's reading is, like Wollen's, partial at best. Nichols suggests that Earp is on his horse saying goodbye to Clementine, who is standing next to the fence (he describes Earp getting on his horse before he describes the farewell scene). Yet, the two characters are face to face, standing on the ground. To suggest the fence is *between* them is straining for credibility (both are, after all, standing on the same side). The issue of the fence is a moot point, because Ford cuts into a closer shot of Earp from behind Clementine's back; Earp moves closer and kisses her on the cheek. The fence is no longer in shot; only the sky appears in the background. Earp talks about returning and visiting her in the schoolhouse. The impression is that this is a temporary departure scene, that Earp will return to the town and to Clementine, and that the formation of the couple will take place sometime in the near future, beyond the end credits.

Nichols's reading downplays the opposition nature/culture (but he nonetheless takes it as a valid opposition in the film, as does Wollen) to emphasize Earp's role as mediator between the opposition. Nichols's reading does not so much refute Wollen's reading as refine it, by focusing on different elements – mediators between the binary oppositions, and the need for a *mise en scène* analysis. (But a *mise en scène* analysis needs to be carried out with more precision and accuracy.)

Question (2b) Non-binary logical relations

Rohdie criticizes Wollen's search for binary oppositions: 'The attempt to decode or perceive artistic productions in terms of a computer-like binary system is more an exercise in control, reduction, impoverishment than it is an understanding of the aesthetic work' (1969, 69). Rohdie's critique links up to a more general assessment of the binary opposition. Anthony Wilden (1980, 8) notes that binary oppositions are only relevant to a system of communication such as verbal language, for they delineate the specific structure of phonemes. They reduce systems down to a duality between two mutually exclusive terms, positing each term as symmetrical opposites. While this is relevant to the semantically empty distinctive features grave/acute, it is not so relevant for positing the relation between (for example) semantically rich 'nature' and 'culture'. Nature and culture are not mutually exclusive, symmetrically opposite terms existing on the same level of reality. A hierarchy exists between them, with culture completely dependent on nature. Representing them as a binary opposition therefore levels them out on the same plane, giving the false impression that they are equal and opposite (see Wilden 1980, xxxiii–xxxv).

Wilden's example of nature and culture shows that other logical relations – besides the crisp case of the binary opposition – exist between two terms. In his understanding, culture is included in nature, is completely dependent on nature for its existence. Other terms can be the reverse of each other (as with 'tie' and 'untie'), or reciprocals (as with 'buy' and 'sell'). More than two terms can also enter into logical relationships, in which they share common features and differ in others (for example, the series 'chair', 'stool', 'bench' share the common feature of furniture to sit on, but differ in their components).

An extension and refinement of Wollen's auteur structuralism could incorporate non-binary relations between two or more terms. It may even be worthwhile, as a way to avoid reductionism, to define these terms in relation to non-classical or fuzzy logic. Whereas the binary opposition categorizes the thematic continuum into two mutually exclusive terms, ignoring all other terms, fuzzy logic deals with matters of degree rather than mutual exclusivity. It studies approximate, inexact, indeterminate categories. Unlike the binary opposition of classic logic, it does not set up a stark threshold between categories (hot/cold, garden/desert), but establishes fuzzy overlapping boundaries between them. (Note, however, that fuzzy logic is not ambiguous, for ambiguity presupposes two or more distinct meanings.)

In terms of Wollen's analysis of Ford, for example, fuzzy logic suggests we do not need to think exclusively in terms of garden or wilderness, nomad or settler, rational legal authority or charismatic authority. It is not a simple matter of classifying a character in terms of the binary logic of either/or. Fuzzy logic enables the analyst to think in more subtle terms, for a character may belong only partially to one category or, more likely, may belong at the same time to several other categories. There are numerous other categories and gradations to take into consideration, a gradation that Wollen in fact acknowledges (but does not implement) in the final pages of his auteur chapter. A director's underlying thematic structure can therefore be categorized more precisely in terms of numerous overlapping, finely graded categories, rather than a few mutually exclusive binary categories.

Question (3) The viability of using of Lévi-Strauss's anthropological methodology in the analysis of film

Like Brian Henderson, Charles Eckert believes that one of the fundamental unresolved problems auteur-structuralism does not address is whether films are like myths. Yet, the structural analysis of film is simply not dependent on drawing analogies between Lévi-Strauss's object of study (myth) and film scholars' object of study (film). That is, the structural analysis of film is not premised on any direct resemblance between film and myth. The similarities lie in *how* films and myths are analysed. For Nowell-Smith: 'The transfer of a "method" from one object to another is a delicate business, but the delicacy does not consist in preserving the purity of the method but in testing its adequacy to the object and the validity of transformations its applications will produce' (1973, 97). Yoshimoto is more direct:

> If Lévi-Strauss's text has any significance for film theorists, it is not because of the object of his reading but because of the structural method he uses to decipher the meaning of the other's discourse. It can even be said that the importance of what Lévi-Strauss reads should be almost negligible compared to the seminal importance of how he reads it. Another way of stating this is to say that the question of whether or not film is myth is irrelevant for the purpose of undertaking the structural analysis of film.
>
> (1990, 57)

In sum, Wollen avoids the obscure concepts of previous auteur theories (interior meaning, personal vision, worldview), but only by adding to the theory a series of highly technical and specialized concepts from linguistics and structural anthropology, concepts that add a new (underlying) level of reality that aims to solve the auteur problem (by carrying out analysis on a director's underlying thematic structures). However, due to a lack of detailed case studies, the auteur problem has yet to be solved, in the sense that no definitive underlying auteur structures have been revealed. Wollen's chapter is simply a first approximation in formulating an auteur structuralism. It needs to go through a series of successive approximations and collect a rich and varied array of data (not just binary thematic oppositions) from a director's films to produce more substantial results, before we can adequately evaluate its validity and significance. Whereas Wollen's reading of *My Darling Clementine* is a first approximation, Nichols's reading offers a second, more accurate approximation, which itself can be subjected to a third approximation.

Do auteur structuralists make a convincing case for approaching their problematic state of affairs and answering it by adding to auteurism a new object of study – an underlying structure of themes? Wollen's auteur structuralism brings order to the 'chaotic' auteur criticism but at the cost of almost losing sight of the director in favour of the impersonal underlying structures – which help us perceive at least one type of basic logical process (the binary opposition) at the root of the films analysed. Only Dudley Andrew's reformulation of the catalyst metaphor carved out a space for the director as individual, an idea at the foundation of non-structuralist theories of auteurism. Wollen's chapter is therefore significant in that it transformed the terms of debate on auteurism, a point Eckert acknowledged: '[Wollen's] faults are many, but they have proven to be seminal faults, spawning ... many ideas and thoughtful reactions ... ' (1973, 46).

Pam Cook agrees:

> But the problems in Wollen's arguments do not detract from the contribution they make to shifting the ground of British film criticism away from empiricism towards a different problematic: the relationship of science and theory to artistic practice and to politics.
>
> (1999, 285)

Notes

1 The book was published in 1969 by Secker and Warburg in association with the British Film Institute; republished in 1970 by Thames & Hudson in association with the British Film Institute; a 'new and enlarged' edition was published in 1972 by Secker and Warburg in association with the British Film Institute (which contains the 1972 postscript); and an 'expanded' edition was published in 1998 by the British Film Institute. This expanded edition contains most of the essays Wollen published (under the pseudonym Lee Russell) in the *New Left Review* from 1964 to 1967, plus an Afterword in which Lee Russell interviews Peter Wollen. I will be quoting from the 1970 edition, which is the same as the 1969 and 1972 editions, except the 1972 edition includes the postscript. All quotations from this edition of the book will be cited in the text with page numbers in parentheses.

2 Foucault makes explicit this assumption in his essay 'What is an Author?':

> the author's name characterizes a particular manner of existence of discourse. Discourse that possesses an author's name is not to be immediately consumed and forgotten; neither is it accorded the momentary attention given to ordinary, fleeting words. Rather, its status and its manner of reception are regulated by the culture in which it circulates.
>
> (Foucault 1981, 284).

3 For Sarris, the auteur theory is based on three premises: technical competence; personal style; and, most importantly, interior meaning. He defined interior meaning as 'the tension between a director's personality and his material' (1962, 7). He adds that interior meaning:

> ... is not quite the vision of the world a director projects nor quite his attitude toward life. It is ambiguous, in any literary sense, because it is imbedded in the stuff of cinema and cannot be rendered in noncinematic terms. Truffaut called it the temperature of the director on the set, and that is a close approximation of its professional aspect. Dare I come out and say what I think it to be is an élan of the soul?
>
> (Sarris 1962, 7)

For Sarris, soul 'is that intangible difference between one personality and another' (7). The term 'interior meaning' is based on Kierkegaard's discussion of shadowgraphs and inner pictures in *Either/Or*, a discussion Sarris quotes as the epigraph to his 1962 essay. Kierkegaard argues that the 'inner picture [is] too delicately drawn to be outwardly visible, woven as it is of the tenderest moods of the soul' (quoted in Sarris, 1). Interior meaning therefore refers to indirect meanings, like an implicit theme.

4 These two short studies were not reprinted in Wollen (1998), presumably because they were superseded by the detailed analysis of Hawks and Ford in the auteur chapter. In an interview, Wollen explains how he began writing film analyses for the *New Left Review*:

> The first things I wrote for the *NLR* were about contemporary politics. But I was interested in film and Perry Anderson, who was the editor, wanted the magazine to be modeled on something like *Les Temps Modernes*, and he wanted cultural coverage as well as political coverage. So the idea came of writing about film and that's when I did my first film pieces, under the name of Lee Russell.
>
> (Quoted in Thomas Elsaesser, 2012, 19)

5 Nonetheless, Wollen indicates that the test of structural analysis lies in the way it treats these peripheral films: 'the test of a structural analysis lies not in the orthodox canon of a director's work, where resemblances are clustered, but in films which at first sight may seem eccentricities' (93). The study of films outside the director's canon became Slavoj Žižek's working method. See Chapter 8.

6 In 'The Structural Study of Myth' Lévi-Strauss wrote: 'Its [myth's] substance does not lie in its style, its original music, or its syntax, but in the *stories* which it tells' (1963, 210). Myth, Lévi-Strauss informs us, is therefore the opposite of poetry, whose substance does lie in its style.

7 In his critique of thematic criticism, David Bordwell lists the small recurrent values it adheres to: 'the meaning of a film [for thematic critics] will often revolve around individual problems (suffering, identity, alienation, the ambiguity of perception, the mystery of behavior) or values (freedom, religious doctrines, enlightenment, creativity, the imagination)' (1989, 108).

8 Jakobson's work on distinctive features was developed from Saussure's notion that language signifies via differential elements, which proposes that linguistic units are only defined in relation to each other.

9 Jakobson's definitive statement on binary oppositions is found in his 1956 volume *Fundamentals of Language*, co-written with Morris Halle:

[E]very phoneme is composed of several distinctive features. The totality of these features is the minimum number of binary selections necessary for the specification of any given phoneme. In reducing the phonemic information contained in the sequence to the smallest number of alternatives, we find the most economical and, consequently, the optimal solution: the minimum of the simplest operations would suffice to encode and decode the whole message. When analyzing a given language into its ultimate constituents, we seek the smallest set of distinctive oppositions which enable us to identify each phoneme of the message framed in this language.

(1956, 58)

10 The last ten pages are excised from the following anthologies: Caughie's *Theories of Authorship*; Grant's *Auteurs and Authorship*; Braudy and Cohen's *Film Theory and Criticism*; most of it is missing from Nichols's *Movies and Methods*, Volume 1.

11 Andrew also describes Lévi-Strauss's structural study of myth as a chemical analysis:

[Lévi-Strauss's] methodology unearths what must be thought of as a chemistry of myth. He finds the values of various mythical elements and measures the overall energy level of the relationships between particles. It can be argued that Lévi-Strauss disrespects stories, seeing them only as structures to be broken down until they speak directly to the ethnographer. It is true at least that he has no interest in, or use for, what literary critics would call the formal aspects of narrative. He has worked at building something like an atomic chart of mythemes, recording atomic weights, stability, and valence.

(Andrew 1984, 78–79)

12 Edmund Leach argues that Lévi-Strauss's model of binary oppositions and mediating middle term 'is little more than the Hegelian triad of thesis, antithesis, synthesis' (1970, 117).

Wollen downplays the use of the mediator in resolving binary oppositions in the films of Hawks and Ford. Furthermore, he does not demonstrate his method – that is, *how* he identifies themes and binary oppositions. Did he, for example, analyse each film by organizing similar elements into paradigms and then establish oppositions between these paradigms? Eckert spends a few paragraphs on method (1973, 48–49), as do the anthropologists Dumont and Monod in their structural analysis of *2001: A Space Odyssey* (1970), and Kinder and Houston in their structural analysis of the films of Nicholas Roeg (1980, 345–74). On the other hand, Jim Kitses' *Horizons West* (1969), a structural analysis of the Westerns of Anthony Mann, Budd Boetticher, and Sam Peckinpah, published in the same year as Wollen's *Signs and Meaning* in the same book series, does not discuss method or even quote Lévi-Strauss. Yet, Kitses structures his analyses around binary oppositions, and (to bring this note back to Leach's point), argues that central to the Western 'we have a philosophical dialectic, an ambiguous cluster of meanings and attitudes that provide the traditional thematic structure of the genre' (1969, 11).

13 Similarly, Robin Wood offers an alternative to Wollen's reading of Hawks's films, in 'Hawks De-Wollenized', in *Personal Views* (1976, 193–206).

2

VISUAL STYLOMETRY

Barry Salt's 'Statistical Style Analysis of Motion Pictures'

> It is nowadays fairly widely accepted that individual styles can be recognized for at least some film directors in the formal aspects of their films as well as in the content. ... The obvious approach in searching for individual characteristics in the formal side of a director's films is to consider those variables that are most directly under the director's control; also to a certain extent those that are easiest to quantify.
>
> (Salt 1974, 13)

Problem-situation

For over 35 years Barry Salt has almost single-handedly established stylometry (or statistical style analysis, as he prefers to call it) as a research paradigm in film studies. Stylometry has traditionally been limited to linguistics, literary studies, and musicology. There are three standard aims of statistical style analysis: (1) to offer a quantitative analysis of style, usually for the purpose of recognizing patterns, a task now made feasible with the use of computer technology. In language texts, the quantitative analysis of style and pattern recognition is usually conducted in the numerical analysis of the following variables: word length, or syllables per word, sentence length, the distribution of parts of speech (the different percentages of nouns, pronouns, verbs, adjectives, and so on in a text), calculating the ratio of parts of speech (for example, the ratio of verbs to adjectives), or by analysing word order, syntax, rhythm, or metre; (2) for the purposes of authorship attribution, in cases of disputed authorship of anonymous or pseudonymous texts (see Foster 2001); and (3) for purposes of identifying the chronology of works, when the sequence of composition is unknown or disputed (e.g. Plato, Shakespeare's plays).

The first aim, the quantitative analysis of style, involves descriptive statistics, and the second and third (authorship attribution and chronology) involve both descriptive and inferential statistics. As its name implies, descriptive statistics simply describes a text as it is, by measuring and quantifying it in terms of its numerical characteristics. The result is a detailed, internal, molecular description of a text's (or group of texts') formal variables. Inferential statistics then employs this formal description to make predictions. That is, it uses this data as an index, primarily an index of an author's style, or to put the author's work into chronological order on the basis of measured changes in style of their work over time. Whereas descriptive statistics produces data

43

with complete certainty, inferential statistics is based on assumptions the statistician makes on the basis of the descriptive data. The assumptions the inferential statistician makes only have degrees of probability rather than certainty.

Salt uses stylometry to quantify film style, especially formal parameters of a shot – such as scale, length, height, and camera movement. In this chapter I rationally reconstruct his essay 'The Statistical Style Analysis of Motion Pictures' published in *Film Quarterly* (1974, 13–22).[1] This is an early and seminal statement of stylometry applied to film. Salt subsequently developed the framework presented in this essay in his first book *Film Style and Technology* (1983; third edition 2009). In 2006 he published his collected essays under the title *Moving into Pictures* (Salt 2006), which contains several papers that push the statistical style analysis of film to an advanced level.

'Statistical Style Analysis of Motion Pictures' is a historically important essay that was published against the grain of the theories prevalent in film studies in the 1970s, which applied semiotics, Althusserian Marxism, and Lacanian psychoanalysis to film. Reflecting on his editorship of *Film Quarterly*, Ernest Callenbach comments on his publication of Salt's essay:

> Theory of a scientific sort depends on quantification, so when a former physicist named Barry Salt sent in an article called 'Statistical Style Analysis of Motion Pictures', it seemed intriguing. Salt had doggedly compiled figures on average shot length, shot scope, and camera movement for hundreds of films. He could demonstrate clear historical trends in these figures, and relate them to interesting stylistic questions. We printed his piece, to the outrage of some humanities people (though statistical analysis had by that time become familiar in linguistic and comparative-literature work). In time, Salt's innovation became a familiar analytic method.
>
> (Callenbach 2008, 64)

Callenbach continued to support Salt's work by publishing his essays in *Film Quarterly*, and by reviewing the first edition of Salt's *Film Style and Technology*, emphasizing its unusual status in film studies by commenting that '[i]t is hardly possible to exaggerate the great gulf between Salt's quantitative style analysis and most film writing' (1985, 46). He went on to comment that Salt's work should nonetheless have a 'salutary cautionary effect' on other film scholars, by 'reining in unsound generalizing' (1985, 47). He also commented on Salt's chapter devoted to the detailed auteurist analysis of the films of Max Ophuls from a statistical perspective. However, Callenbach finds this to be 'fairly dry stuff' (1985, 47). We shall review Salt's analysis of Ophuls at the end of this chapter.

Salt's starting point is Andrew Sarris's auteur theory. We saw in Chapter 1 that Peter Wollen uses structuralism to make the thematic level of auteurism more rigorous and scientific. In this chapter we will see Barry Salt using statistics to achieve the exact same aim – although he makes auteurism more rigorous and scientific on the stylistic level. In other words, statistics makes auteur criticism detached, systematic, and explicit. The auteur critic focuses on the frequency of the common stylistic parameters a director uses – whose uses are independent of the subject matter or context – rather than on a few unusual stylistic traits of a film. In other words, it is possible to describe and identify the series of invariant stylistic traits in a director's work (again, the traits linked to the parameters of the shot, in the first instance). It is imperative to think of a director's unique style not in terms of a few unusual stylistic elements, but in terms of the *combination* of *all* the parameters related to the shot (what statisticians call multivariate analysis).

From his initial, tentative suggestions made in 'The Statistical Style Analysis of Motion Pictures' in 1974 to *Moving into Pictures*, Salt's application of statistics has settled down to a powerful system that includes average shot length, shot scale, camera movement, reverse angles, point-of-view shots, log-normal distribution, theoretical probability curves, correlation coefficient, and several other measures. While auteur criticism is always present in his research, Salt has broadened his scope to include stylistic trends in national cinemas from the early years up to the present. Since his 1974 essay, Salt has continued to make significant advances through his growing database containing several thousand films, and through his increasingly sophisticated application of statistics to those films.

Analysing the problematic state of affairs

Identifying what is problematic

Under this first heading we need to understand the problematic state of affairs Salt addresses in 'The Statistical Style Analysis of Motion Pictures'. In the opening paragraph of his essay, Salt states what is taken to be a truism in auteur criticism – that 'many directors have sharply different styles that are easily recognized' (13). He argues that style can be recognized in terms of form as well as content, although in this essay he delimits his research to film form. He conveys the problematic state of affairs in the same paragraph: 'However, just what constitutes these individualities of style has up to now been more a matter of loose assertion than demonstration' (13). Salt therefore accepts that some film directors have 'sharply different styles' but he finds problematic that this style is easily recognizable. The two interrelated components of Salt's identification of a problematic state of affairs are: (a) existing studies of individual style have been vague and superficial, based on loose assertion; and, (b) a director's individual style is in fact harder to recognize than previous studies acknowledge. In other words, for Salt the problem of identifying a director's individual style has not been formulated and conducted on the correct level. At the end of the paragraph he offers his solution: 'To lend some objectivity to this area, and also in emulation of the statistical analyses of features of literary and musical style that have been in progress since the thirties, the preliminary work reported here has been done' (13; endnote omitted). Salt's solution to identifying an individual director's style is therefore to take the problem to a whole new level – the objectivity of stylometry, or statistical style analysis. This will overcome the loose assertions of previous studies and will reveal that identification of a director's individual style is a more complicated issue than previously assumed.

Background assumptions

Auteur criticism constitutes a major background assumption of Salt's essay. We saw in Chapter 1 that traditional auteur criticism designates the director as the single source of a film's coherence, intentionality, value, and meaning. It was initially formulated in Paris in the 1950s, around the influential journal *Cahiers du Cinéma* (edited by André Bazin). Subsequently, auteur criticism was taken up by *Movie* magazine (London) and by Andrew Sarris (New York), who published *The American Cinema: Directors and Directions 1929–1968* (Sarris 1968) – the standard reference work of traditional auteur criticism. Sarris presents short entries on over 200 American directors, outlining their thematic and stylistic traits. He organized them into a hierarchy consisting of 11 categories, with pantheon directors at the top and minor directors at the bottom. Sarris's influential work constitutes Salt's primary point of comparison and opposition. For Salt, statistics can be used to make auteur criticism more rigorous – that is, detached, systematic, and explicit – thereby correcting the loose and vague assertions auteur critics (especially Sarris) have made in the past. Salt states this point again in the introduction to *Moving into Pictures*:

> Given my scientific background, I thought that [Sarris's] assertions about formal style used by particular directors could do with more solid and detailed empirical support, and it seemed to me that this might be provided by an adapted version of recent work on the statistical style analysis of music.
>
> (2006, 13)

Salt therefore brought auteur criticism in line with one of the major aspects of statistical style analysis – authorship attribution, at least in the way it describes an author's style (rather than infers who the author might be).

Describing the problematic state of affairs

Collecting data

Describing involves collecting data, systematizing it, and symbolizing the results. It is rare for humanities scholars to formally collect, systematize, and symbolize data – these stages of research are usually carried out informally. In particular, data are rarely symbolized, although film historians occasionally use a timeline to formally represent film history and its various stages. However, collecting, systematizing, and symbolizing represent the key stages of Barry Salt's work.

Statistical style analysis makes auteur criticism more explicit and systematic by focusing on the frequency of common stylistic parameters a director uses, rather than on a few unusual stylistic traits of a film. Salt's study of the frequency of common parameters brings film analysis in line with statistical style analyses of language, literature, and music. Salt's working hypothesis is to systematically collect data from the formal parameters of shots.

Salt collects a wide variety of data from the film's formal shot parameters that are under the director's control, and then determines what is most significant in identifying a director's individual style. For Salt, style designates a set of measurable patterns that significantly deviate from contextual norms. He therefore has to establish those norms before he can define how a director deviates from them.

In this early essay he delimits his data collection to the following discrete shot parameters:

- duration of the shot (measured either in terms of feet or seconds);
- shot scale (seven categories, defined in terms of their representation of the body: big close-up [shows the head only]; close-up; medium close-up; medium shot; medium long shot; long shot [full body in the frame]; and very long shot [human figure is small in the frame]); and
- camera movement (six categories: pan; tilt; pan with tilt; track; track with pan; and crane).

Salt recommends for future research collecting data on camera angles (three categories: high, low, eye level) and the more diffuse parameter he calls the strength of a cut, 'the nature of shot transition from each shot to the next' (13).

For the purpose of 'Statistical Style Analysis of Motion Pictures', Salt examines the style of Jean Renoir. He analyses four of his films from the 1930s (*La Chienne* [1931], *Boudu Savre des Eaux* [1932], *Toni* [1934], and *Partie de Campagne* [1936]), and compares them to eight other films (from Europe and Hollywood), ranging from 1917 to 1946. This is a small corpus of films, but they nonetheless establish a minimal context in which to compare the Renoir films. In his book *Film Style and Technology*, Salt carried out statistical tests on several thousand films.

Finally, in terms of data collection, it is important to note that Salt collected the data from 16mm and 35mm prints of the films examined on a film-viewing machine.

Systematizing data (classifying, correlating, ordering, measuring) and symbolizing the results

I shall discuss these two processes together, because Salt organizes and represents his data in one go, using three tables and one bar chart:

- Tables
  - shot length distribution (16);
  - average shot length (17);
  - camera movement (18);

- Chart
  - closeness of shot (shot scale) (19).

The 'shot length distribution' and 'camera movement' tables are reproduced below as Figures 2.1 and 2.2 respectively. The purpose of tables and charts is not only to display the data itself, but also to show patterns and exceptions in the data. Tables and charts are therefore centrally relevant to addressing Salt's problematic state of affairs (of accurately identifying a director's individual style). Whereas tables report actual figures, charts are designed to leave a general impression, rather than communicate exact numbers.

In the shot length distribution table (reproduced here as Figure 2.1), Salt defines shots by referring to the celluloid itself – that is, to the film strip's physical length, measured in feet. This is the most objective (the most physical) way to represent the data. Here, Salt has adopted an 'operational' definition of shot length (and other parameters of the shot). P. W. Bridgman (1927) developed operational definitions in light of Einstein's theory of relativity. Einstein transformed our understanding of previously stable values or reference points: space, time, simultaneity, length, and so on, are not absolute, but are closely linked to each individual perceiver's experience, and cannot be discussed outside the realm of experience. Bridgman argued that a concept should be synonymous with the actual physical activities or operations an individual uses to define it. 'If the concept is physical, as of length, the operations are actual physical operations, namely, those by which length is measured' (1927, 5). For example, 'When we say that space is Euclidean, we mean that the physical space of meter sticks is Euclidean' (1927, 67). The concept of length is not, therefore, definable in terms of abstract intrinsic properties, but is relative to the series of physical operations used to measure and quantify it.[2] Concepts are thereby translated into concrete operations and numerical values, which replace intrinsic properties. And the operations for measuring need to be uniquely specified in order to avoid ambiguity and overlap with other concepts. Bridgman follows the logical positivists' verifiability principle, for a concept is deemed meaningless if it is not measurable in terms of a series of operations.[3] Similarly, he follows Einstein's theory of relativity by analysing concepts in relation to the (operations performed by the) observer. An increase in the accuracy of measurement also changes the concept. Taken together, Salt's precise and systematic measurements, and his resulting quantification of different parameters of the shot, add up to create a new conception of film style.

Nonetheless, Salt's operational definition of shot length is counterintuitive. Very few film spectators or scholars handle celluloid (even in the pre-VHS and DVD days when the essay was published, in 1974); only a few people therefore know (for example) what a shot defined in terms of 8 foot of 35mm celluloid actually means. Defining shots in terms of projection time using seconds is easy to recognize. To say that a shot lasts 5 seconds is more intuitive than saying it is 8 feet long (that is, takes up 8 feet of 35mm celluloid). But this brings us closer to the 'loose assertions' that Salt is criticizing, for to use projection time as a standard of measurement is to assume that projection time is standardized. With sound films, it is standardized to 24 frames per second (sound distortion is clearly evident is a film is projected fractionally faster or slower), whereas silent films are sometimes projected at variable speeds and, because they were hand cranked, they were sometimes made at different speeds. In addition,

35mm feet	0-1	2-8	9-15	16-22	23-29	30-36	37-43	44-50	51-57	58-64	65-71	72-78	79-85	86-92	93-99	100+
THE HIRED MAN	18	720	150	24	12	6										
EROTIKON	9	561	227	31	17											
KAMERADSCHAFT	0	116	147	63	42	42	11	11	11							
THE FRONT PAGE	18	232	13	31	31	9	23	4	9	13	0	0	0	0	4	
THE BIG SLEEP	8	240	101	49	23	21	8	3	8	8	8	0	8	3		

16mm feet	0-½	1-3⅓	4-6½	7-9½	10-12½	13-15½	16-18½	19-21½	22-24½	25-27½	28-30½	31-33½	34-36½	37-39½	40-42½	43-45½	46+
HALLELUJAH	0	276	141	36	44	30	17	5	3								1
THE PUBLIC ENEMY	9	259	119	56	22	16	10	0	0	3	0	0	3	3			
LE MILLION	15	314	137	68	36	18	13	4	5	2	0	1	2	0	1		
LA CHIENNE	2	78	61	42	21	27	15	8	6	7	5	4	2	3	1	3	5
BOUDU	0	122	137	60	34	18	8	5	4	5	5	3	5	1	2	1	
TONI	2	79	53	39	17	17	12	3	15	3	11	4	3	0	0	3	4
PARTIE DE CAMPAGNE	7	171	74	43	41	21	16	16	11	2	0	2	2				4
SYLVIA SCARLETT	24	244	96	36	56	8	8	0	4	4	8	4	4				
HIS GIRL FRIDAY	16	158	50	37	30	18	11	7	9	7	0	5	9				4

Figure 2.1 Barry Salt's shot length distribution table (Salt 1974, 16) © University of California Press. Used with permission

35mm and 16mm films (the two standard widths in which films are made and distributed) cannot be compared directly; the values from one width must be translated into the other. This leads Salt to devise two separate scales for the shot length distribution table – one scale for 35mm film, one for 16mm. There is no absolute length of celluloid corresponding to the length (duration) of a shot.

Furthermore, in the shot length distribution table Salt did not represent individual values for shot lengths. Instead, he grouped together several values of shot length into 17 classes (for 16mm films).[4] Grouped data is still accurate, but less precise than ungrouped data. The shot length distribution table tells us, for example, that in the 16mm print of Renoir's *Partie de Campagne*, a total of 171 shots[5] fall within the range of 1 to 3½ feet. This is an extremely broad range, in which we find a large number of values. The film as a whole contains 397 shots, which means 43 per cent of all values are grouped together in the same class.

In summary, the shot length distribution table has to be studied carefully in order to extract useful information from it, because it is divided into two categories (16mm and 35mm films), the units measuring the data are too specialized, and those units are organized in unsatisfactory groupings. Salt soon recognized the limitations of grouping his data, for he dropped this way of representing it in subsequent research. Only when we look closely and carefully at the shot length distribution table can we discern patterns and exceptions in the data. This table does, therefore, address the essay's problematic, although in a less than ideal way. In Renoir's films, we can discern from the shot length distribution table that his four films under discussion contain a wide distribution of shot lengths. All but *Boudu* reach the end of Salt's scale (46+ feet), and the number of shots in the lower ranges (1–3½ feet and 4–6½ feet) are lower than the other films in the table.

The average shot length table (not reproduced here) simply lists films in the order they were made, and gives one statistical variable – their ASL, or average shot length (the total number of shots in a film divided by the length of the film in seconds). In Salt's sample, average shot length ranges from 4 seconds (*Battleship Potemkin* [1925]) to 21 seconds (*Le Crime de Monsieur Lange* [1936]). This means that, on average, there is a change of shot every 4 seconds in *Battleship Potemkin* and every 21 seconds in *Le Crime de Monsieur Lange*. In the Renoir sample, we would expect from the shot length distribution table that Renoir's ASL would be high. The average shot length table confirms this, with the 4 films ranging at the high end, from 14 to 19 seconds. (The film at the highest end of the scale – *Le Crime de Monsieur Lange* – is in fact another Renoir film.)

Salt's camera movement table (reproduced here as Figure 2.2) is a standard table cross-tabulating films (in rows) and six types of camera movement (in columns). Compared to the shot length distribution table, the camera movement table is easier to read, although Salt does not calculate the total percentage of shots in a film that contain movement. In Renoir's films, I have calculated from Salt's table that camera movement is used in 22–24 per cent of Renoir's shots, except *Boudu*, which has only 13.6 per cent moving shots. This compares with *The Public Enemy* (William Wellman, 1931) (19 per cent) and *Le Million* (René Clair, 1931) (5 per cent). Films can also be compared in terms of individual camera movements. Salt notes, for example, that 'the

Film	Pan	Tilt	Pan with Tilt	Track	Track with Pan	Crane
THOMAS GRAAL'S BEST FILM	0	0	0	0	0	0
THE HIRED MAN	4	7	0	10	0	0
EROTIKON	0	0	0	0	0	0
HALLELUJAH	3	0	0	3	3	0
THE PUBLIC ENEMY	36	3	3	36	18	0
KAMERADSCHAFT	61	25	12	76	51	0
LE MILLION	16	4	2	2	0	2
LA CHIENNE	45	9	3	44	17	0
BOUDU	30	1	0	7	7	0
TONI	45	8	8	23	25	0
PARTIE DE CAMPAGNE	58	12	0	23	21	0
SYLVIA SCARLETT	22	4	0	15	11	0
HIS GIRL FRIDAY	82	0	0	20	9	0
THE BIG SLEEP	77	3	1	36	64	0
THE FRONT PAGE	0	0	6	39	65	0

Figure 2.2 Barry Salt's camera movement table (Salt 1974, 18) © University of California Press. Used with permission

large number of tracks [tracking shots] in *La Chienne* must be noted [9 per cent], and the very small number (for Renoir) in *Boudu* [1.5 per cent]' (18; these figures relate to tracking shots only). The percentage of tracking shots in Renoir's four films averages out at 5 per cent.

The representation of data in charts is more visual, for it immediately reveals patterns and exceptions in the data. It also makes comparison easy. Salt uses bar charts when representing shot scale, which ranges over seven variables from big close-up to very long shot. He places 12 bar charts on the same page (not reproduced here). This enables the reader at a glance to compare the amounts of shot types distributed in a film (that is, we can identify the proportion of each shot type found in each film). It also enables us to compare shot type distribution between films.

Constructing problems

Phenomenological concepts

Salt criticizes attempts by previous auteur critics to resolve the problematic state of affairs (to identify a director's individual formal style). He argues that such attempts are based on weak intuitions – on vague impressions of a director's films usually gained from attending one or two screenings. Salt argues in particular that, when we test Andrew Sarris's impressions about a director's style, they are found to be lacking. Salt quotes Sarris's comparison of Lewis Milestone's *The Front Page* (1931) with Howard Hawks's remake *His Girl Friday* (1940):

> Hawksian fluidity of camera movement and invisibility of editing was actually faster than in Lewis Milestone's classical montage in *The Front Page*.
>
> (Sarris, quoted in Salt, 18)

Salt challenges Sarris's analysis on three counts. First, fluidity. To Sarris's claim that Hawks's camera is more fluid and faster than Milestone's, Salt responds: 'objectively [*The Front Page*] when analyzed has a far greater fluidity of camera movement' (18). When we check the tracking shots in the camera movement table, we note that *The Front Page* is listed with 39 tracking shots against *His Girl Friday*'s 20, and 65 track with pan shots against 9. (In the 'evaluating' section below, we will investigate the link between directly observable, verifiable facts such as 'the number of tracking shots in a film' and epithets such as 'fluidity'.) Second, cutting rate. To Sarris's claim that *His Girl Friday*'s editing is faster, Salt responds: '[t]he average shot length of both movies is the same' (18). The difference between the two films' cutting rates is that *The Front Page* achieves its average via a number of very short and a number of very long shots, whereas *His Girl Friday*'s cutting is more evenly distributed over the middle values. Third, classicism. Salt challenges Sarris's claim that *The Front Page* is more classical than *His Girl Friday*. The concept of 'classicism' is the bedrock in the study of Hollywood cinema, so a lot is at stake in trying to define it from a statistical point of view. In a somewhat tentative interpretation, Salt defines *His Girl Friday* as more classical because its cutting rate is more even. Salt concludes: 'Andrew Sarris is the most perceptive writer on the style of films, but the indulgence of his prejudices and his reliance on screenings only can lead him to make serious mistakes' (20).

Rather than merely watch a film a couple of times, Salt advocates that the auteur critic must examine films carefully on a viewing machine, and must note down the formal parameters of each shot. (The viewing machine is the pre-digital age's equivalent to the non-linear editing systems that professionals now use to cut films.)

Filmic concepts

Salt's essay is primarily about individual films and especially groups of films (grouped around their directors). He analyses parameters of the shot under the director's control, and determines which ones are the most useful in resolving the problematic state of affairs.

In terms of shot length distributions, Salt notes that 'a considerable similarity of overall shape is apparent' (15). He implies that the director's intentionality does not overtly influence shot length distribution. However, Salt soon revises this reading and suggests that there are small deviations from the norm, especially in the way some directors use very short shots and others (such as Renoir) tend towards long shots. This is one indication of a director's style. (As we have already seen, *The Front Page* is also notable for the way its director combines very short and very long shots.) Salt also concludes that, in conjunction with other parameters, ASL may be taken as a guide to a director's style.

In terms of shot scale, Salt concludes that 'Renoir's films are more like each other with respect to this quantity, which we shall call *closeness of shot*, than they are like other directors' films' (15). Directors such as Renoir tend to use the same distribution of shot scale in their films, giving their films a certain unity and distinguishing them from the films of other directors. In other words, frequencies of shot scale in each director's films tend to cluster into groups.

In terms of camera movement, Salt concludes that they 'do not seem, on the evidence available so far, to be so characteristic of a director's work as closeness of shot' (18). Renoir's lack of camera movement in *Boudu* in comparison to the other three films in Salt's sample partly influenced this reading.

Salt concludes by noting that combining parameters can sufficiently address and resolve the problematic state of affairs he set himself:

> At this stage it seems possible that a sufficient characterization of formal style for the films of a director might be obtained from their average shot length, plus two other distributions of numbers of shots according to types of shot (by camera closeness and movement).
>
> (21)

Meta-theoretical concepts

For Salt, research should be guided by the scientific ideals of objectivity. To achieve this ideal, the film scholar should not limit him or herself to analysing a handful of films he or she just happens to like. Instead, a large number of films (both good and bad) need to be examined and compared to one another. Ideally, the sample of films analysed should be chosen randomly.

The data collected should then be subjected to statistical analysis. Salt also subjects his data to statistical sampling, normalizing, and grouping (as well as significance tests). We have already discussed grouping. Salt samples data – he examines the first 30–40 minutes of a film (which he regards as a representative sample) (14), rather than analysing the whole film. He also normalizes his data. Shot lengths '[have] been normalized to correspond to the number there would be if the film was 90 minutes long' (14). 'The distributions of types of shots are analyzed in terms of number of each type per 500 shots' (15). Normalizing is obviously important because films are of different lengths. But why not represent all values as percentages? Salt does not formally apply significant tests to his data. He simply notes that 'differences in quantities have to be well above 10% to be significant for style considerations' (15).

Evaluating data and problems

Genuineness, correctness, and comprehensiveness

Statistical style analysis is data-driven; it privileges data over theoretical concepts. Most of Salt's paper (15–21) is taken up with a comprehensive systematizing of data and with finding patterns in it, patterns that can be attributed to the director. What is beyond doubt is the correctness and genuineness of the data, for the methods of data collection accurately reveal actual physical properties regarding the formal parameters of shots, properties that can be directly verified. Furthermore, the processes of collecting and systematizing data are spelled out and made explicit in the essay. The definition of terms follows on from the operations employed to measure them.

Salt primarily uses descriptive statistics to measure and quantify film style in order to find patterns in it, and these results are directly observable, verifiable, and repeatable by those who follow the same operations. We discover that Milestone's *The Front Page* objectively has a larger number of tracking shots than Hawks's *His Girl Friday*. But the move towards inferential statistics, which goes beyond the data, raises objections. Salt uses his statistical comparison of *The Front Page* and *His Girl Friday* to contradict Sarris's claim that Hawks's film is more fluid. Bill Nichols comments that '[t]hese assessments tend to conflate a statistical "fact" with an aesthetic impression. Frequency of camera movement does not necessarily translate into fluidity' (1985, 692). Dana Polan agrees:

> [A]s the quantitative research of Barry Salt demonstrates, there is a statistically verifiable preponderance of certain shot lengths, camera distances, etc., in Hollywood films of the 1940s. But that doesn't necessarily imply that any particular effect inherently exists in those techniques; all it literally tells us is that those techniques recur to such and such a degree. Any assignation of a particular effect to the forms will have to come either from the projections of interpretations onto form or from historical research on the ways of seeing which adhere in particular viewing situations.
>
> (Polan 1981)

Whereas the number of camera movements is a physical property in the shots, fluidity is not; it is an epithet, a quality attributed to or placed upon the physical properties of the shots, but it does not inhere in them. 'Fluidity' is not based on direct observation, but is a theoretical term used figuratively. In physics, it literally refers to the molecules in a substance moving freely among themselves. This meaning ('moving freely') is carried over from its literal meaning to characterize an experience given by camera movement in the two films. Nichols and Polan are raising objections to Salt's causal link between directly observed facts such as number of camera movements in a film and aesthetic experience. While one would expect correlation, there is no direct cause-and-effect link.

Well-formedness

The problematic of identifying a director's distinct style is well-formed and significant to the extent that auteur criticism is viable – which is still a heavily contested assumption in film studies. Salt does not simply enter the fray but takes the debate to an entirely new level of analysis and attempts to resolve it using statistics. He does not entirely resolve the issue in 'Statistical Style Analysis of Motion Pictures' – and never meant to. Instead, this essay represents the beginnings of Salt's statistical approach to auteur criticism and film form generally.

The rejection of auteur criticism would not invalidate Salt's statistical style analysis, for the data he collects on individual directors can be recontextualized into broader frameworks – to characterize the style of film genres, national cinemas, or historical periods, which Salt carried out in *Film Style and Technology*. Salt does not abandon auteur criticism in this book; he wrote a long and detailed chapter devoted to the statistical style analysis of the films of Max Ophuls. We shall review this chapter to determine if statistical style analysis of a director's films validates auteur criticism.

In a statistical style analysis of Max Ophuls's films (Salt 2009, 379–99), Salt uses standard statistical tests to analyse the distribution of stylistic parameters in each film. First, he uses bar charts to represent the number of each shot type in each film (the number of close-ups, long shots, and so on). Second, he takes equal lengths of film, calculates the expected number of shots and shot types in each section, and then counts the actual number of shots and shot types in that section, to determine if they conform to the average (the mean) or deviate from it. There are several ways to select the equal section intervals:

1. Salt recommends intervals of one minute (i.e. 100ft intervals on 35mm film).
2. If calculating shot types, one can define the intervals in terms of number of shots (e.g. 50) and calculate the expected number of shot types, and the actual number of shot types.
3. Take the ASL of the whole film, and then analyse it scene by scene (each scene is defined in terms of spatio-temporal unity and in terms of events). Work out the expected number of shots and shot types for each scene, and count the actual number of shots. If the ASL is 10 seconds, and the scene lasts 2 minutes, the expected number of shots for that scene is 12.

In his analysis of *Letter from an Unknown Woman* (1948), Salt notes the following: 'For instance, in scene 1 five shots would be expected if the cutting were even throughout every part of the film, but in fact there are only three shots. Contrariwise, in scene no. 5, while only seven shots would be expected, there are actually fourteen' (Salt 2009, 391). This type of analysis can also be applied to the expected number of shot types in each scene and the actual number of shot types. Salt's analysis of Ophuls's film *Caught* (1949) shows how this information can be useful in analysing a film's style:

> *Caught* is the first Max Ophuls film in which there is a very definite reduction in the amount of variation in Scale of Shot and cutting rate from scene to scene, and this becomes very apparent if a breakdown into 100ft sections is made on a 35mm. print. After the point in the film at which Leonora has married Smith-Ohlrig and been left alone in his mansion, we have for the next half hour of screen time very little departure from the average Scale of Shot distribution, and the cutting rate is also very steady for lengths of several minutes at a time, despite the occurrence of scenes of quite varied dramatic nature. It is only in the last 12 minutes of the film, when the most dramatic twitches of the plot take place, that there are any strong deviations from the norms.
>
> (Salt 2009, 393)

Salt is able to determine, not only how the shot lengths and scales are distributed across the whole film, but also how this film compares to Ophuls's other films ('*Caught* is the first Max Ophuls film in which there is a very definite reduction in the amount of variation in Scale of Shot and cutting rate from scene to scene'). Salt develops this historical analysis by considering Ophuls's later films, and notes that the director pares down variation in shot scale even more (relying more and more on the medium long shot), and using longer and longer takes, often combined with extensive camera movements.

For example, in *La Ronde* (1950):

> [W]ith the scene between the Young Man and The Chambermaid we get, after the first 11 shots, long strings of up to 10 shots each with the same camera distance in every shot. Most of these are also in the Medium or Medium Long Shot scale, and the film continues in the same manner after this scene. At one point there is a string of 15 consecutive close ups, which is the sort of thing that just did not happen in other people's films in the same period, as a little checking will show.
>
> (Salt 2009, 394)

This is just a fragment of Salt's long and detailed analysis of Ophuls's film, but it is sufficient to demonstrate that statistical style analysis is a very precise and accurate tool for identifying a director's norms, and for determining both the stability and the change in style that takes place across a film-maker's career. It is this systematic analysis that demonstrates the viability of auteur criticism, which needs to be carried out using statistics, according to Salt, because identifying the uniqueness of a director's style is not a simple task, as previous auteur critics assumed. Several parameters of a film's style need to be systematically quantified in order to discern any directorial patterns in the data.

Significance

In relation to expanding upon existing knowledge, Salt makes significant advances by adding a level of precision and new data that has not existed before in film studies. Salt has made film style amenable to powerful statistical analysis. He does not simply resolve traditional film studies problems concerning auteur criticism using statistics (although he does that as well), but generates new problems, methods of film analysis, and data. He creates a whole new paradigm of film study, one that follows the tradition of statistical style analysis of music, language and literature.

From these early, programmatic beginnings, Salt has continued to collect and analyse data, identify new types of data for resolving various problematic states of affairs, and devise new methods to analyse that data.

Notes

1 All quotations from this essay will be cited in the text with page numbers in parentheses.
2 In addition, measuring an object travelling at high velocity will require a different set of operations, as will measuring an extremely large or small object. Bridgman argues that a different set

of operations leads to the formulation of different concepts, for one is measuring a different kind of entity. That is, the concept of length (and other concepts, such as temperature) cannot be extended indefinitely to cover all instances of measurement.

3 For the early logical positivists, the meaning of a concept such as 'hot' is reducible to the physical sensation of hotness by an observer. For operationalists, the meaning of the concept 'hot' is reducible to the series of operations used to measure it (for example, with a thermometer). Both the logical positivists and the operationalists avoid defining temperature as a transcendental, abstract entity.

4 Except at the beginning and end, the class intervals are the same – for 16mm film, each represent values with a 2½ feet range (1–3½ feet, 4–6½ feet, and so on). The first interval is 0–½ foot and the last one is 46+. Salt therefore uses unequal class interval distributions. Because they are physically larger and therefore longer, Salt divides 35mm films into longer (6-foot) intervals.

5 The number of shots in Salt's tables are, in fact, derived figures, not raw figures, as I explain in the 'meta-theoretical concepts' section.

BETWEEN SHAKESPEARE AND SIRK

Thomas Elsaesser's 'Tales of Sound and Fury: Observations on the Family Melodrama'

> In the Hollywood melodrama characters made for operettas play out the tragedies of mankind which is how they experience the contradictions of American civilisation.
>
> (Elsaesser 1987 [1972], 67)

Problem-situation

'Tales of Sound and Fury: Observations on the Family Melodrama' was published in 1972 in number 4 of *Monogram*, the journal founded and edited by Thomas Elsaesser.[1] This essay not only took *Monogram* to a new level of analysis and sophistication; it influenced a whole generation of film scholars, demonstrating the explanatory power of historically informed criticism and Freudian psychoanalysis in the serious examination of one of the most neglected genres (at that time) in film studies – the Hollywood family melodrama. Just as Robin Wood cited Shakespearean themes in his analysis of Hitchcock's thrillers as a way of conferring legitimacy on what were perceived in the 1960s to be light entertainment films,[2] so Elsaesser cites nineteenth-century forms of European melodrama and Freudian psychoanalysis (and uses a Shakespearean title) to legitimize his study of what appeared to be one of the most frivolous and superficial genres of classical Hollywood cinema.

In *The Melodramatic Imagination*, Peter Brooks, like Elsaesser, defines melodrama as a mode of representing and imagining – a mode they independently called the 'melodramatic imagination'. For both authors, the key characteristics of melodrama are its exteriorization of inner conflict via a heightened, exaggerated visual style and rhythm, in combination with a shift of focus away from public life and duty towards domestic life, personal morals, and responsibility. To explain these characteristics of melodrama, both authors examine its historical context. For Brooks:

> The origins of melodrama can be accurately located within the context of the French Revolution and its aftermath. This is the epistemological moment which it illustrates and to which it contributes: the moment that symbolically, and really, marks the final liquidation of the traditional sacred and its representative institutions (Church and Monarch), the shattering of the

myth of Christendom, the dissolution of an organic and hierarchically cohesive society, and the invalidation of the literary forms – tragedy, comedy of manners – that depended on such a society.

(1995, 14–15)

Brooks identifies the main causes of melodrama's ascendency: the decline of the sacred in the church, monarchy, and aristocratic society – a decline which began with the Renaissance but which ended decisively after the French Revolution. The French Revolution also led to the decline of tragedy, the theatrical mode closely aligned with the sacred. Melodrama replaces the sacred with what Brooks calls the moral occult (1995, 5), the realm of underlying desires that he compares to the unconscious (a comparison central to both Brooks and Elsaesser).

For Elsaesser, the French Revolution is also key to the rise of melodrama. We can speculate that his interest in melodrama stems in part from his PhD thesis: 'A Comparative Study of Imagery in Thomas Carlyle's and Jules Michelet's Histories of the French Revolution' (University of Sussex, 1971), a thesis in Comparative Literature which was completed just one year before the publication of 'Tales of Sound and Fury'. The thesis compares and contrasts two histories of the French Revolution. It is not so much the content of these two histories that influenced 'Tales of Sound and Fury', but the way the histories were written. Both Carlyle and Michelet adopted a literary style to write vivid, dramatic narratives, and Elsaesser uses the structural methods of Roland Barthes together with Gaston Bachelard's study of imagistic energy in poetry to examine the style, structure, imagery, metaphors, and symbols the authors used to dramatize the events of the French Revolution. Carlyle begins his history by creating the metaphor of an artificial, empty, decaying vessel. This visual metaphor, Elsaesser tells us, is used by Carlyle to describe the aristocratic lifestyle, and Versailles in particular:

> this composite image relates first of all to the state of France and its monarchy under the ancien régime, as epitomized by the Court and Versailles. The aristocracy lives in 'hollow langour and vacuity' (I, 13), the reign of Louis XIV is a 'hollow phantasmagory' (I, 16), while ministerial posts 'hang vacant, one may say; extinct, like the Moon in her vacant interlunar cave' (I, 67). The King has 'unspeakable peace within doors, whatever he may have without' (I, 3).

(Elsaesser 1971, 24)[3]

Similarly, Michelet creates a vivid narrative out of the French Revolution using organic and temporal metaphors. Elsaesser analyses Michelet's history using section headings such as 'The Language of Emotion', 'Energy and Movement', and 'The Rhythm of the Revolution'. 'Michelet's metaphors', Elsaesser informs us, construct the events soon after the Revolution in terms of 'a sustained impulse of healthy, creative energy. ... [In Michelet's history,] France seems to pulsate in a regular-regulative rhythm, which promises at once a kind of material consolidation and a living unity' (1971, 300).

Michelet's narration of the storming of the Bastille is 'stylistically indebted to the "gothic horror" tradition and the historical novel' (1971, 312). 'Such scenes', Elsaesser continues, 'convey an emotional intensity which renders the new historical consciousness at once problematic, because it is experienced by "the people" in psychological rather than intellectual terms and thus is subject to all the pressures and "deformations" which Michelet's history so faithfully records' (1971, 312). In sum, Carlyle and Michelet vividly dramatize the French Revolution via visual, organic, and temporal metaphors, stylistic elements they employ to represent emotional intensity, psychological states of mind, and external pressures acting on individuals. In 'Tales of Sound and Fury', Elsaesser switches from analysing these metaphors and themes in histories of the French Revolution to analysing them in the Hollywood melodramas of the 1950s and 1960s. Elsaesser's premise behind this switch is that the nineteenth-century melodrama and Hollywood melodrama both dramatize – embody or exteriorize – a cultural/political crisis. In the nineteenth century, that crisis refers to the bourgeoisie's shaky grip on the state and society, and in Hollywood after the Second World War, middle-class suburban America's shaky grip on the nation. In other words, the crisis is, in one case, the conflict between the high ideals of the enlightenment (liberty, equality, fraternity) and the bourgeois reality of class division, social injustice, and inequality, and in the case of Hollywood, the high ideals of the American Dream, and the high cost – in terms of personal happiness and sexual emancipation – of trying to live up to them.

Analysing the problematic state of affairs

Background assumptions

The essay has a literary title that alludes to the following lines from *Macbeth*:

> … it is a tale
> Told by an idiot, full of sound and fury
> Signifying nothing.

These lines are spoken in one of the films Elsaesser analyses in his essay – *The Bad and the Beautiful* (Minnelli, 1952). The bit part actress Georgia (Lana Turner) is haunted and overshadowed by her famous but now dead actor father. When Jonathan (Kirk Douglas) visits her at 4 a.m., he plays a recording of her father reading these lines (Georgia asks him to switch it off soon after the father reads 'signifying nothing'). The high culture Shakespearean reference is embodied within the low culture Hollywood melodrama; the literary outside is represented in the mass-culture inside. In contrast to the title, the subtitle ('Observations on the Family Melodrama') is less literary and more informative, identifying the main object of investigation – the family melodrama.

After the Shakespearean title, the opening paragraph shifts registers and quotes from a Douglas Sirk interview, in which the director is asked about the colour scheme in his film *Written on the Wind* (1956). Sirk replied:

'Almost throughout the picture I used deep-focus lenses which have the effect of giving a harshness to the objects and a kind of enamelled, hard surface to the colours. I wanted this to bring out the inner violence, the energy of the characters which is all inside them and can't break through.'

(43)

For Elsaesser, this quotation encapsulates 'how closely, in this film, style and technique is related to theme' (43). The Sirk quotation and Elsaesser's comment on it reveal one set of theoretical background assumptions behind 'Tales of Sound and Fury': a traditional auteur analysis focused – as are all auteur analyses – around a particular director's distinctive visual style and thematic concerns. The problem the essay at first seems to address is very common in film criticism, and has already been covered here in Chapters 1 and 2 – the study of theme and style in the work of auteurs. Elsaesser is centrally concerned with the relationship between style and theme in Sirk's films. Yet the subtitle – in the form of the phrase 'Family Melodrama' – suggests the essay will offer a more in-depth investigation into the themes of a film genre, of which Sirk's films are a subclass. The phrase 'Family Melodrama' in fact hints at a different set of theoretical background assumptions behind the essay – it echoes Freud's term 'family romance', thereby suggesting a Freudian reading of the genre's themes. 'Tales of Sound and Fury' therefore aims to transform auteur criticism into a historically informed and psychoanalytically based genre theory, one that enables Elsaesser to speculate on the relation between films and their context. But such speculation raises important questions about whether films simply reflect the dominant psychological and social aspects of their particular historical context (as in sociological reflection theories), or whether they articulate in their own terms their context (semiotic theories). While formulating his problems in reflectionist terms, Elsaesser clearly sides with the semiotic perspective, by stressing throughout the essay that the formal dimension of film centrally contributes to the meaning of its melodramatic plot. (I take up his tension between reflectionist and semiotic models in Chapter 6, where we will see it played out in Laura Mulvey's 'Visual Pleasure and Narrative Cinema'.)

Identifying what is problematic

In the second paragraph of 'Tales of Sound and Fury' Elsaesser identifies the problematic state of affairs he is addressing and the objectives he is pursuing:

My notes want to pursue an elusive subject in two directions: to indicate the development of what one might call the melodramatic imagination across different artistic forms and in different epochs; secondly, Sirk's remark tempts one to look for some structural and stylistic constants in one medium during one particular period (the Hollywood family melodrama between roughly 1940 and 1963) and to speculate on the cultural and psychological context which this form of melodrama so manifestly reflected and helped to articulate.

(43)

Elsaesser tackles his two problematic states of affairs using different methods:

(1) The question of the melodramatic imagination's genealogy is approached through a broadly focused historical analysis that emphasizes change and transformation.
(2) The question of film melodrama's structural and stylistic constants is approached through a narrowly focused, theoretical inquiry into genre.

The first problematic state of affairs, the broad study of the 'melodramatic imagination', is described as elusive, no doubt due to its abstract, conceptual status, and because it has not previously been studied in any depth in film studies. What more can be said about the relation between style and theme, or how characters' interior states of mind are expressed in film style? Elsaesser's primary innovation is to graft the concept of the melodramatic imagination onto this traditional issue in film studies. Rather than abandon the study of style and theme in film, Elsaesser digs deeper: from a comparative perspective, he begins to draw parallels between film melodrama and the history of the European novel and drama, in which individual heroes internalize class conflicts and turn them into personal struggle. He also speculates on the influence of Freudian psychoanalysis on the Hollywood film melodrama, although he draws back from proclaiming any direct influence (59).

The second problematic state of affairs the essay addresses – the specific, focused study of melodrama's structural and stylistic constants – is generated by a property of the data (the colour scheme of *Written on the Wind*), but is not limited to the data. In other words, the essay promises more than a traditional auteur analysis of one of Sirk's films. In the *Brighton Film Review* and *Monogram*, Elsaesser wrote traditional auteur analyses of directors such as Nicholas Ray and Sam Fuller. But from 'Tales of Sound and Fury' onwards, his methods and problems became more general and theoretical.[4]

Describing the problematic state of affairs

Collecting data

One central dimension of film genre criticism is precisely the collecting of data to be classified, correlated, ordered, and measured, and then systematized into a genre or universe of genres, without distorting the data. Elsaesser's primary source of data derives from canonical literary and dramatic texts from Europe, and half a dozen melodramas from Hollywood. There is a clear bifurcation of the essay's direction (signified in the title's Shakespearean overtones and the first paragraph's quotation of Sirk): historical European high culture versus contemporary American mass culture. Justifying their juxtaposition is going to be a fundamental rhetorical strategy of 'Tales of Sound and Fury'. In *The Bad and the Beautiful*, Elsaesser discovered the high culture European discourse embedded in the low culture Hollywood melodrama. This is the strategy he follows throughout the essay.[5]

Elsaesser cites a large number of films in passing (by D. W. Griffith, Vincente Minnelli, Nicholas Ray, Hitchcock, as well as other Hollywood auteurs not specifically associated with the melodrama – from Hawks, Ford, Preminger, Anthony Mann, to Raoul Walsh). He analyses a handful of films in detail: Sirk's *Written on the Wind*, Minnelli's *The Bad and the Beautiful* and *Home from the Hill* (1960), and John Cromwell's *Since You Went Away* (1944).

Written on the Wind epitomizes the Hollywood family melodrama. Elsaesser refers to it several times, not just in the quotation from the interview with Sirk, but also to analyse its *mise en scène*. The film's opening scene (repeated at the end) shows a yellow and chrome sports car driving up to the Hadley mansion, whose Doric columns are made out of stucco plaster. This high angle long shot creates 'a tension of correspondences and dissimilarities in the same image, which perfectly crystallises the decadent affluence and melancholic energy that give the film its uncanny fascination' (53). The same driveway is used again in another scene showing a black servant removing from the front gate a black and green funeral wreath. The camera follows a black ribbon as it falls off the wreath and is blown along the concrete driveway towards the house, where Lauren Bacall, wearing a green dress, looks out of the window. The contrast in texture and materials create an emotional resonance in the scene:

> the colour parallels black/black, green/green, white concrete/white lace curtains provide an extremely strong emotional resonance in which the contrast of soft silk blown along the hard concrete is registered the more forcefully as a disquieting visual association. The desolation of the scene transfers itself onto the Bacall character, and the traditional fatalistic association of the wind remind us of the futility implied in the movie's title.
>
> (53)

Elsaesser also comments on Robert Stack – his anguished voice, the visual composition of his tormented body against a half open window as his wife tells him she is pregnant (after a doctor tells him he is apparently sterile), his drink problem, moments of pathos (when he talks at cross-purposes with his wife). Finally, *Written on the Wind* is also an 'objective' film, that is, it is based on omniscient narration, as it follows several characters, rather than just one.

The Bad and the Beautiful uses décor to express a character's inner turmoil. Elsaesser demonstrates that melodrama creates a rhythm, an extreme clash of emotions from a high point – producer Kirk Douglas discovers Lana Turner, turns her into a star – to extreme low point immediately afterwards, when he rejects her advances on the night of the successful premiere of her first film, leading to her nervous breakdown as she drives away: 'Her nervous breakdown in the car is conveyed by headlights flashing her windscreen like a barrage of footlights and arc-lamps' (60).

Since You Went Away contains an exemplary scene articulating the melodrama's charged relation between décor and character. A historical period of crisis (the Second World War) creates a psychological conflict for the film's heroine. Claudette Colbert is left alone at home after her husband goes to war. The house becomes unbearable to her because it contains objects reminding her of her husband's presence. These everyday objects take on symbolic significance that force repressed emotions to the surface: 'Pressure is generated by things crowding in on [characters] and life becomes increasingly complicated because cluttered with obstacles and objects that invade their personalities, take them over, stand for them, become more real than the human relations or emotions they were intended to symbolise' (62).

The final example discussed in detail is *Home from the Hill*. Rather than focus on individual scenes, Elsaesser analyses its overall plot, and discovers that it is 'structured as a series of mirror-reflections on the themes of fathers and sons, blood ties and natural affinities' (63), but centred on a sensitive adolescent's conflict with his father and upbringing by a hypochondriac mother.

Systematizing data *(classifying, correlating, ordering, and measuring)*

As a study of genre, 'Tales of Sound and Fury' uses classification as a central tool to organize itself as an essay. Genres are classified according to structural and stylistic constants, which Elsaesser studies from a historical perspective. His general concern is to investigate the genealogy of the 'melodramatic imagination' in the novel (especially the eighteenth- and nineteenth-century sentimental novel), various forms of drama (especially the romantic drama), the ballad, street songs, and the opera in England, France, Germany, and Italy between the late medieval period and the early twentieth century (44–45). This broad historical analysis is covered in a condensed opening section called 'How to Make Stones Weep' (43–50) (a heading that would not look out of place in Michelet's history of the French Revolution). Rather than beginning with the French Revolution, this historical section instead identifies the following seven melodramatic traits across artistic practices both before and after the revolution (the first four are pre-revolutionary, the remaining three are post-revolutionary):

- The pre-revolutionary sentimental novel (Richardson's *Clarissa*, Rousseau's *Nouvelle Héloise*) expresses private feelings and interiorized codes of morality (45).
- These private, interior feelings express ideological conflicts, such as class antagonism (46).
- The pre-revolutionary sentimental novel depicts extreme forms of behaviour and feeling, identifying the cause as external constraints placed upon characters (45).
- These novels 'record the struggle of a morally and emancipated bourgeois consciousness against the remnants of feudalism' (45).
- Whereas pre-revolutionary melodramas have tragic endings, the post-revolutionary melodramas have happy endings, for they were able to reconcile the individual to his social position (46).
- The nineteenth-century novel in France (Hugo, Sue, Balzac) and in England (Dickens) combined social reality with melodramatic plots (48–49).
- Dostoyevsky manifested timeless themes – guilt, redemption, justice, innocence, freedom – through melodramatic scenes, while Kafka's novels contain comic and tragically absurd melodramatic scenes centred on family life (50).

64

In addition, we discover other traits used to classify melodrama: in its dictionary definition, 'melodrama is a dramatic narrative in which musical accompaniment marks the emotional effects' (50); melodrama is ambiguous (for it functions either as subversive social and political commentary, or as mere escapism); it is ironic (for it presents a conflict between the moral message and the form in which it is manifest), and expresses 'a particular, historically and socially conditioned *mode of experience*' (49). It does not conform to the genre conventions of realism and naturalism, but is not inferior to them, because it constitutes a complex signifying system with its own history and rich system of genre codes, populated with individual heroes who interiorize conflict and turn it into a personal struggle.

Elsaesser tackles his second question – to identify and classify 'some structural and stylistic constants in one medium during one particular period (the Hollywood family melodrama between roughly 1940 and 1963)' (43) – in the following two sections, 'Putting Melos into Drama' (50–58) and 'Where Freud left his Marx in the American Home' (58–68). In 'Putting Melos into Drama' he argues that while Hollywood melodramas share structural and stylistic constants with previous forms of melodrama, they also present a distinct articulation of the melodramatic mode. He delineates Hollywood's post-Second World War film melodramas in terms of expressive, formal, and structural features of *mise en scène*. These constants serve as the organizing principles behind the data, the underlying traits that confer unity on a series of films within a delimited space and time.

As well as classifying the traits of melodrama, Elsaesser correlates traits from nineteenth-century forms of melodrama to Hollywood films. The traits therefore carry over from one tradition to the other. More specifically, he constructs a historical argument suggesting that many of these structural and stylistic constants can be found equally in nineteenth-century European melodrama and in Hollywood films, implying that both manifest the melodramatic imagination. This historical dimension to his argument offers a plausible explanation for the occurrence of these constants, the historical conditions of their possibility. It also offers a context in which to justify the study of Hollywood melodramas – they are not merely superficial forms of escapist entertainment, for they have roots in European traditions. In addition, Elsaesser argues that the predominance of Freudian psychoanalysis in post-Second World War American culture also influenced the form and themes of the Hollywood family melodrama. From his historical perspective, Elsaesser constructs a system of structural and stylistic constants that define the genre of the Hollywood family melodrama (although it is unclear whether he thinks all of these properties are necessary and sufficient to define this genre). The results are discussed in 'filmic concepts' below.

Constructing problems

Phenomenological concepts

In terms of phenomenological concepts, Elsaesser mentions the 'raw' experience of the melodramatic film: 'when in ordinary language we call something melodramatic, what we often mean is an exaggerated rise-and-fall pattern in human actions and emotional responses, a from-the-sublime-to-the-ridiculous movement, a foreshortening of lived time in favour of intensity – all of which produces a graph of much greater fluctuation, a quicker swing from one extreme to the other than is considered natural, realistic or in conformity with literary standards of verisimilitude' (52). Elsaesser aims to go beyond this experience and explain its occurrence by identifying melodrama's constants, and by arguing that melodrama creates its own specific mode of experience, based on upheaval: Dickens's novels create discontinuity, for they emphasize the 'fissures and ruptures in the fabric of experience' (48), while the film melodramas create a similar experience by compressing long novels into standard feature-length films (especially in the films of Minnelli and Sirk).

Filmic concepts

In terms of filmic concepts, Elsaesser formulates a number of propositions concerning silent films and the function of musical accompaniment that punctuates the silent action, orchestrating the audience's emotional reaction (50–52), before examining the Hollywood family melodrama. In the section 'Putting Melos into Drama', he classifies what he considers to be the dominant structural and stylistic constants of family melodramas made between 1940 and 1963:

- The characters' central dramatic conflicts – or inexpressible internal contradictions – are not externalized as action (as in the Western and *film noir*), but remain internalized, unreconciled, and sublimated 'into décor, colour, gesture and composition of frame, which in the best melodramas is perfectly thematised in terms of the characters' emotional and psychological predicaments' (52).
- This perpetual internalization of inexpressible contradictions leads to 'a conscious use of style as meaning' (54). (The perpetual internalization of inexpressible contradictions also leads to masochistic tendencies of self-pity and self-hatred in the characters – usually in the form of alcoholism [65]).
- The family melodrama 'records the failure of the protagonist to act in a way that could shape the events and influence the emotional environment … : they emerge as lesser human beings for having become wise and acquiescent to the ways of the world' (55).
- The melodramas of Ray, Sirk, and Minnelli deal with 'an intensified symbolism of everyday actions, the heightening of the ordinary gesture and a use of setting and décor so as to reflect the characters' fetishist fixations' (56).

Elsaesser continues this delineation in the essay's third and final section, 'Where Freud Left his Marx in the American Home' (58–68), where he focuses specifically on the influence of Freud on American culture, and Hollywood in particular:[6]

- Gothic romances (or 'Freudian feminist melodrama in the 1940s') show the direct influence of Freud. They depict a persecuted wife plagued by 'strange fantasies of persecution, rape and death' (58) revolving around her husband, who she imagines (or discovers) to be a sadist and murderer. These brief comments inspired Mary Ann Doane's formulation of the 'paranoid woman's film' (1987, 123–54).

- Freud's dream logic of condensation and displacement, latent dream content and manifest dream, can be seen at work in the melodrama: 'certain stylistic and structural features of the sophisticated melodrama may involve principles of symbolisation and coding which Freud conceptualised in his analysis of dreams' (59).
- Parapraxis (or slips of the tongue that manifest inner states of mind). Although not developed in any detail in 'Tales of Sound and Fury' (it is simply mentioned in passing on page 59), this concept took on greater significance in Elsaesser's later work.

This section of 'Tales of Sound and Fury' links up directly with Elsaesser's PhD thesis, particularly the final sections. Influenced by Bachelard and by psychoanalysis, Elsaesser analyses Michelet's account of the unconscious 'energies' and 'forces' unleashed by the French Revolution. Michelet locates these forces in the French people, prompting Elsaesser to explore a psychoanalytic reading of Michelet's history:

> [I am] tempted to investigate Michelet's imagery 'psychoanalytically', rather than to explore it as a controlling artistic device. For at least superficially, the quality which I have mentioned falls into the realm of psychology, designated by such concepts as voyeurism, hypnotic fascination, psycho-pathology, dream-world and nightmare, skoptophilia, vicarious participation and identification – in short, the analysis of 'abnormal' perception.
>
> (1971, 387)

In Elsaesser's reading, this unconscious energy is one of the key elements in Michelet's history, and it migrates into 'Tales of Sound and Fury' in its characterization of melodrama, described less in terms of Bachelard's imagistic energy and more overtly in psychoanalytic terms. 'Tales of Sound and Fury' is therefore important because of its innovative use, in 1972 (three years before Laura Mulvey's influential 'Visual Pleasure and Narrative Cinema'), of Freudian psychoanalysis to analyse the textual structure and underlying themes of a film genre. Elsaesser uses the concept of unconscious, repressed energy to explain how inexpressible internal contradictions become sublimated into the melodrama's setting and décor:

> Melodramas often use middle-class American society, its iconography and the family experience … as their manifest 'material', but 'displace' it into quite different patterns, juxtaposing stereotyped situations in strange con-figurations, provoking clashes and ruptures which not only open up new associations but also redistribute the emotional energies which suspense and tensions have accumulated in disturbingly different directions.
>
> (59–60)

Finally, in this third and final section of 'Tales of Sound and Fury', Elsaesser continues to delineate additional characteristics of the family melodrama:

- The plots of melodramas have a distinct rhythm: 'A typical situation in American melodramas has the plot build up to an evidently catastrophic collision of counter-running sentiments, but a string of delays gets the greatest possible effect from the clash when it does come' (60).
- Extreme dramatic discontinuity (or dramatic reversal), in combination with pressure exerted on characters (60–61) (as in the example from *The Bad and the Beautiful*, mentioned above).
- Minnelli and Sirk in particular are skilful at making multi-protagonist films (62).
- Set in a small town, a suburb and/or a claustrophobic home (62).
- The plot can either be 'objective' (with no central hero, but an ensemble of characters). or 'subjective' (it emanates from a single consciousness) (63).
- Family melodramas 'concentrate on the point of view of the victim' (64).
- 'In Minnelli, Sirk, Ray, Cukor and others, alienation is recognised as a basic condition, fate is secularised into the prison of social conformity and psychological neurosis, and the linear trajectory of self-fulfillment so potent in American ideology is twisted into the downward spiral of a self-destructive urge seemingly possessing a whole social class' (64–65).
- Family melodramas manifest irony or pathos: 'Irony privileges the spectator vis-à-vis the protagonists' (in other words, irony is created by means of omniscient narration); 'Pathos results from non-communication or silence made eloquent ... where highly emotional situations are underplayed to present an ironic discontinuity of feeling or a qualitative difference in intensity, usually visualised in terms of spatial distance and separation' (66).

While most of these observations highlight formal and stylistic aspects of film melodrama, Elsaesser concludes on a more reflectionist note, arguing that characters in Hollywood family melodramas experience the impossible contradictions of the American dream, with the result that these films 'record some of the agonies that have accompanied the demise of the "affirmative culture"' (68).

'Tales of Sound and Fury' is therefore dominated by filmic concepts relating to the structural and stylistic constants of the melodrama, backed up with several examples. Cinematic concepts do not play a significant role in 'Tales of Sound and Fury'.

Meta-theoretical concepts

In terms of meta-theoretical concepts, we have already discovered under the section 'analysing the problematic state of affairs' that Elsaesser pursues his problem – the 'elusive subject' of the melodramatic imagination – in two directions: a general investigation and a focused, delimited investigation. He immediately adds a few meta-theoretical comments: his study is not historical in any strict sense of the term, nor is it exhaustive in its breadth due to the unavailability of the films (back in the pre-video and pre-DVD days of film studies). He therefore delimits his research, by indicating that he will develop a general theoretical argument on the basis of the close viewing of half a dozen films, but especially *Written on the Wind*. His own understanding of these delimitations is twofold: 'it is difficult to see how references to twenty more movies would make the argument any truer. For better or worse, what I want to say should at this stage be taken to be provocative rather than proven' (43). He implies that his argument is to some extent driven by the data, and that the data at this stage is sufficient for supporting the truth conditions of his theoretical hypotheses. But, at the same time, he acknowledges that his theoretical hypotheses (like all hypotheses) are defeasible in nature, alterable upon the discovery of additional data (the viewing of additional films).

The defeasible nature of Elsaesser's argument is most clearly expressed in the tentative way he states his hypotheses and conclusions – which are not logically entailed in the propositions of the argument, but are always open to revision. Elsaesser's tentative stance is expressed in his use of hedges (adverbs and auxiliary verbs that modify the knowledge claims stated in the propositions of the argument). On one single page we find the following hedges (in italics):

> Even if the form *might* act to reinforce attitudes of submission, the actual working-out of the scenes *could* nonetheless present fundamental social evils.
>
> All of this is to say that there *seems* a radical ambiguity attached to the melodrama.
>
> [M]elodrama *would appear* to function either subversively or as escapism.
>
> The persistence of melodrama *might* indicate ...
>
> (47).

In sum, his propositions and conclusions are not meant to be universally true. Instead, they are probable and acceptable according to whether they explain the evidence, and whether they constitute solutions to problems.

Evaluating data and problems

Genuineness, correctness, and comprehensiveness

'Tales of Sound and Fury' presents a small, select number of positive instances of Hollywood melodramas. The analyses are not merely examples that are dropped once a theoretical point is made. Instead, the essay leads up to the analyses, which describe the films in accurate terms – although on occasion infused with numerous adjectives and adverbs. For example, Elsaesser's analysis of the opening scene of *Written on the Wind*, quoted above, describes an image 'which *perfectly* crystallises the *decadent* affluence and *melancholic* energy that give the film its *uncanny* fascination' (53; emphases added). In terms of the four analyses listed above (under the heading 'collecting data'), the theory is not simply restated, but is made to work through the films in order to reveal their meanings. We gain a new perspective on the films, one that justifies their

69

apparent superficiality. That is, 'Tales of Sound and Fury' generates new knowledge as we learn of the significance behind the excesses in the scenes or plots analysed, the unconscious energy that drives the films and their characters. We are also presented with different types of analysis – *mise en scène* analysis of key dramatic scenes (*Written on the Wind, The Bad and the Beautiful, Since You Went Away*), analysis of non-dramatic scenes (the funeral wreath in *Written on the Wind*), or plot analysis of entire films (*Home on the Hill*). The theory is therefore demonstrated to work at different levels. And although the essay still manifests an auteurist inflection, it presents positive instances from several different directors, thereby locating the melodramatic elements in genre, not a single auteur's vision.

Well-formedness

'Tales of Sound and Fury' demonstrates that Hollywood family melodramas certainly do not signify nothing, nor do they consist of tales told by an idiot. Elsaesser successfully established melodrama as a significant and worthwhile object of study in film studies, via a dual historical and theoretical analysis. The rich and detailed historical analysis (partly represented in bullet points in 'systematizing data', above) placed film studies within the context of traditional humanities scholarship, on a more serious level than auteurism could achieve. And the theoretical study of film melodrama's structural and stylistic constants (partly represented in bullet points in 'filmic concepts', above) demonstrated its complex structure and its manifestation of the traits found in European forms of melodrama. Just like the scene from *The Bad and the Beautiful* with which I began, 'Tales of Sound and Fury' reveals European culture to be embedded in Hollywood melodrama.

It is via the lenses of history and theory that Elsaesser formulated a well-formed problem: how and why the melodramatic imagination occurs in the structure and style of a specific Hollywood genre, and how and why its *mise en scène* manifests a character's inexpressible internal contradictions. Elsaesser also helped to legitimize Freudian psychoanalysis as a theory and method of film analysis, mainly by demonstrating that it can account for the unusual textual structure of the Hollywood family melodrama, and generate knowledge on a deeper level than thematic criticism to solve problematic states of affairs.

Significance

As well as formulating a well-formed problem, Elsaesser also formulated a significant problem, one that influenced a whole generation of film scholars, ensuring that 'Tales of Sound and Fury' became a classic reference point for all subsequent studies of film melodrama. Christine Gledhill writes in her anthology on film melodrama:

> Thomas Elsaesser's 'Tales of Sound and Fury' (1972) was the earliest, and remains the most comprehensive, account of film melodrama, attempting to

come to terms not only with the melodramatic nature of Hollywood aesthetics, but with the place of cinema in the total field of European melodramatic forms.

(Gledhill 1987, 7–8)

'Tales of Sound and Fury' became a significant essay because it helped to shift the focus of film studies away from the study of a director's worldview/personal vision and towards the influence on film of cultural and historical modes (such as Western culture's historically distinct forms of melodrama). Elsaesser notes that: 'The auteurs were one polarity of the dialectic: the other was the effort to read the American cinema as symptomatic, as registering the Zeitgeist, the shifts in the cultural history, the rendering explicit of the mass-media unconscious' (Elsaesser 2012).

'Tales of Sound and Fury' forms part of Elsaesser's larger agenda, to take Hollywood seriously – not only through auteurism, but also structuralism, genre study, historical analysis, and psychoanalysis. Melodramas created a problem for auteur critics, because they are full of excess, which challenges any reading of them in terms of aesthetic coherence. But within the psychoanalytically based genre criticism, melodramatic excess can be reclassified as a generic trait.

The essay also made possible the discovery and analysis of a broad array of Hollywood melodramas, since many scholars, such as Pam Cook, pointed out that 'Tales of Sound and Fury' was not a study of the melodrama 'as such', for it only considered a small selection of 'sophisticated' melodramas made by well-known directors, those who were able to create a critical perspective on American society of the 1950s (Cook 1991, 249). 'Tales of Sound and Fury' is not a feminist study of the representation of women in the cinema, nor was it written as one. But it gave feminist film scholars the historical and theoretical framework to seriously study the 'woman's film', a subcategory of the melodrama that privileges the perspective of women. Study of the woman's film became a significant part of a larger debate devoted to the representation of women in the cinema, a debate we examine in Chapter 6.

Notes

1 Thomas Elsaesser, 'Tales of Sound and Fury: Observations on the Family Melodrama'. In: *Monogram*, No. 4, 1972, 4–15. For ease of reference, I shall quote from the version of the essay published in *Home is Where the Heart Is: Studies in Melodrama and the Woman's Film*, edited by Christine Gledhill. London: British Film Institute 1987, 43–69. All quotations from this essay will be cited in the text in parentheses.

2 Robin Wood begins his 1965 book on Hitchcock with the sentence 'Why should we take Hitchcock seriously?' (1965, 9) and references Shakespeare throughout the introduction.

3 All the internal quotes are from Thomas Carlyle's *History of the French Revolution*.

4 Elsaesser's two-part essay on Vincente Minnelli, first published in the *Brighton Film Review* in 1970 (and republished in Elsaesser 2012, 8), is more of a transitional essay between standard auteur criticism and the semiotic-structuralist study of genre.

5 We need to keep in mind that the European culture is already in the films from the start, in the form of the European émigré directors such as Sirk who directed many of the melodramas analysed in 'Tales of Sound and Fury'.

6 Brooks argues that psychoanalysis is the modern fulfilment of melodrama:

> That psychoanalysis has so many points of analogy to melodrama is of course not surprising, it is almost tautological in that our psychic lives are full of melodrama, and our study of melodrama immediately suggested that the form exteriorized a world within. ... What we have called 'the moral occult', the locus of intense ethical forces from which man feels himself cut off, yet which he feels to have a real existence somewhere behind or beyond the façade of reality, and which exerts influence on his secular existence, stands as an abyss or gulf whose depths must, cautiously and with risk, be sounded. ... If melodrama can reach through this abyss behind, bring its overt irruption into existence, it has accomplished part of the work of psychoanalysis.
>
> (1995, 202)

FROM ICONICITY TO SEMIOTIC ARTICULATION

Christian Metz's 'Cinema: Language or Language System?' and *Language and Cinema*

When approaching the cinema from the linguistic point of view, it is difficult to avoid shuttling back and forth between two positions: the cinema as a language; the cinema as infinitely different from verbal language. Perhaps it is impossible to extricate oneself from this dilemma with impunity.

(Metz 1974a, 44)

Problem-situation

Twentieth-century theory and philosophy are marked by a shift from idealist philosophy to the language analysis tradition (see Apel 1976). The structural linguist Ferdinand de Saussure and the American semiotician C. S. Peirce initiated a radical critique of Descartes' and Kant's philosophy of the subject, in which language and signs replaced mental entities as the locus of knowledge. Language analysis therefore rejects idealism, transforming its 'first person perspective' (focus on private mental events, as in Descartes' method of introspection) to the public, 'third person perspective' of language and signs. The problem with introspection, writes Thomas Daddesio, is that 'it was perceived as being unable to provide the objective, repeatable observations that science requires' (1995, 49). Prior to the language analysis tradition, philosophers believed that mental processes founded knowledge (including self-knowledge). 'However', Daddesio adds, 'once this privilege came to be viewed as illusory, introspection was replaced by methods relying on a third-person perspective. From this new perspective, the access individuals have to their own thoughts could no longer be taken as the foundation for knowledge and, consequently, private events were replaced, in discussions of language, meaning, and reason, by events that were open to public scrutiny such as the behavior of others, the words they utter, and the uses to which they put words' (1995, 50). The language analysts' assumption of indirect access to one's thoughts via language and other intersubjective sign systems replaced the idealists' assumption of immediate access to the thoughts in one's own mind.

In the late 1950s cognitive processes made a decisive return *within* the language analysis tradition, beginning with Noam Chomsky's transformational generative grammar (together with his decisive critique of B. F. Skinner's behaviourism). In the form of

Chomsky's linguistics, the language analysis tradition created a synthesis of both idealism and the intersubjective nature of language, thus (in principle at least) avoiding the idealism and first-person perspective and the (quasi) behaviourism of the language analysts' third-person perspective.

This history of twentieth-century theory is reflected in film theory, particularly in the shift from 'classical film theory' (of Arhheim, Bazin, and so on) to 'classical film semiotics' (the early research of Christian Metz, based on structural linguistics) and finally to 'cognitive film semiotics', influenced by Chomsky and cognitive science generally (the research of Dominique Chateau, Michel Colin, Francesco Casetti, and Roger Odin). This chapter outlines the foundations of semiotics, summarizes its institutional context, rationally reconstructs the basic tenets of classical film semiotics, and examines the arguments of a number of its critics (particularly Gregory Currie), before ending on an overview of cognitive film semiotics.

The institutional context of semiotics

Niilo Kauppi (1993) has written a detailed history of the institutional context in which linguistics and semiotics emerged in France in the 1950s. He shows that there were two simultaneous forces shaping French universities during this time: (1) the rapid expansion of higher education, which allowed for the setting up of new university departments, which distinguished themselves from other departments by teaching novel subjects such as semiotics; and (2) the decline of some traditional areas of research, such as Romance philology, history of the French language, and lexicology. Kauppi notes that in the 1950s both Roland Barthes and A. J. Greimas initially worked in lexicology, but were unable to obtain funding. Both, therefore, had to expand their research interests in order to encompass more novel and dynamic subjects such as anthropology, which was well funded partly due to the influence of Lévi-Strauss. To accommodate the rapid increase in university departments, new journals and book series were published. Like the departments they addressed, these new publishing ventures had to distinguish themselves from traditional university research, either by applying novel theories to traditional French culture (Derrida on Rousseau, Barthes on Racine and Michelet), or by combining novel theories with novel subject matter (Barthes's *Mythologies*).

Kauppi also points out that the institutions that introduced semiotics into the university were marginal to the French university system. It was in the Sixth Section of the École Pratique des Hautes Études where semiotics originated in France. This school is unique in that it does not give awards to its students. It therefore attracts students by distinguishing itself from other, more established institutions (such as the University of Paris) by placing itself at the vanguard of intellectual development, functioning primarily as a research institution. It attracts the most innovative researchers to its staff and, uniquely, acts as an intermediary between academics and artists, particularly avant-garde artists. As Kauppi points out, 'in the 1950s the faculty of the Sixth Section included names like Lévi-Strauss, Fernand Braudel, Lucien Febvre, and in the 1960s in semiotics, Barthes, Greimas, Christian Metz as Barthes's assistant,

Barthes's student Gérard Genette, Oswald Ducrot, and Louis Marin' (1993, 190). It is precisely from this innovative context that semiotics emerged in France in the late fifties. The École Pratique also publishes its own journal, *Communications*. It is in this journal that Metz presented much of his most important research, including his essay 'Cinéma: langue ou langage?' (*Communications* 4, 1964), the first version of his *grande syntagmatique* ('La Grande Syntagmatique du Film Narratif', *Communications* 8, 1966), and his essay 'Le signifiant imaginaire' (*Communications* 23, 1975).

We now turn to the activities involved in formulating theoretical problems in two canonical texts by Metz: his essay 'Cinema: Language or Language System?' (published in French in 1964; English translation in Metz 1974a, 31–91), and his book *Language and Cinema* (published in French in 1971; English translation – Metz 1974b). We shall begin with 'Cinema: Language or Language System?'

Analysing the problematic state of affairs

Background assumptions

What type of inquiry is semiotics? What role does linguistic theory play in its study of film? Is there any justification for using semiotics to study an iconic medium such as film? And how does film semiotics analyse, describe, construct, and evaluate problems?

The very idea of 'film language' for film semioticians is not a simple analogy (as it was in the pre-linguistic film-language comparisons of Raymond Spottiswoode, the Filmology movement, and so on), but suggests that film is an intersubjective, coded medium like natural language, and possesses a specific, autonomous, underlying system – again, as does natural language. In principle (if not always in practice), the semioticians' claim that film is a language was therefore made, not through any direct resemblance between film and natural language, but on methodological grounds: film's specific, underlying reality could be reconstructed by the methods of structural linguistics. At least from this methodological viewpoint, film semioticians were justified in using structural linguistics to study film because this discipline is the most sophisticated for analysing a discourse's underlying reality.

As well as offering the most sophisticated method for analysing underlying codes, the work of Ferdinand de Saussure (his *Course in General Linguistics*, first published in 1916, the foundational text of structural linguistics [Saussure 1983]) also enabled linguistics to become an autonomous discipline. For Saussure linguistics can only become autonomous when it identifies and studies a specific object (or dimension of language – *la langue* for Saussure), an object which is not studied by other disciplines, and which can be studied from the 'third person' perspective. Like Saussure, Metz argued that film studies could only become an autonomous discipline by adopting a methodology that studied the irreducible specificity of film (cinematic language).

Structural linguistics and semiotics construct hypotheses and models, founded on the hierarchy between underlying (latent, non-observable) reality and surface (manifest, observable) reality. Structural linguistics is founded on the hierarchy between *langue/parole*, and its ultimate objective is to construct a model of *la langue*.

Some of the concepts semiotics developed to model *la langue* include articulation, arbitrariness, recursivity, language as speech circuit, commutation, plus syntagmatic and paradigmatic relations. These concepts are important because Metz used them to construct his semiotic theory of film.

The concept of articulation is fundamental to structuralism and semiotics. In anatomy and biology, articulation designates 'connection (of bones or skeletal segments) by a joint' (OED). The OED lists a figurative meaning deriving from this anatomical meaning: '*fig.* A conceptual relationship, interaction, or point of juncture, esp. *between* two things'. Articulation also refers to the distinct, basic elements ('signs') that are joined. 'Articulation' therefore refers to the joining together of basic elements, or signs, following rules of combination to create new messages.

In contrast, a non-articulated sign has a direct (iconic) relation to what it represents. Each particular aspect of reality or experience has a corresponding sign. This is an uneconomical, cumbersome way to communicate, for it leads to the proliferation of a long list of signs. Language does not consist of a long list of non-articulated signs, but of a small number of articulated signs organized as a hierarchal system:

> We might imagine a system of communication in which a special cry would correspond to each given situation or fact of experience. But if we think of the infinite variety of such situations and these facts of experience, it will be clear that if such a system were to serve the same purpose as our languages, it would have to comprise so large a number of distinct signs that the memory of man would be incapable of storing it. A few thousand of such units as *tête, mal, ai, la*, freely combinable, enable us to communicate more things than could be done by millions of unarticulated cries.
>
> (Martinet 1964, 23)

Making a message more nuanced or original does not involve the invention of new signs, but the combination of more pre-existing signs into a specific order, or the unusual manipulation of these signs (as in poetry). From a structural-semiotic perspective, language is defined as a finite system of pre-existing signs.

André Martinet argues that language is organized as a double-levelled or doubly articulated system (1964, 22–24). The first articulation involves the minimally meaningful units, where there is a correlation between signifier and signified, creating a sign (Martinet calls these minimally meaningful signs 'monemes'). These monemes in turn are composed of non-signifying significant units (phonemes), which constitute the second level of articulation: 'Thanks to the second articulation language can make do with a few dozen distinct phonic products which are combined to achieve the vocal form of the units of the first articulation' (Martinet 1964, 24).[1] Meaning is generated from the recursive combination of the small number of phonemes to generate a large number of monemes, and the recursive combination of monemes to generate a potentially infinite number of sentences. Double articulation therefore accounts for the extraordinary economy of language, and is, according to Martinet, language's unique, defining characteristic (1964, 22). And because the phonemes on the second level have no direct relation to meaning, then meaning is generated from the inter-relations between phonemes rather than from what they signify. The phonemes are autonomous from reality (they do not 'reflect' reality, but are arbitrary); meaning emerges out of non-meaning – from the selection and combination of phonemes into monemes, rather than simply reflecting a pre-existing meaning.

Saussure delimited the specific object of linguistic study – *la langue* – by the metaphor of speech as a circuit, as Roy Harris explains: 'The *Cours* is the first treatise on language to insist that speech communication is to be viewed as a "circuit," and to attach any theoretical significance to the fact that individuals linked by this circuit act in turn as initiators of spoken messages and as recipients of such messages' (1987, 24–25). The metaphor 'speech circuit' enabled Saussure to conceive of a language as an intersubjective (or social) system of communication.

To study a language as a system of communication, Saussure developed a deductive method to analyse the 'invisible' boundaries within the continuous speech chain, boundaries that confer meaning upon the signs in this chain. This method consisted of the activities of segmentation and classification, which were carried out by means of the commutation test. This test enables linguists to identify the boundaries of a sign. In principle, a commutation involves the correlation between a change on the surface level with a change on the underlying level. A change on the surface may either be a variation of the same sign or a new sign. By means of commutation, linguists are able to identify the changes on the surface level that correlate with the changes on the underlying level.

Before Martinet developed his theory of double articulation, Saussure described *la parole* as an infinitude of manifestations generated by *la langue*, which is necessarily finite. Generating an infinity of utterances with finite means is possible by recognizing that all utterances are composed from the same small number of signs used recursively in different combinations. All the infinite manifestations could thereby be described in terms of the finite system that evoked them. Furthermore – and here Saussure located the 'ultimate law of language' – signs are defined only in terms of their relation, or *difference*, to other signs, both the paradigmatic relations they enter into in *la langue* and the syntagmatic relations they enter into in *la parole*.

Identifying what is problematic

The problem analysed in Metz's first essay in film semiotics is conveniently stated in the essay's very title – is there a filmic equivalent to *la langue* (translated in Metz's essay as 'language system')? An answer to this question would then offer a definition of filmic specificity, the primary objective of film semiotics. In other words, the question in Metz's title assumes that filmic specificity should be defined in terms of an underlying reality (modelled on natural language's underlying reality – *la langue*), not in terms of the immediately perceptible level of film, as classical (pre-semiotic) film theorists had attempted to do. Metz's background assumption in this essay is that film must possess an equivalent to *la langue* to be defined as a language (*langage*). This is the dilemma Metz mentions in this chapter's opening epigraph – the need to compare and distinguish film from natural language when studying it from a semiotic perspective.

Describing the problematic state of affairs

Collecting data

Metz's essay is explicitly formulated in terms of what Francesco Casetti calls a 'methodological theory', the study of a particular aspect of cinema using criteria from a specific theoretical standpoint. Casetti defines 'Cinema: Language or Language System?' as a significant essay because it marks film theory's shift from ontological to methodological theories (1999, 89). The key to understanding how Metz describes his problematic state of affairs is therefore to determine how he turned film into an object of semiotic theory. But one major limitation of the essay is that Metz collects data only from one level – the filmic image.

*Systematizing data (*classifying, correlating, ordering, measuring*)*

Metz systematizes film according to the methodology of a semiotics based on the principles of structural linguistics, outlined above in 'background assumptions'. Not surprisingly, with such background assumptions, and by limiting himself to the filmic image, Metz's semiotic systematization of film came out negatively (he concludes by stating that cinema is a *langage sans langue*). Much of his description involves documenting how the underlying reality of film does *not* resemble *la langue*.

The negative results are not unexpected, for the semiotic language of film does not possess the same system specific to natural language. Metz states: 'the image discourse is an open system, and it is not easily codified, with its non-discrete basic units (the images), its intelligibility (which is too natural), its lack of distance [i.e. lack of arbitrariness] between the [signified] and the signifier' (1974a, 59). Metz emphasized that the image does not derive its meaning in opposition to other images, but from a direct correspondence to pro-filmic events. In other words, film has no paradigm on the level of the image; consequently, it has no *langue*, and no double articulation.

The reasons are twofold: (1) Metz believed, under the influence of the classical film theorist André Bazin, that the image is analogical, not coded, for it is constituted by a continuous, non-articulated resemblance to the thing it represents; and (2) 'The image is always actualized' (1974a, 67). That is, filmic images do not belong to a collective, non-manifest, closed system existing prior to usage; rather, each image is at the outset a complete, manifest, and individual unit of discourse. In Metz's famous example: 'A close-up of a revolver does not mean "revolver" (a purely virtual [non-manifest] lexical unit [moneme]), but at the very least, and without speaking of the connotations, it signifies "Here is a revolver!"' (1974a, 67). This led Metz to state that 'the cinematographic image is primarily speech [*parole*]' (1974a, 69), which is the same as saying that 'The filmic shot is of the *magnitude of the sentence*' (1974a, 86; emphasis in the original).

But the terminology in this quotation – 'magnitude of the sentence' – has often confused the way the linguistic status of the image is understood. Metz merely characterized the relation between image and sentence in *exterior* terms, in which there is no structural similarity between them, because the sentence is also analysable into units that signify paradigmatically: 'The difference [between sentence and image] is that the sentences of natural language eventually break down into words, whereas in the cinema, they do not: A film may be segmented into large units ("shots"), but these shots are not *reducible* (in Jakobson's sense) into small, basic, and specific units' (1974a, 88). The 'irreducibility' of filmic images suggested that they do not involve articulation, because they are potentially infinite in number and each one is unique. This explains why they cannot be theorized in terms of articulation and formed into a closed paradigm.

Metz also concluded that the cinema does not form a speech circuit:

> The cinema is not a language system, because it contradicts three important characteristics of the linguistic fact: a language is a *system* of *signs* used for *intercommunication*. Three elements to the definition. Now, like all the arts, and because it is itself an art, the cinema is one-way communication.
>
> (Metz 1974a, 75)

Language as a 'speech circuit', so crucial for Saussure, does not, therefore, apply to film.

Two reasons explain Metz's failure to establish a film semiotics on the level of the image: (1) the first is a genuine inability to articulate a new perspective on film by means of two fundamental criteria that make linguistics scientific (at least for Saussure) – the arbitrary relationship between signifier and signified, and the metaphor of language as a speech circuit – for these two criteria do not hold on the level of the filmic image. To achieve his objective – to define filmic specificity in semiotic terms – Metz sought the above two criteria on the level of image sequences. (In fact, it was evident that film does not form a speech circuit on any level, so Metz attempted to establish a principle of arbitrariness in the filmic chain.) (2) The second reason has to do with Metz's unnecessary adoption of Barthes's reversal of Saussure's hierarchy between linguistics and semiotics: for Saussure, linguistics is a subset of semiotics, but Barthes asserts that semiotics is part of linguistics (1967, 78–79). This reversal simply forced Metz into a straitjacket; it meant he did not directly apply structural linguistics to film (i.e. the methodological concepts syntagm/paradigm, signifier/signified, and so on) but took the *results* of the analysis of the system of articulation specific to natural language and attempted to find the *same system* (*la langue*) in film. Hence at this stage he did not search for filmic paradigms, for example, but for paradigms organized along double articulation. And because the filmic image does not conform to the same system of articulation as that revealed by the structural linguistic analysis of natural language, Metz concluded that the structural linguistic research into the specificity of film language on the level of the image is an inappropriate starting point at which to establish a film semiotics. This is because, for him, semiotics must operate within the narrow confines of structural linguistics, which is geared exclusively to the study of systems such as *la langue*, rather than to analogical systems (such as *la parole*), to a system of arbitrary signs systematically organized into paradigms. He believed all semiotic systems to be regulated by *la langue* composed of non-signifying – that is, purely differential – units (such as phonemes), which constitute *la langue* as a doubly articulated system. The lack of all these features on the level of the image forced Metz to conclude that film is, in some sense, a '*langage sans langue*'. And in later essays, he attempted to clarify this statement by arguing that the specific system of filmic language begins on the level of the syntagm, or sequence of images.

Constructing problems

Phenomenological concepts

Film semiotics does not conceive 'film' to be a pre-given, unproblematic entity. Instead, it defines film's specificity – its uniqueness – in terms of its underlying reality, rather than its immediately perceptible qualities. The role of theory is to make visible this invisible reality by constructing a model of it. Like other semiotic studies, film semiotics adopted the two-tier semiotic hierarchy (between manifest/latent levels of reality), and formulated hypotheses describing that underlying reality. One way to justify the linguistic analysis of film is to determine if it carries out its own agenda – modelling film's underlying reality. But one problem with the film semiotics developed in 'Cinema: Language or Language System?', as we have just seen, is that Metz modelled film's underlying system directly in terms of natural language's underlying system.

Cinematic concepts

Filmic concepts do not play a significant role in Metz's essay, so we shall summarize some of the conclusions reached concerning Metz's early semiotic study of cinematic concepts. Stephen Heath writes that, for Metz in 'Cinema: Language or Language System?', 'cinema lacks any equivalent to the double articulation of linguistic *langue*, its very economy, the combination of systematically defined units of a lower level (phonemes) to form units of a higher level (monemes); instead of articulation, duplication, instead of economy, an infinity of analogical resemblance' (1981b, 142). Because Metz could not codify the filmic image in terms of *la langue*, he concluded that it is completely uncoded, a mechanical duplication, or analogical resemblance. Metz thought of images as uncoded actualized discourse. Furthermore, he concluded that cinema is a *langage sans langue* because it is one-way communication (or expression, rather than communication), unlike natural language, which is two-way communication; it lacks signs (since filmic images are motivated, not arbitrary); and it does not form a system (precisely because filmic images are motivated – they derive meaning from outside film, in terms of what is represented – they do not require a system of signs in paradigmatic and syntagmatic relations to generate meaning). There is no system of virtual, or non-manifest images that a film then manifests; instead, each image is an invention. In one sentence, cinema suffers from a paradigmatic poverty. This wasn't the most promising start for initiating a semiotics of the cinema!

Meta-theoretical concepts

'Cinema: Language or Language System?' is a pioneering, exploratory essay that transformed the way film theory is carried out. For that reason, much of the essay reflects upon the activity of theorizing film from a semiotic perspective (a stance Metz adopted again in another pioneering essay, 'The Imaginary Signifier' [Metz 1975], which opens with him reflecting on the theorizing of film from a psychoanalytic perspective). In the section 'Film and Linguistics' (1974a, 60–61), Metz discusses the relationship between linguistics and semiotics. He privileges linguistics in his semiotic analysis because semiotics derives from linguistics, and linguistics is a more advanced discipline than semiotics. But he also notes that linguistics can help the theorist delineate what film (or filmic specificity) is not, before defining what film is. Both stances, he argues, are legitimate approaches to studying film.

Evaluating data and problems

Genuineness, correctness, and comprehensiveness

'Cinema: Language or Language System?' employs in a tentative manner the hierarchy between underlying/manifest levels and defines the aim of film semiotics as the identification of pertinent underlying elements, where filmic specificity is to be found. To that extent, Metz's essay is written from a genuine semiotic perspective, although he struggled at this stage of his research to identify genuine underlying elements. More problems arise in terms of correctness and comprehensiveness. One fundamental difference between the various underlying realities studied by linguists and by semioticians is that natural language's underlying system, *la langue*, is of a much higher level of organization than the underlying systems of other semiotic languages. Care needs to be taken to qualify the term 'language' to indicate whether we mean natural language (a narrow use of the word 'language') or semiotic language (a much broader use of the word). To argue that a semiotic language is the same as natural language is to commit a category mistake, one that confuses the logical type of the semiotic language under discussion. In transposing linguistic concepts to film, Metz confused filmic concepts with linguistic concepts (the background assumptions concerning the nature of film with the background assumptions concerning the nature of natural language). In other words, he believed (following Martinet and Barthes) that the reality underlying all languages should conform to the reality underlying natural language, the doubly articulated system of *la langue*. Finally, Metz's theory at this stage is not comprehensive because it is too narrowly focused – the object of analysis (the filmic image) is too restricted.

Well-formedness and significance

It is doubtful whether 'Cinema: Language or Language System?' formulated a well-formed and significant problem, since it is not a significant problem whether film conforms to *la langue*, for the simple reason that *la langue* is unique to natural language – it is natural language's underlying reality. Metz did not perceive that film has its own underlying reality that does not resemble the structure of *la langue* (Metz therefore directly compared film to natural language, an erroneous activity which inspired pre-semiotic film theorists). In effect, Metz was attempting to define filmic specificity in terms of the specificity of natural language as formulated by structural linguistics, since he believed that double articulation is the only form of articulation. He even ended up contradicting the basic semiotic premise that the aim of film semiotics is to define filmic specificity in terms of an underlying reality – since he argued that film is always actualized. But if film has no underlying reality, what is actualized? Surely, to say that film is actualized implied a prior set of terms that are actualized. However, Metz did manage to identify a pre-existing underlying reality in his subsequent work.

In 'Problems of Denotation in the Fiction Film' (1974a, 108–46), Metz moved on to explore the syntagmatic dimension of film, under the background assumption that filmic specificity is to be identified with narrativity (a single, super-structural code): '*it is precisely to the extent that the cinema confronted the problems of narration* that ... it came to produce a body of specific signifying procedures' (1974a, 95; emphasis in the original). The main purpose of the essay is to employ the structural linguistic method of segmentation and classification to identify a prior set of sequence (or syntagmatic) types operative in classical cinema, a paradigm of syntagms from which a film-maker can choose to represent pro-filmic events in a particular sequence. Each syntagma is identifiable by the particular way it structures the spatio-temporal relations between the pro-filmic events it depicts. Syntagmas are commutable because the same events depicted by means of a different syntagma will have a different meaning.

These spatio-temporal relationships between the images constitute filmic specificity for Metz because they articulate the pro-filmic events in terms of a *specific* cinematic space and time. In other words, this cinematic space and time confers upon these events a meaning that *goes beyond* their analogical relation to the image. These image orderings therefore conform to the principle of arbitrariness, since there is no strict motivation governing the choice of one syntagma over another in representing a particular pro-filmic event.[2]

Metz detected eight different spatio-temporal relationships in total, which constitute eight different forms of image ordering (*syntagmas*). Metz called the resulting 'paradigm of syntagmas' the *grande syntagmatique* of the image track. These image syntagmas form a paradigm to the extent that they offer eight different commutable ways of constructing an image sequence. As Metz himself has said: 'These montage figures [film syntagmas] derive their meaning to a large extent in relation to one another. One, then, has to deal, so to speak, with a paradigm of syntagmas. It is only by a sort of *commutation* that one can identify and enumerate them' (Metz 1976, 587).

The *grande syntagmatique* identifies syntagmatic units only when a change in shot produces a change in meaning – that is, when a spatio-temporal transition (the cut, etc.) on the level of the filmic signifier correlates with a change in meaning on the level of the signified (= the spatio-temporal relationship between the pro-filmic events). Each filmic syntagma is constituted by the same spatio-temporal relationship between its images. As long as the same relationship holds across cuts, there is no commutation. A commutation, or change in meaning, therefore occurs when a spatio-temporal transition on the level of the filmic signifier is correlated with a *new* spatio-temporal relation between pro-filmic events, for a new relation signals the end of one syntagma and the beginning of another. (See Metz 1974a, 124–33, for an outline of the eight syntagmatic types.)

Metz employs the hierarchy between underlying/manifest levels (the syntagmas constitute an underlying system of discrete codes upon which is based film's illusion of continuity) and specifies the aim of film semiotics as the activity of identifying pertinent underlying units (codes) and their rules of combination. Metz makes the assumption that film language is to be equated with narrative. This is one of the major limitations of the *grande syntagmatique*, with the result that Metz equated narrative with filmic specificity, because narrative in the cinema conforms to the principle of arbitrariness. In other words, narrative is presented as being intrinsic, rather than contingent, to film form.

'Problems of Denotation in the Fiction Film' successfully identifies an autonomous level of articulation in the cinema (syntagmas) and constructs a paradigm of eight syntagms (thus overcoming cinema's paradigmatic poverty). As Heath points out: 'The focus on syntagmatic relations "saves" semiology (in so far as it is held in the *langue* or *langage* debate) in the face of the paradigmatic poverty of cinema' (1981b, 144). Yet two problems remain: Metz's identification of filmic specificity with narrativity (confusion of types), and the uncoded, transparent nature conferred on the image (a problem carried over from 'Cinema: Language or Language System?', and merely displaced in the *grande syntagmatique*). Metz approached both problems in *Language and Cinema* (1974b).

Language and Cinema: analysing the problematic state of affairs

Identifying what is problematic

In *Language and Cinema* Metz continues to pursue the question: What is the specificity of film from a semiotic perspective? But he answers it by distinguishing between film and cinema and then defining specificity in terms of a combination of cinematic codes and sub-codes:[3]

> We shall call *filmic* ... all the traits which appear in films (i.e., in the messages of the cinema), whether they are or are not peculiar to this means of expression, and no matter what idea one has of this specificity or of its absence. We shall call *cinematic* certain filmic facts which are supposed to play a part ... in one or the other of the codes specific to the cinema. The cinematic is but a part of the filmic. Certain phenomena are filmic and cinematic, others filmic but not cinematic.
>
> (Metz 1974b, 47)

Metz now regards the study of singular filmic systems to be an equally important dimension of film semiotics. In other words, he no longer limits film semiotics to the study of an underlying system constituting filmic specificity, but also includes study of the way specific and non-specific codes combine in single films.

The study of film (the filmic) involves the analysis of singular textual systems, while the study of cinema (the cinematic) involves the analysis of codes: 'In this sense, film and cinema are opposed as a real object to an ideal one, as an *utterance* to a *language system*' (Metz 1974b, 24). In *Language and Cinema* Metz no longer uses the term *la langue* to discuss cinematic language, but replaces it with the more general term *code*, which constitutes an underlying system but which has no linguistic connotations; there is therefore no obligation to search for double articulation.

Cinematic language refers to a generality not exhausted by any film, whereas singular textual system refers to the specific organization of one film. A singular textual system therefore lacks the generality of a code, and is not concerned with cinematic specificity, but with the way specific and non-specific codes combine in a particular film.

Background assumptions

Two background assumptions of *Language and Cinema*, not evident in Metz's previous film semiotics, are: that filmic specificity (cinematic language) can only be defined in terms of a combination of codes, and: specificity can only be defined by referring to a language's material of expression (to use Louis Hjelmslev's term):

> [T]he position which is adopted here includes two elements, not one: (1) the specificity which interests semiotics is the specificity of codes, not the 'crude' specificity of physical signifiers; (2) the specificity of specific codes nevertheless refers to certain features of the material of expression.
>
> (Metz 1974b, 219)

Earlier, Metz stated:

> [T]here is a great difference between a specificity defined directly according to material criteria and one that is defined in terms of codes, even if the specification of codes cannot be accomplished without a consideration of certain traits of the material of the signifier (and not of this material itself, taken as a whole and without further analysis).
>
> (Metz 1974b, 43)

No single code is unique to the cinema, although this does not prevent Metz from defining codes as specific: 'A code may ... be specific for *several* languages. ... This notion of an *obviously multiple specificity* is paradoxical only in appearance. Sameness is not the only form of specificity, and a circumscribed multiplicity also forms a specific group; a specific field is not necessarily a very small one' (1974b, 224). Instead, he defines cinematic language in terms of a *combination* of (more or less) specific codes.

A consequence of this is that Metz identifies a hierarchy of specificity amongst these codes, a hierarchy defined in terms of material of expression.

Language and Cinema: describing the problematic state of affairs

*Systematizing data (*classifying, correlating, ordering, measuring*)*

Metz systematizes his data (cinematic and filmic codes, and their relation to film's matter of expression) in the form of concentric circles, which enables him to establish classes of codes and define their relation to one another. Each circle represents a code and also a group of languages associated with it. In chapter 10.4 of *Language and Cinema*, Metz defines the specificity of film's image track in terms of a specific combination of the following codes: iconicity, mechanical duplication, multiplicity, and movement. Metz's several-page description can be symbolized or represented visually in a Venn diagram (see Figure 4.1), a practice Metz would have done well to follow.

This description of the problematic state of affairs in film semiotics is motivated by the fact that the relationship between these codes is one of inclusion (as well as intersection). Iconicity is a code specific to all visual languages; its degree of specificity therefore remains rather low. More specific is the fact that filmic images are produced

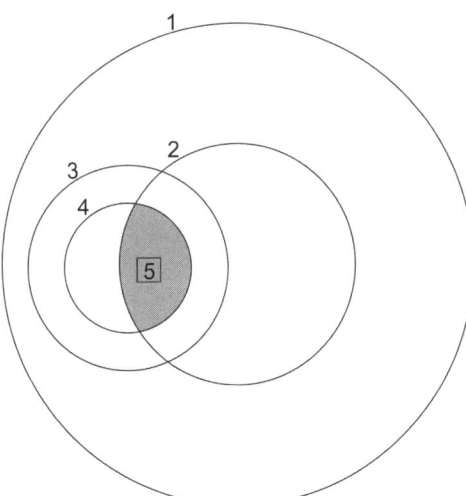

1. Iconicity
2. Mechanical duplication
3. Multiplicity
4. Movement
5. Mechanically produced multiple moving images

Figure 4.1 The five codes of cinematic language

by mechanical duplication (circle 2) and are multiple (circle 3). The combination of these three codes attains a high degree of specificity, but does not define film's unique specificity. Moreover, multiplicity is not included within circle 2, but intersects with it, because some languages (such as cartoons) are made up of a multiplicity of non-mechanically produced images. A fourth characteristic of filmic specificity is that its multiple mechanical images move. Because movement depends upon a multiplicity of images, it is included within circle 3 (multiplicity) and also intersects mechanical duplication and iconicity (circles 2 and 1 respectively). Film belongs to a fifth group of languages included within circle 4 – namely, mechanically produced multiple moving images (the area labelled '5' in Figure 4.1). This fifth group is the logical product of 4 and 2.

In terms of the image track, filmic specificity has been defined by a combination of codes and their material of expression. Because all these codes can be manifest in film's material of expression, they attain a degree of specificity. However, both film and television images belong to the shaded area of Figure 4.1. It seems, then, that cinema has no unique codification. Metz (1974b, 235–40) resorts to a technological criterion to distinguish them – a televisual image is electronically produced, rather than photographically produced, although both modes of production function to manifest the same code – that of movement. Furthermore, there is, of course, a purely perceptual difference, in that filmic images are initially projected on a large screen, whereas televisual images are electronically transmitted on a small screen. Nonetheless, what appears on the big and small screen are still the same set of codes.

Language and Cinema: constructing problems

Phenomenological concepts

Language and Cinema rigorously employs the hierarchy between underlying/manifest levels (cinema and film respectively) and continues to identify the aim of film semiotics as the activity of identifying pertinent underlying elements (codes) and their rules of combination. However, phenomenology makes a return within film semiotics, for some of the codes Metz analyses are defined in terms of the matter of expression – film's sensory dimension – they are manifest in.

Filmic concepts

The nature of film is significantly expanded in *Language and Cinema*, overcoming the two problems identified in 'Cinema: Language or Language System?' and 'Problems of Denotation in the Fiction Film': iconicity is defined as coded, and film consists of a combination of codes (rather than one code – *la langue*, or narrativity).

Defining iconicity as coded and film as a combination of codes are significant additions to film semiotics, in that they show Metz tackling the issue of iconicity within a semiotic framework. In 'Cinema: Language or Language System?' and 'Problems of Denotation in the Fiction Film', Metz worked with the realist conception of the image-as-analogue (as a mechanical duplication of reality). Heath called this 'the blind spot of Metz's formulations' for it is 'the point at which the articulation of significance collapses in the face of analogy' (1981b, 141). Metz overcame this blind spot under the influence of Umberto Eco. Eco was one of the first semioticians to successfully study the image in terms of codes, which enabled him to define its apparent analogical (non-semiotic) nature as a system of iconic codes organized into a triple hierarchy (Eco 1976a).[4]

Once semiotic analysis had overcome the problem of analogy, the rich semiotic field of the cinema was opened up to analysis because film theorists were able to analyse the multiple systems of codes that constitute the complex act of filmic signification. Within this framework the social and ideological determination of all semiotic systems were finally recognized. Heath commented that: 'It is this recognition of codes at work in the image, of the possibility of analogy being itself the result of codes, which marks a decisive process of rethinking in Metz's writings' (1981b, 143). *Language and Cinema* represents this process of rethinking. In earlier work, Metz preferred to reject the status of film as a complete semiotic system rather than challenge the realist status of the photographic image. But using the concept of code in *Language and Cinema* developed 'a response to cinema as a complexity of codes of differing kind and degree of systematicity' (Heath 1981b, 144).

Language and Cinema: evaluating data and problems

Well-formedness and significance

It is arguable whether all the answers Metz formulates to the problems he poses in *Language and Cinema* are well-formed, since some of the logic is dubious (his argument that some codes are not specific to one language, and that there is a hierarchy of specificity amongst codes). In *Language and Cinema* Metz reached the limits of the question of filmic specificity, and also reached the limitations of a structuralist answer to this question. (These two limitations are, of course, interrelated, since the study of filmic specificity – of an autonomous realm of film – is approached by film semioticians with the methodology of structural linguistics.) These two limitations are evident in Metz's use of classical set theory to represent filmic specificity, which gives the impression that it can be defined simply in terms of an addition, or culmination, of codes. That is, the single component codes are seen to culminate into a complex set of component codes. But such a representation of information can be misleading, as George Lakoff has shown (1987, Chapter 9). He gives many examples showing how the intersection of two components does not necessarily add up to form a complex set of components. For one of his examples, 'pet fish', he writes that 'A guppy might be a good example of a pet fish, but a bad example of a pet, and a bad example of a fish' (1987, 141). 'Pet fish' is not therefore a simple combination of 'pet' and 'fish'.

This criticism also applies to Metz's representation of filmic specificity in *Language and Cinema*. Iconicity, mechanical duplication, movement, and multiple images do not simply overlap and intersect with one another (i.e. culminate) to form filmic specificity. Instead, these component codes interact in more dynamic ways to form filmic specificity. Metz did in fact begin to explore this issue at the end of *Language and Cinema*, with the concept of 'filmic writing', in which the codes are thought to displace one another rather than simply culminate. But the whole book is built upon a classical theory of classification, and the theory of filmic writing sits uneasily within that context.

In conclusion, we can say that, in *Language and Cinema*, Metz attempted to develop a complex definition of filmic specificity (based on a combination of codes) using the methodology employed to develop a simple definition of filmic specificity (defined in terms of a single, master code). But such a methodology is not equipped to develop a complex definition (since it cannot adequately represent the way the multiple codes combine without resorting to the simple principle of culmination).

Despite the limited success of his results, Metz established a new object of study, new problematics to be confronted, and a new methodology with which to approach film, therefore making it possible to identify and establish film studies as an autonomous discipline. The new object of study was of a new level of filmic reality – the unobservable, latent level that makes filmic meaning possible and which defines its specificity.

My criticism of Metz's research is based on identifying and clarifying its internal logic and inconsistencies. However, it is now fashionable to reject film semiotics outright. Gregory Currie does not regard film semiotics to be either well-formed or significant. He considers two hypotheses from film semiotics to reject: the strong hypothesis that film is like a natural language, and the weak hypothesis that film is a semiotic system. Most of Chapter 4 of his book *Image and Mind* (Currie 1995) is devoted to refuting the strong hypothesis. Currie has made an unfortunate choice because he is simply repeating the arguments Metz presented back in 1964, in 'Cinéma: langue ou langage?' As we saw above, in this essay Metz compared film images with natural language (= *un langage avec langue*), and found that no similarities exist, which led him to conclude that film is a *langage sans langue* (that film is not a natural language).

Metz abandoned the direct comparison between film and natural language's underlying system (*langue*) and argued, in his subsequent work on image sequences, that film is a language in the sense of a semiotic system (the second hypothesis that Currie does not attempt to reject, even though it characterizes the dominant position in film semiotics). Currie has not considered the history of film semiotics, nor has he adequately characterized its basic hypotheses. When Currie writes: 'I shall argue that, in crucial respects, film is very unlike natural language' (1995, 119), he is simply repeating Metz's statement that film is a *langage sans langue*. There is no disagreement between Metz and Currie, simply Currie's misunderstanding, caused by his failure to grasp the status of Metz's arguments and the history of film semiotics.

Even though Metz tried without success to compare film to natural language, he never argued that film is like a natural language (he did compare them, with negative results). He did not commit the category mistake of arguing that film has the same status as English, French, Japanese, and so on. Yet Currie attributes this view to film semiotics. To repeat: film semiotics argues that film is a language (a semiotic system) but does not argue that film is like a natural language, such as English, French, or Japanese.

By attributing the proposition 'film is like a natural language' to film semiotics, Currie has simply constructed his own straw man to attack. This is due to his narrow definition of the term 'language', in which it always means 'natural language'. Film is not a language for Currie because it is not like a natural language. But for Metz, even though film is not like a natural language, it is still a language (a semiotic system).

The clearest moment when Currie collapses the distinction between language and natural language is in the last section of Chapter 4 of *Image and Mind*, when he briefly considers whether the comparison between film and natural language can be made in the study of image sequences:

> Perhaps the claim that there is a language of cinematic images is not the claim that these images themselves have a language-like structure, but rather that these images enter into language-like combinations with each other. In films, there are combinations of images; sometimes these combinations form identifiable and recurrent patterns, and these combinations can have a meaning which partly depends on the manner of their combination. Isn't there something here like the articulated structure of a sentence? No. As many film theorists have recognized, the representational content of a cinema image cannot be equated with that of a name, predicate, or other sub-sentential part of speech.
>
> (Currie 1995, 134)

I agree with Currie that we can only give the answer 'no' to the question 'Isn't there something here [in the recurrent patterns of image combinations] like the articulated structure of a sentence?' But this is because it is the wrong question, since film semioticians do not fall into the trap of making comparisons between the specific structure of natural language sentences and image combinations. (Or if they do, their results are negative.) If Currie asked: 'Isn't there something here [in the recurrent patterns of image combinations] like semiotic articulation?' (that is, articulation not reducible to natural language's specific system of codes, *la langue*) the answer would be 'yes, there is something like semiotic articulation in the recurrent patterns of image combinations'. Metz's *grande syntagmatique* is a model of the eight recurrent types of image combinations (syntagmas) that dominate classical cinema. The problem here is Currie's purely argumentative engagement with film semiotics, an engagement that only offers decontextualized criticism. Similarly, Murray Smith's claim that 'Currie's argument [in Chapter 4 of *Image and Mind*] is in stark contrast to the lingering and vague belief in the language-like structure of film among semiotic thinkers, and constitutes perhaps the most comprehensive demolition of this article of faith to date' (1998, 326) is also misplaced.

Cognitive film semiotics

The problem Metz addressed in 'Cinema: Language or Language System?' and *Language and Cinema* – defining filmic specificity in semiotic terms – was only partly well-formed, because the structural linguistic theory he employed to solve this problem was limited in its capacity to address filmic problems. Nonetheless, it is a significant problem that demanded more sophisticated theories to address the complex semiotic nature of film. A more sophisticated theory was developed in the 1980s, under the influence of the generative linguistics of Noam Chomsky and cognitive science.

David Bordwell has noted the absence of references to the work of Chomsky in film theory: 'it is surprising that theorists who assign language a key role in determining subjectivity have almost completely ignored the two most important contemporary developments in linguistic theory: Chomsky's Transformational Generative Grammar and his Principles-and-Parameters theory' (1996a, 22). He adds that: 'no film theorist has mounted an argument for *why* the comparatively informal theories of Saussure, Émile Benveniste, or Bakhtin are superior to the Chomskyan paradigm. For over two decades film theorists have made pronouncements about language without engaging with the major theoretical rival to their position' (1996a, 22). The truth of the matter is that since the 1980s a number of film theorists have been engaging with Chomskyan linguistics and, furthermore, have deemed it to be superior to structural linguistics. Here I shall briefly chart the relation between classical film semiotics and cognitive film semiotics. (For a more detailed overview, see Buckland 2000.)

During the 1970s and 1980s Metz's classical film semiotics was modified and transformed. Its fundamental problems lay in its total reliance upon structural linguistics. One major transformation came from post-structural film theory, which did not draw upon autonomous linguistic theories, but based itself primarily upon the Marxism of Louis Althusser and the psychoanalysis of Jacques Lacan.

The second transformation was carried out by cognitive film semiotics. For most Anglo-American film scholars, film semiotics takes only one form – namely, Metz's early film semiotics, represented by the research analysed above. But as Metz himself acknowledged in the opening chapter of *Language and Cinema*: 'By its very nature, the semiotic enterprise must expand or disappear' (1974b, 19). Although *Language and Cinema* marks the logical conclusion to the classical era of film semiotics, it does not mark the end of film semiotics per se. In his subsequent work – particularly his essay 'The Imaginary Signifier' (1975) – Metz adopted a psychoanalytical framework, which aided the formation of post-structural film theory. However, many of his students and colleagues continued to work within a semiotic framework, which they combined with cognitive science. Research in film semiotics has continued unabated, especially in Europe. Far from disappearing, film semiotics has expanded into a new framework, one that overcomes the problems of classical film semiotics by embracing three new theories: (1) transformational generative grammar and cognitive science generally (in the work of Dominique Chateau [e.g. 1987] and Michel Colin [1985; 1995]); (2) a renewed interest in enunciation theory (particularly in the work of Francesco Casetti [1998] and Metz of *L'Énonciation impersonnelle ou le site du film* [1991]), and (3) pragmatics (in the work of Roger Odin [1988; 1995a; 1995b]).[5]

In his essay 'The *Grande Syntagmatique* Revisited' (Colin 1995) Michel Colin redefined Metz's eight syntagmatic types in terms of selectional (or semantic) features. Selectional features represent the inherent grammatical and semantic components of

CHRISTIAN METZ'S *LANGUAGE AND CINEMA*

lexical items (or 'words'). For example, the lexical item 'cat' can be represented in terms of the following selectional features: +Common, +Count, +Animate, −Human. Every lexical item can be characterized in terms of these and other selectional features. The most remarkable results of Colin's rereading of Metz's work is that, as with all generative models, the actual, manifest syntagmatic types are posited as merely the result (the epiphenomenon) of the generative process. Within the generative framework, we can identify and analyse, not only actual syntagmas, but also possible (i.e. potential) syntagmas and impossible syntagmas. Once all the finite selectional features have been identified, the potentially infinite number of syntagmatic types can be conceived and generated. These selectional features constitute the finite underlying level of filmic discourse (or its system of codes) from which a potentially infinite number of film sequences can be generated. For Colin, then, the primary aim of the *grande syntagmatique* is not to identify actual syntagmatic types, but to identify the more fundamental selectional features that combine to form these syntagmatic types.

In linguistics, cognitive pragmatics designates a discipline that describes a type of linguistic competence that governs the relation between utterances and the appropriate contexts in which they are uttered. Cognitive pragmatics is therefore a study of the immediate discursive nature of language. Roger Odin (1995a; 1995b) develops a cognitive-pragmatic theory of film semiotics. Odin develops a threefold distinction between institutions, modes, and operations in order to characterize the film spectator's pragmatic competence in comprehending films. From this Odin identifies the different filmic institutions, modes, and operations, with particular focus on fiction films, documentaries, home movies, and what Odin calls the 'dynamic' mode of film-making (1988).

Enunciation designates the activity that results in speech, in the production of utterances (*énoncés*). Émile Benveniste identified two forms of utterance: discourse (*discours*) and story (*histoire*). *Discours* employs deictic categories – words such as personal, possessive, and demonstrative pronouns that grammaticalize within the utterance particular aspects of its spatio-temporal context (e.g. the speaker and hearer), whereas *histoire* is a form of utterance that excludes deixis. (Benveniste's theory of enunciation is discussed in more detail in Chapters 5 and 8.) Francesco Casetti (1998) takes to its logical conclusions the analysis of the deictic dimension of film – of film as *discours*. Using the deictic categories *I*, *you*, and *he*, he develops a seminal typology of four shot types, which aim to describe the way film orients itself in relation to the spectator. However, in his final published book Metz (1991) disputes this deictic theory of film, and instead argues that film can only be studied as *histoire*.

The psychologist Karl Bühler (1990) used the term deixis to refer to systems of orientation that position an individual's body and consciousness in relation to his or her environment. In the sense of systems of orientation, deixis refers to a general cognitive process. Deictic systems of orientation include bodily gestures (e.g. pointing), language expressions, and imagination. Casetti conducted his research within the framework of one of these general systems of orientation – personal pronouns in linguistic expressions. Metz criticizes Casetti's use of personal pronouns to describe how the spectator is oriented in relation to film. (Metz is therefore criticizing Casetti's overreliance on linguistic concepts.) Metz then replaces orientation by means of personal pronouns with orientation by means of anaphora – a narrow system of orientation in which one textual element points to another textual element. Moreover, Metz identifies anaphora as a reflexive moment in a film, which results in his identifying filmic enunciation with reflexivity.

The work of the cognitive film semioticians represents the current state of film semiotics, which is united by the same project – to combine film semiotics and cognitive science with the aim of modelling filmic competence. Far from disappearing, film semiotics has continued to expand, even though its results haven't been in the spotlight of Anglo-American film theory.

Notes

1 As we saw in Chapter 1, Jakobson and Halle (1956) then identified in the phonemes a small number of distinctive features, organized into binary oppositions.

2 Gianfranco Bettetini presents an extreme example:

> [I]n the scenes of the protagonist's erotic relations with her husband and her lover from Jean-Luc Godard's *Une femme mariée*, the presence of the medium makes itself felt with considerable expressive relevance. In fact, the cutting of the various shots creates autonomous relationships and a fictitious reality that is almost independent of the one that gave birth to the images; furthermore, the very gestures of the actors conform to the expressive ends imposed upon them by the director and, hieratically unreal, incredible in their fragmentariness, lend themselves to the formation of a poetic universe that is real and completely credible, but absolutely unrepeatable and not even remotely comparable to the objective one that gave life to them.
>
> (Bettetini 1973, 68–69).

3 The distinction between cinematic codes and sub-codes is irrelevant to my discussion here. But briefly, cinematic codes are codes specific to film, whereas cinematic sub-codes, while also specific to film, are specific to only some films. Moreover, whereas codes syntagmatically combine with one another (lighting, montage, and so on) sub-codes (of the same code) are in a paradigmatic relation of substitution. Hence, the code of punctuation is a cinematic code, whereas the fade and the dissolve are sub-codes of this code. As such, they cannot appear at the same time in the same film (this being due to their paradigmatic nature), and may not appear in a film at all (this being due to their nature as sub-codes).

4 For additional semiotic studies of iconicity, see Eco (1976b, 191–217) and Kjørup (1978).

5 Robert Stam argues that Bakhtin's translinguistics, written in the 1920s, 'both anticipated and superseded the structuralist project' (1989, 28). In particular, it can overcome the blind spots of structural linguistics that Metz inherited. See Stam (1989, Chapter 1) for more details.

5

FILM AS A SPECIFIC SIGNIFYING PRACTICE

Stephen Heath's 'On Screen, In Frame: Film and Ideology'

Specificity here is semiotic, and a semiotic analysis of film – of film as signifying practice – is the analysis of a heterogeneity, the range of codes and systems at work in the film text. [A semiotic analysis also involves the study of] the heterogeneity in its particular effects, its particular inscriptions of subject and ideology, of the subject in ideology.

(Stephen Heath 1976, 257)

Problem-situation

Like other 'contemporary film theorists' of the 1970s, Stephen Heath sought to combine Saussurean semiotics, Lacanian psychoanalysis, and Althusserian Marxism in an attempt to develop a materialist knowledge of the ideology perpetuated by mainstream cinema, and to map out a political agenda for an oppositional, avant-garde cinema that would transform the mainstream. Heath's important essay 'On Screen, in Frame: Film and Ideology', first published in the *Quarterly Review of Film Studies* in 1976, is a programmatic essay, a prolegomenon outlining the agenda of contemporary film theory, which perhaps explains why Heath republished it as the opening chapter of his seminal collection *Questions of Cinema* (1981a). The essay outlines the main problems that contemporary film theory needed to address in the 1970s, but without working out any detailed solutions (Heath's essays in the rest of the volume – and elsewhere – try to achieve that). Moreover, Heath does not provide any exposition of the theoretical concepts used in his work.[1] Instead, his essays are performative, about their own act of theorizing, delivery, and construction. They are about the juxtaposition of semiotic, psychoanalytic, and Marxist concepts and the application of them (usually for the first time) to the cinema. Heath is not so much reporting or describing the end result of these juxtapositions, but stages them in the act of writing. To that extent his essays are experimental. They carry out the radical practice of avant-garde writing, possibly inspired by Joyce's *Finnegans Wake* and the French Nouveau Roman (topics on which he had written extensively in the past [Heath 1972a, b; 1973]).

'On Screen, in Frame' was Heath's opening address at the 'International Symposium on Film Theory and Criticism', held at the Center for Twentieth Century Studies, University of Wisconsin-Milwaukee, 19–22 November 1975.[2] An announcement for the conference noted that: 'Main addresses and workshops will be presented on: semiotics of film, film and ideology, approaches to film history, film and narration, film and the visual arts, and experimental cine-video' (Anon 1975, 19). In a note at the end of the *Quarterly Review of Film Studies* version of the essay, Heath wrote: 'This paper has been left in the form in which it was delivered; as the opening address, its aim was to suggest the problems involved in the analysis of film and ideology and, in doing so, to touch on a number of issues raised by the various sections into which the Symposium was divided (narration, history, semiotics, etc.)' (1976, 264–65). This original context in which the paper was written and delivered gives us insight into its structure and content – especially its use of numerous historical anecdotes to make theoretical points concerning film semiotics, and film and ideology. These historical interludes do not sit comfortably in the essay; they seem to have been added for the purposes of the conference. We just need to look at the way the essay begins:

> Something changes between 22 March and 28 December 1895. Between the scientific and industrial presentation (the first Lumière demonstration of the cinématographe for the Société d'encouragement à l'industrie nationale) and the start of commercial exploitation (the first public performance in the Grand Café), the screen is fixed in what will come to be its definitive place. ... *cinema* begins.
>
> (251)

This is a dramatic history of origins, reminiscent of traditional film histories. The opening does not prepare the reader for the dense theoretical text that follows.

In addition to the above note at the end of the *Quarterly Review of Film Studies* version of the essay, Heath listed in one paragraph his main influences (since this version of the essay does not contain any endnotes). These include Althusser, Lacan, Brecht, three theorists of suture (Jacques-Alain Miller, Jean-Pierre Oudart, Daniel Dayan), the film semiotics of Christian Metz (*Language and Cinema*, 'The Imaginary Signifier'), plus an unpublished paper by Jacqueline Rose, called 'The Imaginary – the Insufficient Signifier'. (This was subsequently published in 1981 under the title 'The Imaginary' in MacCabe [1981, 132–61].) The version of 'On Screen, in Frame' published in *Questions of Cinema* does contain endnotes, plus a general note listing two other papers Heath wrote on Brecht and film (1974; 1975/6).

What's in a title?

The title of Heath's essay is dominated by two spatial prepositions – *on* screen, *in* frame. Prepositions set up spatial configurations. *On* sets up the screen not only as a surface, but also as a support that determines the position of the object placed upon it. However, the object is not spelled out in the title – we do not know what is 'on screen'. *In* sets up a boundary between an interior and exterior space, and privileges the interior. It suggests a container surrounding an object. As with *on*, the object is not spelled out in the title – we do not know what is 'in frame'. What is important for Heath is that the semantics of *on* and *in* signify position and containment, carried out by the screen and frame respectively.

But we can also detect an opposition between the two prepositions, with *on* emphasizing that the screen is literally a two-dimensional surface and *in* suggesting that the frame is metaphorically a three-dimensional volume, a container. The title therefore references one of the main features of the cinema – the projection of an apparent three-dimensional image onto a two-dimensional screen. This projection of image on screen negates the screen's two-dimensional materiality as it gives way to the apparently three-dimensional image. In the 1930s, classical film theorist Rudolf Arnheim in fact wrote about the experience of cinema as a combination of two and three dimensions. He argued the experience is 'neither absolutely two-dimensional nor absolutely three-dimensional, but something in between' (Arnheim 1957, 12).

Whereas the essay's title simply uses a comma to separate *screen* and *frame*, the subtitle uses *and* to conjoin the two terms *film* and *ideology*. Does Heath use a comma to avoid repetition of the word *and* ('On Screen and In Frame: Film and Ideology')? Or does the comma serve a rhetorical purpose? If we assume the latter, we can see that the comma brings the terms closer together than if they were separated by *and*. That is, *screen* and *frame* are conceived almost simultaneously, as if Heath finds it difficult to separate them. *Film* and *ideology*, on the other hand, are easier to conceive separately. Indeed, it will take a lot of theoretical work to show that they are intertwined.

The title uses two specific terms, while the subtitle uses more general terms. Part of the essay's function is to explain the link between the two general terms (*film* and *ideology*) via the two specific terms (*screen, frame*). In other words, to the problem of how ideology functions in film, we need to take into consideration the screen and frame, which function to position and contain. For, in response to the question: What is on screen and in frame? The answer is, precisely, film and ideology. Moreover, the spatial prepositions in the title hint at one reasoning strategy Heath uses to bridge the gap between the general and the specific – namely, spatial metaphors. As we shall see below, Heath borrows spatial metaphors from Marx and Freud.

But, what exactly is Heath's essay about? Towards the end he brings together his main themes and concepts:

> Cinema, with its screen, its frames, its binding memory, is perhaps *the* image machine; not because it is a 'good object' … but because it holds the subject – on screen, in frame – in the exact turning of symbolic and suture, negativity and coherence, flow and image. …
>
> (263)

In the following reconstruction, I shall unpack these concepts and the language Heath uses to formulate them, and spell out the essay's theoretical agenda. At the end, I will return to this quotation to determine if it constitutes and formulates significant theoretical problems.

Analysing the problematic state of affairs

Identifying what is problematic (1)

I point out above that 'On Screen, In Frame' is a programmatic essay, a prolegomenon outlining the agenda of contemporary film theory. To that extent, this first stage of formulating problems in film theory – analysing the problematic state of affairs – is the main purpose of the essay. The following quotations point towards the problematic states of affairs Heath wishes to address:

> What is the role of cinema in capitalist society as a point of investment and a form of representation and meaning production?
>
> (256)

> From the analysis of cinema, of film, we may be able to engage with theoretical issues of a more general scope, issues crucial for a materialist analysis of ideological institutions and practices.
>
> (253)

The opening of the first quotation spells out the obvious – the analysis of film and ideology must examine 'the role of cinema in capitalist society'. The rest of the sentence points out that this needs to be carried out in conjunction with a study of representation and meaning. In the second extract, Heath places his analysis of film and ideology within a wider context – historical materialist analysis of all ideological practices. Because Heath does not make explicit his theoretical background assumptions, I shall briefly outline a few of them here.

Background assumptions

The concept of ideology is clearly central to Heath's essay. Ideology emerged from traditional critiques of religion (Feuerbach) and, more generally, from the need to conceal the contradictions inherent in capitalism's exploitative relations of production; the process of concealing ensures the reproduction of those relations of production. Ideology was therefore initially defined negatively from a critical perspective, represented by Marx and Engels in *The German Ideology* (1970). Marx and Engels argue that ideology is a non-coercive form of persuasion that distorts thought, that it is a series of mistaken ideas that alienate individuals, leading to false consciousness. In the twentieth century, this negative definition was displaced by a more positive one, developed by Gramsci and Lenin. They developed an 'enabling' theory, which states that ideology forms social consciousness – the worldview of each class in society.

Heath was directly influenced by Althusser's theory of ideology. Althusser criticizes Marx and Engels's negative theory for being idealist, empiricist, and humanist. It is idealist in that it confines the discussion of ideology to the realm of ideas, not material reality; it is psychological, not social. It is empiricist because it suggests that individuals can gain direct, unmediated experience of reality outside the realm of ideology. And it is based on the humanist notion of the free individual who is subsequently imprisoned by a cloud of false ideas. This negative definition posits that reality exists outside of ideology. Against this, Althusser posits that ideology has a material existence, is a form of representation supported by apparatuses, and is enabling (is involved in the creation of consciousness, in the manufacture of subject positions for individuals to occupy).

Yet, the positive definition by itself downplays ideology's function: to conceal the contradictions of capitalism from individuals so that the capitalist relations of production can be reproduced. Althusser therefore attempts to reconcile the two theories, by developing a theory of ideology in general (a positive definition) plus a theory of particular ideologies (negative). Althusser's most famous formulations – 'Ideology interpellates individuals as subjects' (1971, 170) and 'Ideology represents the imaginary relationship of individuals to their real conditions of existence' (1971, 162) – use Lacan's concept of the imaginary. This, in fact, has led to much confusion amongst Althusser's interpreters, since an opposition between the imaginary and the real suggests that the real exists outside the imaginary (an idealist and empiricist formulation). Larrain writes: 'For those who continue to maintain a negative version, ideology "interpellates" individuals as subjects in a fundamental misrecognition which is bound to reproduce the system' (1983, 95). But Althusser also argues that the imaginary relation is constant, or universal; we cannot escape it. Our access to reality is always mediated through the imaginary and through ideology. Paul Hirst writes: 'The imaginary modality of living is necessary because men's conditions of existence can never be given to them in experience. … There can never be any true or false *consciousness* because there is no basis for a correspondence between the experience of the subject and his social relations' (1979, 32–33). In addition, the imaginary is constant because it forms the basis of man's relation to the world, and constitutes that relation as a narcissistic orientation towards reality: as soon as we wake, we always and only see the world only from our own perspective. For Althusser, the only escape from the imaginary and ideology is through science, or theoretical practice – another formulation that has led to much confusion amongst Althusser's interpreters.

Identifying what is problematic (2)

This short detour through the theory of ideology reveals that Heath's essay emerges from a real problem at the core of Marxism – the role of ideology in concealing contradictions. Nicos Poulantzas makes clear what is at stake: 'ideology has the precise function of hiding the real contradictions and of reconstituting on an imaginary level a relatively coherent discourse which serves as the horizon of agents' experience' (quoted in Larrain 1979, 46). Moreover, ideology comes at a cost of prescribing or imposing one meaning on experience against others.

Heath and other contemporary film theorists use the Marxist theory of historical materialism to reverse this process of ideological concealment. They analyse this ideological process of concealment in mainstream cinema by examining the way the impression of a coherent filmic discourse is produced. Heath in particular uses a number of concepts – the impression of reality, subject position, suture, film as specific signifying practice – to address this Marxist problem in film theory.

We can now begin to identify the problematics Heath's essay addresses:

> [This essay examines] the articulation of film and ideology on the figure of the subject.
>
> (261) (Problematic 1)

This is the clearest statement of the essay's problematic – 'the articulation of film and ideology', to be worked out via 'the figure of the subject'. Here we see Althusser's direct influence on Heath; for Althusser, 'the decisive central term on which everything else depends [is] the notion of the *subject*' (1971, 170).

But *analysis* of film and ideology is only half the problematic. From his Marxist perspective, Heath also addressed the problem of how to *transform* the state of affairs his ideological analysis uncovered. This is where science, or theoretical practice, becomes crucial:

> The aim now must be [the] … transformation of the cinematic institution in its ideological effects.
>
> (257)

> The problem, the political problem, for film in its intervention can be given as the transformation of the relations of subject and ideology.
>
> (264) (Problematic 2)

This transformation involves a change in the material conditions of film production, one where the cinema no longer functions as a vehicle for dominant ideology, but instead investigates its own materiality, contradictions, and conditions of production, resulting in a political avant-garde cinema. By exposing, rather than concealing, contradictions, this political cinema deconstructs the impression of a coherent filmic discourse that ideology sets up. In addition, both statements of Problematic 2 crucially posit that the political transformation of cinema must take place through the subject. This means that a political cinema must also challenge the impression of a coherent subject that ideology sets up. In the end, the aim of political cinema is to dissolve ideology and its effects.

Heath only touches on Problematic 2 in 'On Screen, In Frame'. He examines the role of political cinema as a transformative practice – new production practices ranging from a political modernist art cinema (Jean-Luc Godard, Nagisa Oshima, and so on) to a materialist avant-garde cinema (Peter Gidal, Michael Snow) – throughout the other essays in *Questions of Cinema*.

Describing the problematic state of affairs

Collecting data

Heath, then, identifies his main problematic as the articulation of film and ideology on the figure of the subject. He addresses this problematic by: referring to a few – mainly early – films; through anecdotes; and via metaphors borrowed from Marx and Freud.

Metaphors

In his opening pages Heath addresses his problematic state of affairs head on by discussing visual metaphors in Marx and Freud: 'important here are the images of screen and position in Marx and Freud and what they have to suggest for a consideration of film and ideology' (251). In *The German Ideology*, Marx famously used the metaphor of the camera obscura to characterize ideology's effect of falsifying consciousness. Heath quotes from *The German Ideology*:

> Consciousness can never be anything else than conscious existence, and the existence of men in their actual life-process. If in all ideology, men and their circumstances appear upside down as in a camera obscura, this phenomenon arises from the historical life-processes just as the inversion of the retina does from their physical life process.
>
> (251)

Heath is quick to point out the inadequacies of this metaphor:

> Men and their circumstances appear upside down as in a camera obscura –
> everything is projected in a darkened room but inverted. The conception is clear
> but difficult in the comparison with the camera obscura: the match between
> idea and model, as it were, *makes the problem, shows the work to be done.*
>
> (252; emphasis added)

'The match between idea [ideology] and model [camera obscura] makes the problem': in other words, Marx's camera obscura metaphor does not so much clarify, for Heath, the problem of film and ideology, but actually adds to the problem. The metaphor creates too many disanalogies to be useful to Heath in addressing his main problematic, the articulation of film and ideology on the figure of the subject.

Before considering these disanalogies, let us remember that Marx uses the figure of inversion to explain how ideology conceals contradictions. The metaphor is useful to Marx because the figure of inversion 'is commonly associated with the realm of the negative, the abnormal, the wrong-sided' (Cassar 2008, 2), qualities Marx wishes to confer on ideology. But the metaphor is not sufficient on a number of accounts. For Heath, Marx's metaphor fetishizes an instant, a static image of a subject in front of an inverted reality:

> The model of the camera obscura stops on the screen, hypothesizes subject
> and reality in the simple figure of inversion at the very moment that it seeks
> to stress the relations of their production, a process that crosses subject and
> reality in ideology.
>
> (252)

The metaphor is static and shallow. One of Heath's main tasks in his essay, as we shall see below, is to transform this static metaphor into a dynamic one.

Cassar reminds us that, in a camera obscura, the image is not only inverted, but reversed from left to right as well (2008, 2). Yet Marx does not consider this aspect of the metaphor; he simplifies an already simple metaphor.

The metaphor also sets up a sharp division between inside and outside – the inverted image is inside the camera, sealed off from reality outside; there is no direct contact between reality and ideology. The camera obscura metaphor therefore perpetuates the idealist and empiricist theories of ideology.

In addition, the metaphor suggests that the reality outside ideology/the camera obscura is free from politics and economics. In place of this naïve thesis, we need to realize that the reality 'outside' has already been transformed. Ideology is already reflecting a reflection: 'Instead of holding to a reproduction of life ... [film] holds to a reproduction of the image of life' (Heath 1976, 253).

Finally, Marx uses a specular metaphor to describe a social process: he reduces a complex social phenomenon involving invisible processes to a purely visual analogy involving relations between immediately visible objects, which (as both Heath and Sarah Kofman point out[3]) creates the problem, rather than solving it. The metaphor of the camera obscura is itself ideological. Heath's strategy, as we shall see below, is to focus on the frame implicit in the metaphor as a way of explaining ideology, rather than the inverted image.

Heath finds Freud's metaphor, describing the unconscious in spatial and photographic terms, to be more productive for film theory. In an attempt to describe the unconscious in his *Introductory Lectures*, Freud compared it to an inaccessible room full of negative photographic images.[4] Only those images that are able to get past the threshold of the room into consciousness become positive images that can be perceived. The other images remain repressed.

Freud's metaphor privileges negativity, for the unconscious naturally evokes the negative (the non-conscious, the unknown, the disowned, the necessity of ambivalence), just as the camera obscura naturally evokes inversion. The metaphor is based on the passage from unconscious to consciousness being similar to the transition from negative to positive image. It also suggests that both camera and psyche produce images.

At first, Freud's metaphor sounds as unpromising as Marx's camera obscura. It is a spatial metaphor that has the tendency to 'nominalize' the word *unconscious*: that is, to present the unconscious as a pre-existing object, a storeroom full of instinctual or primordial impulses, located in a separate space from consciousness. (Compare this to Lacan's emphasis on the unconscious as an inference the analyst makes from interpreting disruptions [slips of the tongue, parapraxes] in language.)

Sarah Kofman argues that '[t]he difference between these two models is minimal, the physical image in one [the camera obscura] becoming a chemical impression in the other [the photographic negative]' (1998, 21). But Heath sees beyond the similarities between Marx and Freud's metaphors, because Freud presents a split subject, rather than a coherent one (whether imaginary or not): 'The subject is no longer given in front of the screen of ideology but divided in the very process of its construction for that confrontation. The camera obscura becomes a series of chambers with negatives and positives, movements and repressions, screenings for and from the eye of consciousness' (252–53). The split subject becomes just as important to Heath's formulations as does his emphasis on a dynamic subject (the subject-in-process), as we shall see below.

Film references

In terms of films discussed, Heath mentions: *La Sortie des ouvriers* (1895), *Le Repas de bébé* (1895), *L'Arroseur arosé* (1895) (three early Lumière films), *Uncle Josh at the Moving Picture Show* (1902), *Grandma's Reading Glass* (1901), *Ramona* (1910), and Godard's *Les Carabiniers* (1963). Only *Uncle Josh* is discussed in any detail, particularly the moment when Uncle Josh, who is attending a film screening for the first time, tears down the screen to help the heroine in the film who is being kissed by her (presumed) fiancé. When Uncle Josh tears down the screen, he finds the projectionist behind it; both then engage in a slapstick fight.

Uncle Josh displays a naïve attitude toward film – he is unable to distinguish between film and reality. What seems to be important for Heath is that 'Uncle Josh can see well enough that it is the screen that is at stake, but then he only sees its images (which he loves) and so misses it completely, passes through it. The image goes on, *continues* … ' (254). Heath again evokes the distinction between two-dimensional screen and an imaginary three-dimensional image, and notes that the image negates the materiality of the screen. Uncle Josh seems to be an ideal spectator for Heath, one who is completely taken in by the cinematic illusion.[5] Curiously, Heath goes on to say that to attack the image, 'Uncle Josh should have turned, as we must turn, in the other direction' (254). Heath does not state what we must face when turning, but presumably he means the film projector, the apparatus that produces the image. But in the case of Uncle Josh, the projector is *behind* the screen. Although the point remains (we must confront the apparatus when questioning cinematic illusion), one wonders why Heath does not mention that the projectionist is situated behind the screen, not in front of it.

Anecdotes

The same applies to the anecdotes Heath mentions in passing, which are mainly concentrated in the opening pages: the origins of cinema's beginnings in the Grand Café (251); the necessity to explain to early Japanese film audiences how projection worked (251); in shadow theatre, men, but not women, could move behind the screen (251); Samuel Goldwyn's unsuccessful attempt to persuade Freud to write a screenplay (253); Carl Laemmle asking Eisenstein if his friend Trotsky could write a screenplay (253); and the apocryphal story of a spectator standing up in the Grand Café at the first public film screening in December 1895 and shouting 'The discovery of the universal language!' (253). In the last few pages Heath mentions D. W. Griffith's apparent dislike of pan shots (because he thought they exposed the mechanisms of film) (263); and Griffith's infamous advert he took out in the *New York Dramatic Mirror* in 1913, announcing his break with his former production company Biograph, and also claiming he invented most of the language of cinema – the close-up, the 'switch-back' (or parallel editing), and the fade (263). All of these anecdotes are simply inserted into Heath's text, with no attempt to integrate them. They are present in the essay as a second (popular) discourse, in complete contrast to his dense theoretical arguments. As the opening address at the first film studies conference held at the Center for Twentieth Century Studies, perhaps Heath felt the need to insert a few popular, traditional anecdotes to assuage an audience unfamiliar (at that time) with contemporary film theory.

Systematizing data (classifying, correlating, ordering, measuring)

Heath draws upon a number of core Marxist concepts to classify and organize his data – classifying films as dominant or subversive; classical or avant-garde; a cinema of realism (representation, illusion) versus a modernist cinema (non-representational, anti-illusionistic); of unreflexive/reflexive practice; acquiescence to dominant ideology/ resistance to dominant ideology; a cinema that constructs coherent, centred subject positions/a cinema of decentred, fragmented subject positions (the subject-in-process, discussed below). These oppositions, founded on the philosophical positions of idealism and materialism respectively, clarify Heath's two problematics by spelling out what makes mainstream cinema ideological, and what a political avant-garde cinema must do to oppose the mainstream.

But Heath not only valorizes the radical potential of avant-garde cinema against the mainstream; following a Brechtian agenda, he also celebrates the disruption of ideology (the disruption of imaginary, coherent subject positions) in mainstream cinema (for example, his famous analysis of Hitchcock's *Suspicion* (1941) [1981a, 19–24]), and in international art cinema as well (such as Oshima's *Death by Hanging* (1976) [1981a, 65–69] and *Empire of the Senses* (1976) [1981a, chapter 6]). In these examples, there is a shift from the dramatic (engagement with the fiction) to the epic (exposing the dramatic illusion), to use Brecht's terms.

Brecht became a key influence on theorizing political avant-garde film-making in the 1970s, despite his own 'fundamental reproach' against the cinema. Rather than advocate a purely formal modernism in which artworks explore their own medium specificity, a reified form of art that appealed only to the educated elite, Brecht encouraged a genuine political activism for a mass audience. Rather than simply advocate emotional involvement in a story, he also proposed interrupting this emotional involvement with moments of critical detachment, thereby creating a mixture of pleasure and political awareness. Heath mentions Brecht on five occasions in 'On Screen, In Frame': quoting him to the effect that critical art can create a break with the past by exploring alternative possibilities to the way things are (256); a mention of Brecht's fundamental reproach that Hollywood cinema is inevitably regressive, leading to the importance of the *Lehrstück* (learning play) to Brecht's theatrical work (257–58); a brief allusion to Brecht and Walter Benjamin's valuation of the cinema as 'a new mode of organizing and defining artistic production and, in fact, as a potentially epic mode' (259); towards the end Heath proclaims his essay to be a response to Brecht's principle: 'For as long as one does not criticize the social function of cinema, all film criticism is only a criticism of symptoms and has itself a merely symptomatic character' (Brecht, quoted on 264). In other words, Heath is attempting to indicate that his essay is not purely academic, but has real political consequences. Heath's essay ends on another quote from Brecht, in which he again promotes an alternative to the pre-existing order.

In 'On Screen, In Frame', Brecht therefore gets the last word, seems to define the essay's – and Heath's – horizon. It is all the more surprising, therefore, that Heath decided not to reproduce his two essays on film and Brecht (Heath 1974; 1975/6) in *Questions of Cinema*. What is completely missing in Heath's essay and his book is any discussion of Third Cinema (explicitly political films committed to activism and revolution).

Symbolizing the results

It is rare for humanities scholars to formally symbolize their results. Heath sets up an opposition between dominant and avant-garde cinema, an opposition that in 1972 Peter Wollen (1972) symbolized in terms of a table of seven oppositions:

- narrative transitivity versus narrative intransitivity
- identification versus estrangement
- transparency versus foregrounding
- single diegesis versus multiple diegesis
- closure versus aperture
- pleasure versus un-pleasure
- fiction versus reality.

A little earlier, in 1969, Jean-Louis Comolli and Jean Narboni employed Althusser's theory of ideology to distinguish seven categories of film (symbolized into the categories [a] to [g]) according to how their form and content relate to ideology. To give just a few examples: category (a) films promote the dominant ideology on both form and content; category (c) films contain a subversive form but reactionary content; category (d) films contain reactionary form but radical content; and category (e) films are 'films which seem at first sight to belong firmly within the ideology and to be completely under its sway, but which turn out to be so only in an ambiguous manner' (Comolli and Narboni 1990, 62).

Constructing problems

In constructing problems, Heath's focus falls on the cinematic, although he begins with phenomenological concepts. Because he is not analysing individual films per se, the filmic plays a negligible role in the essay.

Phenomenological concepts

Intuitions are pre-reflective (non-theoretical) judgements common sense holds about the cinema. Heath interrogates these intuitions and transforms them into theoretical statements via a series of concepts. The problematic data includes what in everyday life (the ideology of common sense) is regarded as being unproblematic ('natural') about the cinema: the film frame, the screen, the spectator's physical position in front of the screen, the realism of the photographic image, and narrative. It is only from Heath's theoretical assumptions – informed by semiotics, Marxism and psychoanalysis – that these intuitive aspects of the cinema become problematic. For Heath, these elements of cinema work to create a coherent subject position, a sense of realism, continuity, coherence of meaning (the signified), against dispersion, contradiction, materiality, the signifier.

As Heath's title indicates, he privileges the screen and frame in this essay. The screen is only discussed briefly. It is the support of the image (which Uncle Josh tears down in his over-investment in the image): 'The screen is the projection of the film frame which it holds and grounds' (258). Heath then devotes three pages to the frame, gradually transforming it from an intuitive to a theoretical concept. He begins by offering the etymology of the verb form of *frame* ('to advance, to further, to gain ground' [258]), although if we look at the OED, we see that Heath has limited himself to *frama*, the Old Norse origins of the word, and not considered *framian*, the Old English origins ('to be helpful or profitable, to make progress, f. *fram* forward'). I wonder how useful is Heath's etymological investigation, since the meanings associated with the word's origins (whether Old Norse or Old English) are all listed in the dictionary as obsolete. Definition 5 of the verb form of *frame* in the OED seems to be more useful: 'To shape, give shape to; to fashion, form'.

Heath then lists the various meanings of the term *frame* in film studies, and compares the film frame to painting's frame, and to theatre. He initially discovers four fairly conventional meanings: (i) physically, the frame is a single transparent photograph printed on the strip of film; (ii) it also names the boundary of the photographic image projected onto the screen; (iii) the term is also used to talk about the passage of the film through the projector (the image is in or out of frame, just as it is in or out of focus); (iv) it also refers to the activity of filming, of framing a scene (it names the camera's viewpoint) (258). But towards the end of his discussion of the frame, he adds more theoretical definitions: (v) 'frame, framing, is the very basis of disposition – German *Einstellung*: adjustment, centering, framing, moral attitude, the correct position' (260). He also links up the frame to the rhetorical figure of metaphor: (vi) 'the frame itself is the constant metaphor' (260). Metaphor involves the transfer of meaning from one object to another. For Heath, the frame transfers the spectator's vision from the film theatre to the film's fictional world, or diegesis. He develops this idea of transfer further:

> The stake of the frame is clear (it is this that is finally crucial in Marx's camera obscura, not the inversion): the frame is the reconstitution of the scene of the signifier, of the symbolic, into that of the signified, the passage through [the soundtrack and] the image from other scene to seen; it ensures distance as correct position, the summit of the eye, *representation*.
>
> (260)

This extract emphasizes cinema's fiction effect. The fiction film creates a representation – the film's diegesis, an alternative fictional world, an imaginary scene, the film's signified. The camera's frame (at the time of filming) and the frame projected on screen at the cinema both function simultaneously to position the spectator at the correct distance in front of that diegesis, allowing them to see through the filmic signifier, the materiality of film, to the diegesis. But, for Heath, this alignment of spectator and fictional world involves more framing: (vii) 'Analysis ... must trace the windowing identity of subject and camera, the setting of the gaze to accompany the play of "point of view" between characters in the diegetic space of the film (always the drama of the eye) which organizes the images in the coherence of the fiction' (260). In other words, some camera framings are aligned to the characters' point of view in the fictional world. No longer is that diegesis as a whole simply being framed; but inside that diegesis, certain frames represent the look of characters. These point-of-view framings located inside the diegesis help to centre the spectator's eye within that diegesis.

Heath introduces one final meaning of frame – (viii) as narrative: 'Narrative, that is, may be seen as a decisive instance of framing in film' (261). This is because narrative, like the frame, functions as a form of containment; both contain the subject in place in front of the film's diegesis.

Edward Branigan has gone further than Heath in identifying fifteen different meanings of the word *frame* in film studies (2006, 102–16). Branigan's fifteen meanings encompass Heath's. For example (and I follow Branigan's numbering and wording):

(1)   The literal frame; the real edge of an image created by limits imposed on the celluloid inside a physical camera and projector. In his first category, Branigan brings together Heath's first three categories (i), (ii) and (iii).

(5)   The frame is the overall composition of an image; critics using this meaning speak about how a shot is framed—that is, talk about its arrangement of figures, forms, colors, lighting, angle, perspective, etc. this links up with Heath's number (iv), the framing of a scene.

(9)   The frame is a view of the film's fictional world given from within that world; a point-of-view shot, representing a character's perspective on the fictional world, is the privileged example of this usage of the term 'frame'. This meaning links up with Heath's definition number (vii).

(10)   The frame is a rhetorical figure; clearly a parallel to Heath's idea (vi) of frame as a metaphor.

(12)   The frame is the narrative structure that contains the story; and

(13)   the frame is the narration that generates the story. Narrative and narration therefore organize, deform and generally manipulate the story. These two interrelated definitions link up to Heath's number (viii), which means that Heath does not sufficiently separate out narrative and narration.

(15)   Finally, the frame acts as a form of world knowledge needed to understand the film; we come to know the world of the film through a particular frame. This definition has certain affinities with Heath's frame number (v) *Einstellung*: moral attitude, the correct position.

Like Heath, Branigan establishes a hierarchical relationship between the fifteen conceptions of frame. He identifies (1) (Heath's [i], [ii] and [iii]) as the literal definition, which is then projected onto the other 14, in an increasingly metaphorical and abstract manner: 'while a frame may be literally rectangular in definition 1, it is being projected by definitions 2–15 into numerous other "rectangular" shapes as well as non-geometric shapes' (2006, 116). There is no simple parity between Heath and Branigan; for example, Heath's first three categories can be subsumed under Branigan's first category, while Heath's eighth category covers Branigan's 12 and 13. Furthermore, Branigan identifies additional meanings of the word *frame* in film theory that do not appear in Heath's essay. Branigan's discussion of frame is therefore invaluable for understanding Heath's theory in more detail.

In comparing the film frame to painting's frame, Heath challenges the numerous typical studies that emphasize the two mediums' differences (the painting's frame follows classical rules of composition and invites contemplation because it frames a still scene, whereas the cinema typically frames a constantly moving scene, breaking rules of composition and the spectator's contemplation). Instead, Heath emphasizes the similarities: in both painting and film, the frame 'stays in view throughout the comparison, in place, the constant screen' (259). Heath presents the same view regarding film and theatre: whereas theorists such as Bazin stressed the differences between the two media (theatre has wings, which are fundamentally different to the stage, whereas the cinema has off-screen space, which is a continuation of screen space outside the frame). For Heath, it is the similarity between stage and frame that is important: both delimit the scope of the action taking place in the story.

Cinematic concepts

Most of the concepts Heath formulates to address his two problematic states of affairs are cinematic, indicating that he is theorizing the cinema, or 'film' as such (rather than individual films).

His most significant cinematic concepts are of:

(1) film as a specific signifying practice;
(2) suture;
(3) film as a (i) reproductive practice (reproducing capitalist subject positions); and
    (ii) revolutionary practice (a materialist avant-garde).

(1) Before introducing the concept of film as a specific signifying practice, Heath contextualizes this concept by distinguishing industry, text, and machine. (The following discussion is mapped out in Figure 5.1.) '*Industry* refers to the direct economic system of cinema, the organization of the structure of production, distribution, and consumption' (256). Heath defines the text simply as the film, 'a particular product of that industry' (256). His main focus is cinema as machine. In this essay at least, 'machine' does not refer to film technology but to the cinematic apparatus, where apparatus designates the mental machinery of the spectator (*le dispositif*) (cf. Baudry

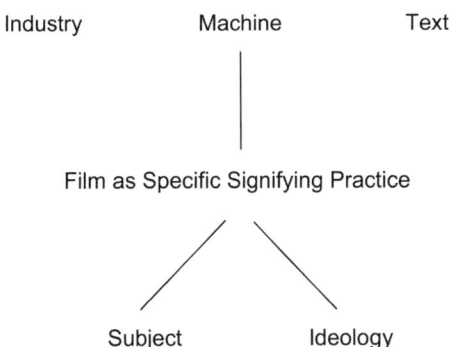

Industry   Machine   Text

Film as Specific Signifying Practice

Subject   Ideology

Figure 5.1 Film as specific signifying practice

1976; Copjec 1982). For Heath, cinema as machine is positioned precisely between cinema as industry and as text. It is within the cinema as machine that Heath locates film as a specific signifying practice.

As before, Heath defines the three terms one by one: '*Signifying* indicates the recognition of film as system or series of systems of meaning, film as articulation' (256). This formulation is influenced by two stages of Christian Metz's linguistic-based film semiotics. In his *grande syntagmatique*, Metz attempted to identify film's system of articulation in one code – its narrative units (1974a). In *Language and Cinema* (1974b) Metz recognized that the filmic text is made up of several systems of meaning, not just one. We see the influence of *Language and Cinema* again in Heath's definition of the specific: 'specificity ... is the analysis of a heterogeneity, the range of codes and systems at work in the film text' (257). Finally, practice 'takes film as a work of production of meanings' (256); it stresses the process of meaning production.

Film does not, therefore, simply represent and replicate pre-existent meanings; it is a practice or process that manufactures or produces meanings. Yet Heath does not sufficiently develop the concept of practice, even though it is fundamental to the Marxist theory of historical materialism. Practice is a mediator between individuals and the material world; it is a process that guides humans in transforming matter into products. Marxism identifies three forms of practice: economic, political, and ideological. Economic practice produces from raw materials, machinery, and a workforce, the material conditions of subsistence. Political practice produces and organizes social relations between different social groups – in capitalism, the antagonistic relation between the middle class and the working class. Ideological practice is a practice of representation that produces a subjectivity for individuals. Althusser stresses the interdependence of practices, subjects, and ideology: '1. There is no practice except by and in an ideology; 2. There is no ideology except by the subject and for subjects' (1971, 170). Ideological practice therefore entails the manufacture of subject positions, which play an active, determining role in the successful functioning of ideology. These subject positions, in turn, ensure that individuals play their role in reproducing economic and political practices. Ideological practice in Althusser's formulation is both enabling (positive) and limiting (negative): it enables individuals to function in society, but it also prescribes how they should act and think.

It was Julia Kristeva who formulated the concept of signifying practices, which she developed in the late 1960s after joining the editorial board of the influential journal *Tel Quel*. We can only grasp the radical potential of this concept by taking into account another influential concept she developed, which also had a deep impact on Heath: the notion of the subject-in-process. 'This subject ... accentuates *process* rather than identification, *projection* rather than desire, the *heterogeneous* rather than the signifier, *struggle* rather than structure' (Kristeva, quoted in Coward and Ellis, 145–46). The subject-in-process challenges Western philosophy's focus on a unified, fixed identity existing outside of contradiction, separate from otherness. For Kristeva, this unified subject represents a fragile equilibrium, a strictly temporary moment of stasis that is always vulnerable to what she calls 'the semiotic' – meaning, in her case, otherness, specifically primal, unconscious drives – because the subject by its very nature is in process, is founded on alterity. This moment of stasis, of the fixed subject, is a temporary effect of the imaginary and symbolic – of law, ideology, the Oedipus complex, the state, language, and analytic logic. These apparatuses of the symbolic attempt to censor, repress, or restrain/contain the primal drives of the semiotic. Literary avant-garde texts liberate (or unsettle) language and the reader's drives from the rigid subject positions set up by ideological apparatuses: 'Through a specific practice affecting the mechanisms of language itself (in Mallarmé, Joyce or Artaud) or affecting mythical or religious systems of representation (Lautréamont, Bataille), the "literary avant garde" presents society – even if only in its margins – with a subject in process, attacking all the stases of the unitary subject' (Kristeva 1998, 136–37). This means that signifying practices derive their specificity from primary drives of the semiotic rather than from the symbolic's unified subject. Or, more precisely, signifying practices are founded on the constant dialectic between the semiotic (heterogeneity) and the symbolic (unity), between the process and fixity of the subject. It is through this dialectic that the literary avant-garde continually destroys/renews meaning and explores the infinite possibilities of language. (Kristeva's dialectic is different from Hegel's dialectic in that hers is never-ending; there is no *Aufhebung.*) Kristeva's dialectic is resolutely materialistic, not only because it avoids Hegel's belief in a universal history inevitably progressing towards and culminating in a final consciousness of freedom, but also because its formulation of a fragile, fleeting subjectivity expunges all traces of idealism: 'the work of Kristeva on the process of signification as the process of the subject itself can be said to offer a real challenge to the "metaphysical appurtenance of the sign" [Derrida], and to be the real beginning of a materialist theory of language, signification, and ideology' (Coward and Ellis 1977, 152).

Kristeva (and more generally the *Tel Quel* group's theory and practice of the literary text) significantly influenced Heath. In his work on the French Nouveau Roman (1972a) and his essays on Joyce – which he published in *Tel Quel* (1972b; 1973) – Heath acknowledges the influence of Kristeva. However, her name does not appear anywhere in *Questions of Cinema* (except as co-editor of the volume *Langue, discours, societe* [see Heath 1981a, 71 n.27]), and there is only one reference to *Tel Quel* – a citation of Godard and Gorin's 'Enquête sur une image', *Tel Quel* 52 (1972) (see Heath 1981a, 193 n.17).[6] This suggests that, with the publication of *Questions of Cinema* in 1981, Heath wished to move on from his *Tel Quel* days, a sentiment he expresses in the English translation of his *Tel Quel* essay 'Ambiviolences', where he states on the opening page: 'As far as I am concerned, the piece is … entirely past – which does not mean that I dissociate myself from it but only that I could not now write it in the same way' (1984, 31).

Kristeva complements Heath's Althusserian Marxism (and, in fact, undermines it), for she places emphasis on psychoanalysis and linguistics, and their interrelation. She influenced his formulation of film as a specific signifying practice and also the radical potentials of the term 'practice', based as they are on the subject-in-process (which is the concept that undermines Althusser). The outcome of Heath's study of film as a signifying practice is to identify the role of the subject-in-process in the production of filmic meaning. Heath carries this out via the concept of suture.

(2) Suture is crucial to Heath, because it articulates the subject's relation to film and ideology. Heath presents the subject as an effect of film's heterogeneous codes: that is, an analysis of film's heterogeneous codes also involves a study of 'the heterogeneity in its particular effects, its particular inscriptions of subject and ideology, of the subject in ideology' (257).

Heath's use of the word *inscription* is of interest. The verb *inscribe* is a compound made up of *in* plus *scribe*, to write. Inscribing involves: 'To write, mark, or delineate (words, a name, characters, etc.) in or on something; esp. so as to be conspicuous or durable, as on a monument, tablet, etc.' (OED). The inscription of the subject in ideology therefore involves marking out a durable place in ideology for individuals to occupy.

Heath goes on to say that:

> These effects of inscription are fundamental, the area of the intersection of film in ideology by industry and machine as institution of the subject, as institution of image and position, and their shifting regulation *on* the figure of the subject.
>
> (257)

Intersection is a term from Boolean logic and from set theory denoting conjunction, an area of partial overlap between concepts. In this instance, Heath is indicating an area of partial overlap between 'film in ideology by industry' (the industrial-economic-technological system of cinema) on the one hand, and the 'machine as institution of the subject' (the spectator's mental machinery [*dispositif*]) on the other. The importance of this intersection is that it links, in the area of overlap, materialism (physical technology) and consciousness, or thinking (mental machinery). From Heath's Marxist perspective, we can set up a hierarchy between these two terms, in which materialism precedes and determines consciousness. Consciousness is not, therefore, autonomous, but emerges from materialism, from external reality, and remains dependent on it. Heath theorizes the concept of subject positioning from a materialist perspective. What this means is that the subject position is a material form that determines the individual's conscious disposition towards a film. The subject position for individuals to occupy therefore takes shape/is manufactured at the conjuncture of technology and psychology (mind and matter). We can therefore understand a subject position to be a form of consciousness created by material reality – in Heath's essay, film as a specific signifying practice/an ideological apparatus. If we combine this analysis of intersection with the definition of inscription, we can see that the manufacture of subject positions involves a physical marking in material practices that addresses, positions, and shapes an individual's consciousness.

This physical marking, or inscription, in the discourse is an empty location, a stand-in, which the individual comes to occupy. Although Heath does not mention it in this essay, such formulations were influenced by linguistic theories of enunciation (especially Benveniste 1971). These theories argue that language is oriented towards, or centred around, its users and their spatio-temporal context. It identifies a series of deictic terms – including personal pronouns such as *I* and *You*, or adverbs of place such as *here* and *there* – which link utterances to the speaker and hearer or to the context of the utterance. The deictic words inscribe in the utterance these reference points: the letter *I* quite literally defines the speaker's position in the utterance. This is analogous to the theory of subject positioning, for the subject position inscribes the spectator's place and position in the film.

But crucially, for Heath, the manufacture of subject positions is not a one-time, static process. He writes about the '*shifting* regulation on the figure of the subject' (257; emphasis added). The inscription of the subject position is not complete, but is an ongoing process:

> The hypothesis, in short, is that an important – determining – part of ideological systems in a capitalist mode of production is the achievement of a number of machines (institutions) which move – which *movie* – the individual as subject – shifting and placing desire, the energy of contradiction – in a perpetual retotalisation of the imaginary.
>
> (257)

Heath's sudden shift from *move* to *movie* seems purely gratuitous (or an attempt at avant-garde wordplay), for it simply emphasizes the fact that *movie* is a colloquial term for *moving* picture; this fact does not clarify the difficult concept Heath is attempting to explain (in fact, it detracts from the sentence's meaning). The main premise behind

110

this sentence is based on Althusser's argument that ideology is perpetuated in capitalist societies through apparatuses. These apparatuses, in Heath's words, 'move the individual as subject'. Heath's use of the verb 'to move' suggests to set in motion, to change the position of, to influence, affect. It denotes the individual's mobility and the ability to undergo a change of position via external influence. This emphasis on the movement of the subject suggests why Heath rejected Marx's static metaphor of the camera obscura.

But it is not so much the individual as such which undergoes a change of position. Instead, it is what Kristeva calls the semiotic – the drives, the energy of contradiction – that is shifted and repositioned. Excess energy, in other words, is (partly) contained by the apparatuses, with the aim of creating a sense of coherence and fullness of identity. It is in this creation of an imaginary, coherent subject position for individuals, via the (partial, strategic) suppression of desire, contradiction, and the symbolic, sexual difference, that the ideological force of apparatuses – including the cinema – is to be located.

But this process of containment is never complete or completely successful – it is 'perpetual'. The 'retotalisation of the imaginary' against desire, contradiction, and the symbolic is an ongoing process. For Heath, as for Kristeva and Slavoj Žižek (as we shall see in Chapter 8), the subject is in process. Following the Lacanian psychoanalyst Jacques-Alain Miller, Heath calls this ongoing process 'suture':

> In psychoanalysis, 'suture' names the relation of the individual-as-subject to the chain of its discourse where it figures missing in the guise of a stand-in (its place is taken and it takes that place); the subject is an effect of the signifier in which it is represented, stood in for.
>
> (261)

Heath goes on to emphasize that suture is a never-ending dialectical process:

> What must be emphasized ... is that the stopping – the functioning of the suture in imaginary, frame, narrative etc. – is exactly a *process*: it counters a productivity, an excess, that it states and restates in the very moment of rejection in the interests of coherence – thus the film frame, for example, mined from within by the outside it delimits and poses and has ceaselessly to recontain. The process never ends, the construction-reconstruction has always to be restarted: the machines, cinema included, are there for that. Ideology is *in* the suture.
>
> (262)

The process of suturing individuals into the text by making them take up the subject position inscribed in the text is an ideological process, is the way that ideology works in apparatuses such as the cinema. Heath's italicized preposition *in* is quite precise in locating the operation of ideology in the cinema.

Like Marx's static metaphor of the camera obscura, Althusser's theory of interpellation posits a static coherent subject. Heath advances beyond Marx and Althusser by emphasizing the *process* of subject construction and by theorizing the subject as *split*, not coherent. Ideology therefore functions, never 100 per cent successfully, to cover up this split and close off the individual from contradictions. Heath's development was due primarily to his integration – under the influence of Kristeva – of psychoanalysis into Marxism, which goes far beyond Althusser's limited borrowing of Lacan's concept of the imaginary. According to Heath, we must progress to the symbolic, where the individual enters the realm of language and social norms, but at the expense of repression, leading to the formation of the unconscious and, therefore, the split subject. Freud's photographic metaphor tentatively hinted at the split subject; but Heath's use of Kristeva's work, plus the concept of suture (in which Heath advances beyond previous applications of it to cinema by Jean-Pierre Oudart and Daniel Dayan) took the theory of subject positioning in the cinema to a new level. We shall see in Chapter 8 that Žižek takes the concept of suture beyond the realm of the symbolic and into the Lacanian Real.

(3) Heath's theory of suture demonstrates how film as a specific signifying practice and as an ideological apparatus functions as a reproductive practice, one that continually produces and reproduces capitalist subject positions. To the extent that those subject positions suppress desire, contradictions, and the symbolic, they lead to alienation.

Marxism challenges and transforms ideology through revolutionary practice, rather than through the realm of ideas; the contradictions of capitalism can only be resolved on a practical level. For Heath, the ideology of mainstream cinema can be overcome via a revolutionary filmic practice – politically modernist, avant-garde film. But where does this leave Heath's theoretical writing? Althusser introduced a new form of practice – theoretical practice – in which theory transforms ideology into scientific knowledge. Heath's written work (and that of the contemporary film theorists in general) constitutes a theoretical practice, in Althusser's sense of the term. A few contemporary film theorists – notably Peter Wollen and Laura Mulvey – also put their 'theoretical practice' into practice, by making avant-garde films, including: *Penthesilea: Queen of the Amazons* (1974), *Riddles of the Sphinx* (1977), and *Amy!* (1980).

Meta-theoretical concepts

In 'On Screen, In Frame' Heath does not spend time reflecting on the aims and nature of theoretical inquiry; as I pointed out above, his main aim is performative. Or, in Dana Polan's terms, Heath's essays are written 'within a discursivity of process' (1985, 163). Heath's questioning of cinema is also presented as a questioning of his own writing: '[this questioning] shows up most immediately in a certain deliberate hesitation of his writing, its allusiveness, its non-linearity, a slippage and drift not unlike that he searches for in a cinema directed against narrative representation' (1985, 169). Through his writing style, Heath therefore avoids a theoretically neutral stance and instead enacts the materialist avant-garde practice he is theorizing. He avoids reproducing a simple, unified, fixed, subject position outside of contradiction from which a simple, unified, fixed meaning can be read from his essay. 'On Screen, In Frame' puts the reader (the subject) in process.

But Heath does ask a meta-theoretical question: 'At what levels – how – does analysis need to operate?' (256). This question leads him to a precise formulation – film should be analysed as a specific signifying practice, which necessarily entails examining ideology and the subject in relation to that practice. In addition, the introduction of the subject leads Heath to formulate the following meta-theoretical statement: it is necessary to integrate psychoanalysis into an ideological analysis: 'Cinema brings historical materialism and psychoanalysis together in such a way that the consideration of film and ideology begins from and constantly returns us to the conjuncture' (253). Heath's attempts to integrate Marxism and psychoanalysis (via semiotics) were inspired by Althusser's use of Lacan and, more fundamentally, Kristeva's work of the 1970s.

Evaluating data and problems

Genuineness, correctness, and comprehensiveness

Heath presents a careful analysis of metaphors in Marx and Freud. He does not simply repeat these well-worn metaphors, but critically interrogates their function and blind spots. Heath's film examples and anecdotes are perfunctory; they do not feel genuine. The anecdotes are not sufficiently integrated into the essay and, except for *Uncle Josh at the Moving Picture Show,* the films Heath mentions are not comprehensively discussed; they only have a very limited value in addressing his problematic states of affairs. We also need to consider if *Uncle Josh at the Moving Picture Show* has been correctly described, since the projectionist depicted in that particular film is situated behind the screen, not in front of it.

Well-formedness and significance

Heath's essay emerges from a real problem at the core of Marxism – exposing the role of ideology in concealing the contradictions of capitalism, and the need to develop a revolutionary practice. To that extent, his theory is well-formed, for it makes sense within a Marxist perspective. And his theory is significant in that it makes funda-mental advances in addressing this problem by developing a materialist theory of the subject – a theory that focuses, moreover, on the subject constructed in process and division.

Within the specific context of film theory in the 1970s, Heath's essay is well-formed, significant, and innovative in the way it deploys the semiotic concept of a specific signifying practice, the Marxist (Althusserian) concept of the ideological appa-ratus, and the psychoanalytic (Lacanian) concepts of suture and the subject-in-process to analyse 'the articulation of film and ideology on the figure of the subject' (261). His second problematic, following the Marxist agenda of revolutionary practice, is mapped out in the essay, but is not addressed in any detail: 'The aim now must be [the] ... transformation of the cinematic institution in its ideological effects' (257). But he says enough within his semiotic-Marxist-psychoanalytic theory to indicate that establishing a revolutionary cinematic practice, one based on de-alienation, involves promoting a materialist avant-garde filmic practice, one that promotes excess, desire, and contradictions, at the expense of rigid, static, coherent subject positions perpetuated by dominant cinema.

The quotation I used in the opening to outline what Heath's essay is about should now make more sense: 'Cinema ... holds the subject – on screen, in frame' (263). Heath precisely locates the ideological function of cinema in the way it holds the subject in place via the screen and frame (or various types of frame), within a perpetual dialectic between 'symbolic and suture, negativity and coherence, flow and image' (263).

Nonetheless, Heath's agenda has been criticized from different theoretical perspectives. Rodowick, in many respects sympathetic to Heath's political modernist agenda, finds his theory to be too formalist: 'To the extent that the destiny of the subject is decided "in the text" it can be none other than a formal problem' (1988, 208). In other words, the problem Heath identifies and his solution are worked out only in terms of an aesthetic text (the unity/disunity of a formal subject position), not in terms of political practices. The text, whether mainstream or avant-garde, is conceived as the sole factor in the determination of the film spectator's consciousness. This is a problem with the scope of Heath's theory. The beginnings of theory building necessarily involve the simplification of the problems in order to make them manageable. But the progress of a theory is dependent on its ability to expand and take account of new phenomena. What we witness in 'On Screen, In Frame' is an *initial* attempt to theorize subject positioning in the cinema as a subject-in-process. This is where the value of Heath's essay lies in the history of film theory. Once we move beyond the essay's immediate time frame, we can perceive (as Rodowick does) its limitations, including its formalism.

A more fundamental critique emerged from cognitive film theory in the 1980s. Cognitive film theorists such as David Bordwell (1985) rejected the reliability of Heath's theoretical statements. Bordwell returned to some of the intuitions he interrogates and transformed them using cognitive concepts. For Bordwell, the Marxist agenda of exposing the role of ideology in concealing contradictions, and the need to develop a revolutionary practice, are not his concern. The problems Bordwell addresses lie elsewhere. For cognitivists, consciousness is not a mere superstructure on top of a hidden, repressed unconscious. Instead, it is the basis of identity. Bordwell therefore argues that film theorists should begin with cognitive explanations of film phenomena, and should move on to psychoanalytic explanations only if the cognitive account is found wanting: 'The theory I advance attends to the perceptual and cognitive aspects of film viewing. While I do not deny the usefulness of psychoanalytic approaches to the spectator, I see no reason to claim for the unconscious any activities which can be explained on other grounds' (1985, 30). In analysing the way spectators comprehend films, Bordwell argues that they do not passively take up a subject position and absorb the film's finalized, preconstituted meaning; instead, films (even classical narrative films) are fragmentary, and spectators are actively involved in constructing their meaning. At the same time, he argues that spectators are not free agents who can construct a film's meaning in any way they wish; instead, they process the fragmented film guided by schemata – norms and principles in the mind that organize the film into a coherent mental representation. (See Bordwell 1985, Chapters 3 and 4, for a detailed outline of his cognitive theory of filmic comprehension.) Much of Bordwell's work involves applying his cognitive theory to distinct historical periods of film-making, resulting in what he calls a historical poetics of cinema.

The most devastating critique of Heath's theory emerged from analytic philosophy. Noël Carroll wrote an acerbic 74-page review of Heath's *Questions of Cinema* (Carroll 1982; subsequently revised and turned into a book: Carroll 1988b). I will only hint at the flavour of this review essay by quoting Carroll's critique of Heath's language:

> The style of *Questions of Cinema* is dense. The book is packed with neologisms, pleonasms, misuses, and strained uses of words and grammar – Heath, one surmises, enjoys calling things by the wrong name – and the book has strong tendencies toward formulaic repetition and belletristic rambling. If *Questions of Cinema* fails to become a favorite of graduate film students, this will undoubtedly be a consequence of his prose style. Throughout, the tone of the book is bullying. Heath liberally peppers his commentary with *thus*, and *therefore* – words that ordinarily signal the conclusion of a piece of reasoning – where there is no argument in the vicinity. The reader searches for nonexistent premises until he gives up – staring blankly at the poker-faced text. Heath also tends to overuse words like *precisely* and *exactly* at just those points in the exposition where he is least precise and exact.
>
> (1982, 153)

At some point in the reading of 74 pages of Carroll's review, readers will come to the conclusion that Carroll is not even attempting to understand Heath's work on its own terms. Carroll's intervention is far more polemical: he wants to demonstrate that Heath's theory is fundamentally flawed and should be discarded completely. But his polemicism makes meaningful disagreement impossible. It fails to follow what Donald Davidson called the principle of charity: 'We make maximum sense of the words and thoughts of others when we interpret in a way that optimizes agreement. ... [W]e improve the clarity and bite of declaration of difference, whether scheme or shared opinion, by enlarging the basis of shared language or shared opinion' (1973–74, 19). And: '[This] method is not designed to eliminate disagreement, nor can it; its purpose is to make meaningful disagreement possible, and this depends entirely on a foundation – *some* foundation – in agreement' (1973–74, 19). It is clear that Carroll does not observe the principle of charity in his review of Heath's book.[7]

Part of interpreting Heath's theory charitably would involve realizing that, as I pointed out above, it is the initial formulation of an ambitious project, an initial formulation that needed to be developed. But Heath did not develop the theory further; he simply wrote a long response to Carroll's review – which he called (amongst other things) a 'solid block of error' (Heath 1983, 65). One effect of Carroll's review was that film studies bifurcated, with contemporary film theorists deepening their theories of subjectivity, merging film into cultural studies, while an alliance between analytic philosophy and cognitive theory took on board Carroll's critique of contemporary film theory and developed Bordwell's alternative theory: 'on one side stood a politicized cultural studies and, on the other, the more formalist cognitive film theory (including historical poetics [and analytic philosophy]). While the former profits from sliding away from the medium to examine whatever it finds of interest around it, the latter resolutely holds onto the specificity of film' (Andrew 2009, 906). Heath's concept of film as a specific signifying practice is valuable for representing a brief, historical moment in film theory when these two (now bifurcated) positions found a temporary balance, for Heath offered a politicized theory of film that remains grounded in the semiotic study of filmic specificity.

Notes

1 For an authoritative exposition of the problems, concepts, debates, and agendas that dominated this fertile period of theoretical activity, see Rosalind Coward and John Ellis's *Language and Materialism* (1977).

2 Michael Benamou, the director of the Center in the 1970s, stated the Center's aims: 'The Center for Twentieth Century Studies is a community of scholars in the humanities whose research focuses on ethnic studies, mass media (including film and video) and artistic/technological alternatives to print culture. In 1975 the Center organized its first international Symposium on Film Theory and in 1976 a Conference on the Teaching of Film. Papers from these two conferences are published in special issues of the *Quarterly Review of Film Studies* (vol. 1, nos 3 & 4)' (1977, 2).

   Questions of Cinema contains a total of three addresses Heath made at The Center for Twentieth Century Studies: in addition to 'On Screen, In Frame' (presented in November 1975), he presented 'Film Performance' in February 1977 (Chapter 4 of *Questions of Cinema*) and 'The Cinematic Apparatus: Technology as Historical and Cultural Form' (February 1978; Chapter 10).

3 'To describe ideology as a camera obscura – is this not to remain, as Marx reproaches Feuerbach, at the level of speculative criticism … ?' (Kofman 1998, 5).

4 In an endnote to 'Freud and the scene of writing', Derrida points out that the metaphor of the photographic negative occurs frequently in Freud (1978, 330 n.18).

5 Thomas Elsaesser points out that these 'rube' films create a superior form of spectatorship – but at the expense of self-censorship and self-restraint: 'The audience laughs at a simpleton and village idiot, who is kept at a distance and ridiculed, and thereby it can flatter itself with a self-image of urban sophistication. The punishment meted out to Uncle Josh by the projectionist is both allegorized as the reverse side of cinematic pleasure … and internalized as self-control: in the cinema … the rule is "you may look but don't touch" (2006, 213). Elsaesser quotes Walter Benjamin at the end of this extract.

6 I would argue that *Questions of Cinema* is primarily a work of *Tel Quel* theory applied to cinema and, more specifically, of Kristeva's theories of 'specific signifying practices' and the 'subject-in-process'. D. N. Rodowick has noted the influence of *Tel Quel*/Kristeva on Heath's *Questions of Cinema*: 'Paradoxically, the directness of Heath's relation to Kristeva is all the more profound for the almost complete absence of reference to her. Neither the name of Kristeva nor the concept of negativity are indexed in *Questions of Cinema*, for example, although at least the latter is repeatedly invoked in his work. Nevertheless, I hope to demonstrate the pervasiveness of Kristeva's work in relation to Heath's' (1988, 214 n.4). See Rodowick (1988, Chapter 7) for his analysis of the influence of Kristeva on Heath's film theory.

7 I review Carroll's book in more detail in Buckland (1989).

6

AGAINST THEORIES OF REFLECTION

Laura Mulvey's 'Visual Pleasure and Narrative Cinema'

Psychoanalytic theory opened up the possibility of understanding the mechanics of popular mythology and its raw materials: images of sexual difference, instincts and their vicissitudes, primal fantasy. Structuralism and semiotics opened up the possibility of understanding the way images work as signs and symptoms, patterns of rhetoric, narrative and narration. A previously invisible world whose images, sensations and inklings had previously evaded one's grasp materialised with the language that could name its objects, like the appearance of invisible ink in front of a flame.

(Laura Mulvey 1989, xiii)

Problem-situation

The work of the British feminists – including Elizabeth Cowie, Claire Johnston, Pam Cook, and Laura Mulvey – constitutes a dominant aspect of contemporary film theory, and shares its dense web of theoretical influences: Marxism; psychoanalysis (Freud and Lacan); semiotics (especially Barthes's study of myth, and the concept of specific signifying practice); structuralism (Lévi-Strauss's study of kinship systems and of woman-as-sign); plus the feminism of Juliet Mitchell (*Psychoanalysis and Feminism* [1974]). The British feminists employed these theories to develop a critique of patriarchal values in cinema, and also to criticize the sociological 'image-of-women' approach to film analysis. Claire Johnston discovered this sociological bias at work in three pioneering feminist film books published in the early 1970s: Marjorie Rosen's *Popcorn Venus* (1974), Molly Haskell's *From Reverence to Rape* (1974), and Joan Mellen's *Women and their Sexuality in New Film* (1973). 'All three', Johnston writes, 'derive essentially from the dominant traditions of practical criticism based on personal response and subjectivity' (1975, 115). Furthermore, they are impressionistic, anecdotal, and adopt a reflectionist theory of the cinema, 'which see[s] the world created in films as a mirror of the real world, albeit a distorting mirror' (116). The success or failure of this one-to-one mirroring between image and reality is judged as either true or false, positive or negative. These authors therefore talk about positive-correct-accurate images versus negative-incorrect-inaccurate ones, which are then condemned. The problem-situation for the British feminists therefore emerged from their criticism of known solutions, the sociological image-of-women approach (from now on, the 'images approach'), using a new theoretical perspective. A similar critique took place in literary studies.[1]

117

The underlying assumptions behind the images approach are causal determinism plus an empirical aesthetics. Causal determinism is a logocentric notion: it posits a fixed, unchanging, direct mechanical link between an external cause (reality) and effect (the cinematic image of that reality); the reality is seen to directly cause the image and to be fully present in the image. This causal link can be distorted, leading to biased images. But this assumption is based on the further notions of a direct, non-distorted causal link, and that a pre-existing referent exists fully formed, simply waiting to be represented, and that representation can potentially offer a full, accurate image of women. The British feminists challenged these notions:

> The work of film is not ... the simple representation of an already constituted meaning or content. As a consequence, therefore, it must be involved in producing meanings, and hence in producing specific definitions of women. ... 'Woman' is not given, biologically or psychologically, but is a category produced by signifying practices.
>
> (Cowie 1997, 19; 25)

The way Rosen, Haskell, and Mellen talk about the different stereotypes/images of women suggests a full representation of the stereotype. They posit a pre-given fixed referent fully present in the image, rather than examine the filmic text's production of that stereotype.

The images approach is empirical in its rejection of abstract levels of meaning. It valorizes immediately observable content (stereotypes on screen) and meaning as external, pre-given, and stable. It ignores film's material textuality, relegating it to a phantom status, and fails to analyse in depth abstract elements such as the film's overall patriarchal narrative structure – which, like all structures, is not immediately given in experience, and cannot be reduced to experience. The patriarchal values are not immediately visible in the image.[2]

To counter causal determinism and empiricism, Cowie took her cue from Lévi-Strauss's study of myth. She quotes his analysis of the sun as a symbol (a mytheme) in myths. The anthropologist does not, of course, study the sun scientifically, as a pre-existing referent, a star. Nor should he or she posit fixed, eternal meanings for the sun's appearance in myths. Instead, Lévi-Strauss argues,

> The mytheme 'sun' does not, taken in and for itself, have any meaning. Depending on the particular myths under consideration it can range over a whole variety of different ideal contents. In fact nobody coming across 'sun' in a myth, would be able to say in advance just what specific content, nature or functions were in that myth. Its meaning could only be identified from the relations of correlation and opposition in which it stands to other mythemes within this myth.
>
> (Lévi-Strauss, quoted in Cowie 1997, 27)

This structural definition of the mytheme 'sun' offers a suitable analogy for understanding how the British feminist film theorists rejected the images approach and proposed to study woman as sign. Building upon Marxism, psychoanalysis, and semiotics, they developed a critique of the image and the reflectionist approach to representation by conceptualizing the film as text/medium/discourse/specific signifying practice, which examines film's production of meaning rather than simple reproduction of it. They took from semiotics the notion that meaning emerges out of non-meaning, from the selection and combination of codes on the level of the filmic text. Like Metz and other film semioticians, they advocated the need to identify and analyse those meanings generated specifically in the filmic text: 'Playing on the tension between film as controlling the dimension of time (editing, narrative) and film as controlling the dimension of space (changes in distance, editing), cinematic codes create a gaze, a world, and an object, thereby producing an illusion cut to the measure of desire' (Mulvey 1975, 17). Here we are far from the images approach to film, for Mulvey is talking about cinema's specific *creation* of a gaze, a world, and an object, not its simple reproduction.

Cowie, Johnston, Cook, and Mulvey therefore rejected the positions that locate meaning purely and simply outside the film – either a historical reality, or in a real author expressing him or herself. They shifted film feminism to the study of images *as* images, their appeal as images rather than simply for what they represent. The image was conferred its own materiality, its own signifying power. They also expanded the object of study: not just a critique of the image, for they also examined the unconscious ideological-patriarchal nature of the cinematic apparatus – its creation of a male gaze, of gendered (masculine) subject positions, and patriarchal narrative forms. It is not merely what is represented in films, but the realism of representation and the apparatus supporting that representation which constitute the new problematic state of affairs to be addressed. The problem, Mulvey argued, lies in patriarchy and the male psyche: 'I argued, with the help of psychoanalytic theory, that the sexualised image of woman says little or nothing about women's reality, but is symptomatic of male fantasy and anxiety that are projected on to the female image. ... The direction of the gaze shifted, satisfyingly, from woman as spectacle to the psyche that had need of such a spectacle' (1989, xiii–xiv).

Two examples of the way the British feminists changed the study of women in film: Cowie re-examined Wollen's analysis of women in Howard Hawks's films (1997, 26–35). She argued that, although he avoids the images approach by studying women as signs rather than referents within a textual system, he assigns them a fixed meaning:

> Hawks does not have, as Wollen argued, a general system of sexual difference, of either man in control of nature and woman in his adventure films, or woman as nature in control of man in the comedies. The binary oppositions Hawks sets into play are not a fixed structure which is then inverted, rather each film works a set of distinctions around sexual difference producing definitions of masculinity and femin[in]ity.
>
> (Cowie 1997, 31)

Cowie objects to Wollen positing a series of pre-existing static structures that simply become manifest in a director's films. Instead, drawing upon the same sources as

Wollen – semiotics and Lévi-Strauss's structural anthropology – Cowie argues that specific meanings, including masculinity and femininity, are created from the play of codes and structures at work in each film. Cowie acknowledges a continuity of structure and codes from one director's film to the next, but challenges Wollen's idea that these structures are a priori and unchanging from film to film.

In their analysis of *The Revolt of Mamie Stover* (Raoul Walsh, 1956), Cook and Johnston go beyond the surface appearance of the central female character (Stover), who seems to be strong and independent: 'It has often been argued that there are a number of films directed by Raoul Walsh which appear to present women as strong and independent characters. The authors of the following essay take issue with this type of reading and attempt to demonstrate that women (e.g., Mamie Stover) in fact function as a signifier in a circuit of exchange where the values exchanged have been fixed by/in a patriarchal culture' (Cook and Johnston 1974, 94). On the surface, Mamie Stover appears to be autonomous, the subject rather than object of desire, defined outside of patriarchy. But, with the aid of semiotics, Marxism, and psycho-analysis, Cook and Johnston go beyond this surface appearance and reveal 'the central contradiction of [Mamie Stover's] situation' (1974, 100), that she can only become the subject of desire by defining herself in terms of patriarchal values, which she is unable to escape. These include her job as a hostess/showgirl at The Bungalow (a fetishized image of woman), and the fact that her desire is defined by the male lead, Jimmy (who rejects her in the end, leading to her downfall).

In summary, because it constitutes meaning as outside and pre-existing cinema, the image-of-women approach 'does not have to confront the essential question of how ideology is inscribed into the actual material practices of the cinema, such as the structuring of the narrative, the production of the "realism" effect, etc' (Johnston 1975, 117). This approach does not question the issue of the image as representation; it takes the image for granted. The image is posited as transitive, transparent, and neutral; the biased representation derives from outside the cinema. Women in the cinema are discussed in the same way as women outside cinema.[3]

Counter cinema

The British feminists' critique of the causal determinism and empirical aesthetics in the images approach also influenced their conception of what women's cinema should consist of. They argued that ideology is to be challenged and transformed through revolutionary practice, rather than in the realm of ideas, and that the contradictions of capitalism can only be resolved on a practical level. As we saw in the previous chapter, on Stephen Heath, this transformation involves a change in the material conditions of film production and system of representation, one where the cinema no longer functions as a vehicle for dominant ideology, but instead investigates its own materiality. From this Marxist perspective, the British film feminists argued that a women's cinema cannot simply record on camera, cinéma vérité style, women's oppressive experiences, for this also presupposes a stable referent: 'the "truth" of our repression cannot be captured on celluloid with the "innocence" of the camera: it has to be constructed/manufactured' (Johnston 1973, 28). The counter cinema images of women do not have stable referents that can simply be captured by the camera, but must be constructed: 'Any revolutionary strategy must challenge the depiction of reality; it is not enough to discuss the oppression of women within the text of the film; the language of the cinema/the depiction of reality must also be interrogated, so that a break between ideology and text is effected' (1973, 29). Like Heath, Johnston draws upon the radical potential of the term 'practice' by focusing on process, a film's production of meaning, rather than its reproduction of pre-existing fixed meanings.

But does the formation of a women's counter cinema have to be purely negative? We shall see below that Mulvey initially said yes: patriarchy can only be challenged through the destruction of dominant cinema's visual pleasure. While also advocating radical film practices, Johnston was more accommodating to conventional forms of film-making. She argued, for example, that within Hollywood, women directors such as Dorothy Arzner and Ida Lupino successfully created critiques of patriarchal ideology. They infiltrated the dominant system and subverted it from within, whereas Mulvey sought an alternative system, a new type of practice outside of dominant systems of representation. Johnston's work conforms to a search for minor cinema, analogous to Deleuze and Guattari's analysis of minor literature.[4]

'Visual Pleasure and Narrative Cinema'

Mandy Merck (2007) presents a comprehensive account of the origins of Mulvey's essay. (For an outline of Mulvey's essay, see the box on p. 122.) She emphasizes that it was not in fact an academic essay, but was written in the mode of a modernist manifesto, emerging out of the Women's Movement of the 1970s and from organizations such as the British Film Institute and the Society for Education in Film and Television (populated not with lecturers from the university sector, but with intellectuals and cinéphiles). Its prescriptive statements, polemical, vivid language, and call for the destruction of visual pleasure align it with the manifesto format, and it avoids some of the trappings of the academic essay (no descriptive subtitle complementing a playful rhetorical title, no direct quotes, few footnotes). The essay was published in Screen (vol. 16, no. 3, 1975: 6–18), the journal of SEFT mainly funded by the BFI (see Bolas 2009 for a history of these institutions).

Mulvey was also a member of 'The Lacan Women's Study Group', along with Juliet Mitchell, Mary Kelly, and Jacqueline Rose. Mulvey's psychoanalytic concepts emerged mainly from Freud's *Three Essays on the Theory of Sexuality* and from his essay 'Instincts and their Vicissitudes'. Perhaps she was partly influenced by Mitchell's juxtaposition of psychoanalysis and feminism in her 1974 book *Psychoanalysis and Feminism*.

An Outline of 'Visual Pleasure and Narrative Cinema'

I Introduction

A A political use of psychoanalysis: 'Psychoanalytic theory is ... appropriated here as a political weapon, demonstrating the way the unconscious of patriarchal society has structured film form' (6).

B Destruction of pleasure as a radical weapon: A feminist avant-garde cinema can challenge the patriarchal assumptions of mainstream narrative cinema (for the mainstream operates at the expense of women); similarly, psychoanalytic theory can destroy the male pleasure perpetuated by mainstream cinema.

II Pleasure in Looking/Fascination with the Human Form

A Cinema offers several visual pleasures, including scopophilia – an active and controlling pleasure in using another person as an object of sexual stimulation through sight.

B Another visual pleasure involves narcissism, taking the self-image (the ego) as an object of pleasure: either in the mirror image, or in the idealized human forms on the movie screen.

C Freud posited a fundamental contradiction between A (sexual libido) and B (ego). Mainstream narrative cinema is able to keep these two contradictory visual pleasures in balance (the male spectator identifies with his like on screen [B] and, through him, takes visual possession of the woman within the diegesis [A]).

III Woman as Image, Man as Bearer of the Look

A Introduction of the binary oppositions: active/passive, male/female, plus a discussion of woman as a spectacle for the active male gaze.

B The opposite of spectacle: narrative, controlled and motivated by the male characters.

C1 Woman is not simply a spectacle (creating male pleasure); she also signifies castration (creating male unpleasure). This unpleasure is disavowed via voyeurism (a temporalized, sadistic narrative investigation of the woman as bearer of guilt) or fetishism (a static, over-valuation of woman as fetish object).

C2 Filmic examples: Sternberg (fetishism in *Morocco* and *Dishonoured*) and Hitchcock (fetishism but especially voyeurism in *Rear Window*, *Vertigo*, and *Marnie*).

Mulvey was almost certainly inspired by Mitchell's and other feminists' appropriation of psychoanalysis as a political weapon:

> Psychoanalysis is not a recommendation *for* a patriarchal society, but an analysis *of* one. If we are interested in understanding and challenging the oppression of women, we cannot afford to neglect it.
>
> (Mitchell 1974, xv)

I am interested not in what Freud did, but in what we can get from him, a political rather than an academic exploration.

(Mitchell 1974, xx)

Psychoanalytic theory is … appropriated here as a political weapon, demonstrating the way the unconscious of patriarchal society has structured film form.

(Mulvey 1975, 6)[5]

The title of Mulvey's essay is premised on narrative cinema's 'skilled and satisfying manipulation of visual pleasure' (8). The title's two concepts ('visual pleasure', 'narrative cinema') are simply linked together by 'and', suggesting equality and close affinity between them (we can reverse them, for example, without loss of meaning). Within the essay, visual pleasure is conferred more technical names (scopophilia, voyeurism, narcissism), while narrative cinema remains the same, although it is sometimes called a variation of mainstream illusionistic Hollywood film. I have already mentioned that there is no subtitle offering a more descriptive account of the essay's content. This is because the title itself is fairly descriptive; section headings offer more description of the essay's content ('Pleasure in Looking/Fascination with the Human Form'; 'Woman as Image, Man as Bearer of the Look').

Analysing the problematic state of affairs

Identifying what is problematic

A gap in knowledge can be generated by the emergence of new (problematic) data, from the identification of conceptual paradoxes/contradictions, or by criticizing known solutions to problems from a different theoretical perspective. In 'Visual Pleasure and Narrative Cinema' (1975), when identifying exactly what is problematic, Mulvey chooses the second and third options. She implies that the existing theories (the logocentric or reflectionist image-of-women approach) and its solutions cannot adequately account for the patriarchal representation of women in film. For that, one needs psychoanalysis, which feminists can use as a political weapon to reveal the contradictions at the centre of patriarchal society.

Yet Mulvey opens her paper apparently using the reflectionist theory of representation: 'This paper intends to use psychoanalysis to discover where and how the fascination of film is reinforced by pre-existing patterns of fascination already at work within the individual subject and the social formations that have moulded him' (6). The essay begins with pre-existing patterns of fascination and social formations that exist outside film. The next sentence uses the word 'reflects' to relate film and social formation: '[This essay] takes as starting point the way film reflects, reveals and even plays on the straight, socially established interpretation of sexual difference which controls images, erotic ways of looking and spectacle' (6). Again, film is posited as simply reflecting and revealing a pre-existing external force (socially established interpretation of sexual difference) – although film also 'plays' with this force, suggesting that it is not completely transparent. This is confirmed in the final sentence of the opening paragraph, in which Mulvey states her intention to use psychoanalytic theory to demonstrate 'the way the unconscious of patriarchal society structures film form' (6). This final sentence is crucial in many respects, not least because it shifts the essay away from theories of reflection towards a materialist theory of film, where Mulvey makes her most significant contribution to feminist film theory.

Mulvey formulates the problematic state of affairs to be addressed in her second paragraph:

> Recent wr[i]ting in *Screen* about psychoanalysis and the cinema has not suffi-ciently brought out the importance of the representation of the female form in a symbolic order in which, in the last resort, it speaks of castration and nothing else.
>
> (6)

While unidentified, this 'recent writing' in *Screen* (and elsewhere in the early 1970s) suffers from remaining too much on the surface level of film, thereby keeping a number of patriarchal values unknown and unchallenged. (This problem, of course, is based on the background assumption that the patriarchal symbolic order – and its values such as castration – determines the representation of women in the cinema.) Remaining on the surface creates the problematic data. The problematic state of affairs Mulvey identifies is therefore a gap in knowledge concerning the way patriarchal values such as castration define women negatively. This gap is partly filled through psychoanalysis, which becomes a political tool in raising awareness of how women are defined and repressed: '[psychoanalysis] gets us nearer to the roots of our oppression' (7).

The second problem becomes one of challenging that patriarchal definition of woman by conceiving an alternative, while still being caught up in it:

> the ultimate challenge: how to fight the unconscious structured like a language (formed critically at the moment of arrival in language) while still caught within the language of patriarchy.
>
> (7)

Mulvey locates the problematic state of affairs at a repressed, unconscious level, and identifies it as an issue, not of biology or sociology, but of language and discourse (by following Lacan in defining the unconscious as structured like a language). The problem, through, is one of distance – of maintaining critical distance from patriarchal values that nonetheless structure identity. We have already encountered this problem in the previous chapter in regards to ideological analysis. Althusser's concept of 'theoretical practice', in particular, attempted to address this issue of distance. Mulvey draws upon psychoanalysis to address this issue: 'psychoanalytic theory as it now stands can at least advance our understanding of the status quo, of the patriarchal order in which we are caught' (7). Like Althusser and Marx, she identifies concealed contradictions and paradoxes at the centre of the patriarchal social formation she analyses (see 'constructing problems', below).

Background assumptions

As we have already seen, the problematic state of affairs Mulvey addresses in 'Visual Pleasure' is based on the background assumption that patriarchal concepts such as castration determine the representation of women in the cinema. Mulvey makes this assumption central to her essay: 'woman as representation signifies castration, inducing voyeuristic or fetishistic mechanisms to circumvent her threat' (17). Ultimately, the essay is about the possibility of theorizing the female body image. Psychoanalysis made this theorizing possible: it enabled Mulvey to conceptualize patriarchy's negative definition of woman as castrated, and the way the cinema at the same time perpetuates that definition and employs voyeuristic and fetishistic mechanisms to circumvent this negativity, the threat she poses to the male psyche.

Moreover, by making explicit the background assumption that patriarchy is founded on the image of the woman as castrated (an assumption not found in the images approach), Mulvey changes the *level* at which a feminist analysis needs to operate: feminist film theorists must dig further than the images approach and discover the *repressed* values that determine 'the representation of the female form': 'Psychoanalytic theory provided [the] investigative gaze with the ability to see through the surface of cultural phenomena as though with intellectual X-ray eyes. The images and received ideas of run of the mill sexism were transformed into a series of clues for deciphering a nether world, seething with displaced drives and misrecognised desire' (1989, xiv). Mulvey therefore goes far beyond the images approach by employing a series of underlying abstract concepts from psychoanalysis to develop a more adequate account – especially Freud's concepts of castration, voyeurism, and fetishism. Like other contemporary film theorists, Mulvey sets up a two-tier hierarchy (surface/underlying reality) and privileges the underlying level, for while the surface level manifests the problematic data, it can only be resolved on the abstract, underlying level.

Describing the problematic state of affairs

Collecting data

Mulvey's data derives initially from Hollywood mainstream cinema, which she condemns as a monolithic discourse that perpetuates – and is structured by – patriarchal values: 'However self-conscious and ironic Hollywood managed to be, it always restricted itself to a formal mise-en-scène reflecting the dominant ideological concept of the cinema' (7). (Note again that Mulvey mediates between film form and social context via the word 'reflect'.) She briefly mentions two films by Hawks (*Only Angels Have Wings* and *To Have and Have Not*) before analysing five films by two well-known auteurs – Josef von Sternberg's *Morocco* (1930), and *Dishonored* (1931), and Hitchcock's *Rear Window* (1954), *Vertigo* (1958), and *Marnie* (1964).

Mulvey notes that a cheap alternative, in the form of 16mm, is now (in the 1970s) possible as a way to challenge the political and aesthetic assumptions of mainstream cinema (8). While Mulvey only notes the role of the avant-garde in passing (as does Heath in 'On Screen, In Frame'), this point is significant for she made, with Peter Wollen, a series of radical avant-garde films in the 1970s, including *Penthesilea* (1974) and *Riddles of the Sphinx* (1977): 'In [these] films, theory and politics could be juxtaposed with narrative and visual poetics. ... The films could confront questions of film criticism with film itself, debate images with counter-images, intellectual strategies with visual play' (Mulvey 1989, ix).

Systematizing data *(*classifying, correlating, ordering, measuring*)*

Like other contemporary film theorists, Mulvey classifies film-making into a binary opposition: mainstream (Hollywood)/political avant-garde. Mainstream cinema is capitalist; avant-garde practice is artisanal (7). The avant-garde can 'only exist as a counterpoint' to the mainstream (8). Whereas the mainstream generates erotic pleasure for the male psyche, feminist film theory and avant-garde practice aim to destroy that pleasure. Within Hollywood, Mulvey distinguishes between films that privilege different types of male pleasure: fetishism (e.g. Sternberg) and those that privilege voyeurism-sadism (Hitchcock – although Mulvey points out that Hitchcock also employs fetishism).

Constructing problems

Phenomenological concepts

Like other contemporary film theorists, Mulvey's essay is formulated against phenomen-ology, since the immediate lived experience is regarded as being ideological (patriarchal). This is apparent in her implicit rejection of the images approach, as well as her replacement of auteurism and cinéphilia with psychoanalytic concepts. The 'love' of and 'pleasure' generated by mainstream cinema, celebrated by auteur critics and cinéphiles at the film's surface level, is redefined on an underlying level with psycho-analytic concepts such as castration, voyeurism, and fetishism, and is recoded as an exclusively male pleasure. Mulvey's call for a destruction of pleasure is therefore a reaction against the male pleasure of cinéphilia: 'Women, whose image has continually been stolen and used for [voyeuristic mechanisms] cannot view the decline of the traditional film form with anything much more than sentimental regret' (18).[6]

Cinematic concepts

Mulvey begins her essay (section I A) by outlining external social forces that have shaped the idea of women in patriarchal societies: 'The paradox of phallocentrism in all its manifestations is that it depends on the image of the castrated woman to give order and meaning to its world' (6). The patriarchal definition of woman as castrated is the central concept, or 'lynch pin' (6), in both patriarchal societies and in Mulvey's argument (she refers to the concept of castration no less than 13 times in a relatively

126

short essay). In section I B, Mulvey begins to outline how these external social forces structure Hollywood film form, and how a psychoanalytically informed critical theory and a political avant-garde film-making practice must challenge and destroy the male pleasure created by that film form.

That pleasure is primarily visual, based on different types of looking, which constitute the main problematic object of study in the essay. By going beyond the surface, Mulvey discovers several underlying material contradictions and paradoxes that constitute the visual meanings in narrative cinema:

(1) We have already seen that, on the opening page, Mulvey identifies a paradox in phallocentrism: that it depends on the image of the castrated woman (6). This insight derives from the new theoretical paradigm Mulvey has introduced into the study of women in the cinema – psychoanalysis, which identifies the castrated woman as the ultimate absent cause or empty signifier at the centre of the patri-archal symbolic order. Mulvey (and Juliet Mitchell before her) emphasizes that she is not describing a reality, but a symbolic-semiotic definition of woman.

(2) Mulvey next identifies two contradictory aspects of looking: scopophilia (a trans-lation of Freud's *Schaulust*), based on separation and the sexual libido; and narcis-sism, identification with one's own ego: 'During its history, the cinema seems to have evolved a particular illusion of reality in which this contradiction between libido and ego has found a beautifully complementary phantasy world' (11). Mulvey also expresses this contradiction as a split between narrative and spectacle.

(3) Building on from (1), Mulvey notes that underneath the surface image of woman in film lies an underlying meaning, one that brings unpleasure: castration. She sum-marizes this argument on the final page: 'the structure of looking in narrative fiction film contains a contradiction in its own premises: the female image as a castration threat constantly endangers the unity of the diegesis and bursts through the world of illusion as an intrusive, static, one-dimensional fetish' (18). The narrative cinema's visual pleasure is therefore based on an underlying unpleasure (castration), and on attempts to disavow this underlying unpleasure.

(4) The two psychic mechanisms open to the male ego in coping with castration anxiety are voyeurism and fetishism. Mulvey notes that this opposition leads to contradictions, and that 'these contradictions and ambiguities can be illustrated more simply by using works by Hitchcock and Sternberg, both of whom take the look almost as the content or subject matter of many of their films' (14). I will briefly mention Mulvey's treatment of Hitchcock and Sternberg under 'filmic concepts' below.[7]

(5) One final contradiction emerges from Hitchcock's films: 'The hero portrays the con-tradictions and tensions experienced by the spectator. In *Vertigo* in particular, but also in *Marnie* and *Rear Window*, the look is central to the plot, oscillating between voyeurism and fetishistic fascination' (15). For Mulvey, these films are reflexive because their male leads possess the controlling gaze and confront the same castration anxieties as the male spectators watching these films.

For much of the essay, Mulvey focuses on scopophilia, which gains additional values as the essay progresses: male, active, narrative, voyeuristic, sadistic.[8] This is in opposition

127

to narcissism, coded as female, passive, ego, libido, and fetishistic (although one would expect voyeurism to be paired with exhibitionism and sadism with masochism).

Filmic concepts

Mulvey sets up an opposition between Sternberg and Hitchcock: 'While Hitchcock goes into the investigative side of voyeurism, Sternberg produces the ultimate fetish' (14). Sternberg downplays scopophilia – narrative suspense, voyeurism, sadism, and guilt – in favour of creating a perfect static image of the woman for the film's spectator: 'Sternberg plays down the illusion of screen depth; his screen tends to be one-dimensional, as light and shade, lace, steam, foliage, net, streamers, etc, reduce the visual field' (14). Sternberg's fetishism downplays the look within the film by presenting the image directly to the spectator. Hitchcock, by contrast, builds his narratives around the male hero's sadistic investigation of the female characters: Jeff's investigation of Lisa (*Rear Window*); Scottie's investigation of Madeleine/Judy (*Vertigo*); and Mark's investigation of Marnie (*Marnie*). All three investigations combine voyeurism, fetishism, and guilt/punishment. In *Rear Window*, when Lisa goes into Thorwald's apartment to steal evidence of Mrs Thorwald's murder, Jeff watches her from his apartment through his camera lens, including the moment Thorwald returns and discovers her in his apartment: 'He does not merely watch her through his lens, as a distant meaningful image, he also sees her as a guilty intruder exposed by a dangerous man threatening her with punishment, and thus finally saves her' (16). Mulvey points out the same narrative structure in *Marnie* and *Vertigo*, although in the latter film the 'guilty' woman cannot be saved, but is punished. The theoretical concepts Mulvey introduces into feminist film analysis are therefore illustrated with film examples where these concepts (scopophilia, fetishism, and so on) are thematized in the films. The films become examples of the way 'pre-existing patterns of fascination already at work within the individual subject and the social formations that have moulded him' (6) have structured film form and influenced its themes.

Meta-theoretical concepts

Implicit in Mulvey's essay is the need to maintain a balance between the study of film form, on the one hand, and patriarchy on the other – that is, between an internal approach to film analysis and an external approach, one focused on social and political structures of sexual inequality. There is also the need to adequately theorize the interface or mediation between internal and external. As we have already seen, the reflectionist images approach does not offer a satisfactory concept of mediation, for it suffers from causal determinism and empirical aesthetics.

Fredric Jameson finds one possible solution in Lévi-Strauss's interpretation of the facial decorations of the Caduveo Indians:

> The starting-point will be an immanent description of the formal and structural peculiarities of this body art; yet it must be a description already

pre-prepared and oriented towards transcending the purely formalistic, a movement which is achieved, not by abandoning the formal level for something extrinsic to it – such as some inertly social 'content' – but rather immanently, by construing purely formal patterns as a symbolic enactment of the social within the formal and the aesthetic.

(Jameson 1981, 77)

Lévi-Strauss begins with a formal analysis, but not one enclosed in upon itself; instead, it is oriented towards the external, yet remains a formal analysis that seeks textual patterns that 'enact' aspects of the external (particularly formal solutions to real external contradictions). Lévi-Strauss therefore supports the study of texts as signifying practices (as Cowie demonstrated in her discussion of Lévi-Strauss's example of the mytheme 'sun'), generating meaning through the interaction of codes, an interaction that symbolically enacts the social. By privileging film's creation of a gaze through its specific manipulation of space and time, Mulvey goes some way to specifying how film form enacts patriarchal values.

Evaluating data and problems

Genuineness, correctness, and comprehensiveness

Mulvey characterizes the unconscious phenomena that she discusses as 'shifting', 'ambiguous', and 'contradictory'. Towards the end of the essay she notes that '[t]hese contradictions and ambiguities can be illustrated more simply by using works by Hitchcock and Sternberg' (14). Mulvey begins her analysis of Sternberg with an anecdote about the director: 'It is well known that Sternberg once said he would welcome his films being projected upside down so that the story and character involvement would not interfere with the spectator's undiluted appreciation of the screen image' (14). Like Elsaesser in 'Tales of Sound and Fury' (see Chapter 3), Mulvey quotes a director discussing the aesthetic qualities of his films. Sternberg's comment partly strengthens Mulvey's analysis of his films as creating the ultimate fetish. But in the remainder of her analyses, Mulvey relies exclusively on the films themselves. She describes the one-dimensionality of Sternberg's images before subjecting them to a psychoanalytical reading. She then turns to Hitchcock, whose films illustrate the concepts of voyeurism as well as fetishism. Mulvey only analyses films in which the look is the subject matter of the film (*Rear Window*, *Vertigo*, *Marnie*). In effect, abstract theoretical concepts that name contradictory, ambiguous phenomena are simplified and made concrete via carefully selected examples,[9] all of which are described in accurate terms. Mulvey's essay is taking well-known films and subjecting them to a new theoretical reading. Her film analyses fulfil the aims of the essay – using psychoanalysis as a political weapon against mainstream film – for she exposes the patriarchal bias in films considered to be 'neutral' and 'unproblematic' (as escapist entertainment). Her essay therefore uses theory in a novel way (in the early 1970s) to transform perception of two auteurs. But her theory also had broad scope, and could, in principle, be applied to any mainstream film. The concepts of broad scope, transformative power, and novelty will be discussed under 'significance'.

Significance

A whole book could be written on reactions to and reformulations of 'Visual Pleasure and Narrative Cinema'. I shall leave it to Merck and Rodowick to state a few well-known truths about the significance of Mulvey's essay:

> By far the most cited work in its field, paradigmatic in cultural studies at large, Mulvey's essay has been applied, elaborated, interrogated, revised, refuted, and endlessly reiterated in the years since its publication.
>
> (Merck 2007, 1)

> Without doubt, it is and will remain one of the most important essays in contemporary film theory. 'Visual Pleasure and Narrative Cinema' has indeed been successful in its original, polemical objective: to place questions of sexual difference at the center of the debate concerning film theory's appeal to psychoanalysis.
>
> (Rodowick 1991, 4)

We have just seen that there are at least three overlapping reasons Mulvey's essay became significant: because of its broad scope, its transformative power, and its novelty. First, Mulvey's theory has a broad scope of applicability, for it can be applied to any narrative film (Hollywood alone furnishes a rich source of popular films open to psychoanalysis). However, this generality has also led to criticisms. In his attempt to develop an affective-somatic theory of film, Steven Shaviro argued that castration, voyeurism, and fetishism do not have such a systematic, all-encompassing, inflexible hold over mainstream cinema as Mulvey suggests (Shaviro 1993, 12) (a point developed by Rodowick and Cowie from the perspective of theories of fantasy, discussed below, and a point also made by Slavoj Žižek from his New Lacanian perspective, discussed in Chapter 8). The second reason Mulvey's essay became significant is that, beforehand, images of women on screen simply were not conceived in terms of the technically defined psychoanalytic concepts of fetishism, voyeurism, or castration. Mulvey's use of psychoanalysis transformed the anecdotal approach of previous feminist discussions of film. Mulvey's exemplary analyses (especially of the canonical films of Hitchcock) promoted the psychoanalytic study of the way 'the unconscious of patriarchal society has structured film form', which transformed the way cinéphiles and auteur critics in particular perceived their formerly beloved Hollywood films. And third, Mulvey's essay has novelty value, for it invokes highly anti-intuitive concepts such as castration, it defines the look in the cinema as inherently male, and it invents new terminology (such as woman's 'to-be-looked-at-ness').

One main problem with the essay's reception, Rodowick points out, is that it was generally read as a final, definitive statement on mainstream cinema's perpetuation of patriarchy, and the role of psychoanalysis in that analysis, rather than an initial opening statement on the problem. Those who read it as a definitive statement were quick to criticize it, while others saw it as opening up new research programmes. We can consider these new programmes in more detail by evaluating the well-formedness of the essay's theoretical arguments.

Well-formedness

We shall first restate the two interrelated problems Mulvey's essay addresses:

(1) previous research has not highlighted the 'importance of the representation of the female form in a symbolic order in which, in the last resort, it speaks of castration and nothing else'; and
(2) how to fight the patriarchal unconscious, which defines women as castrated.

Both problems are premised on the viability of psychoanalytic theory as a critical tool for feminists to expose the values of patriarchy.

In relation to problem (2), Mulvey, looking back from the late 1980s, perceived it as unsolvable; it was formulated in 'a high moment of Utopian optimism, when a new cinema seemed possible. ... During the 1970s it had seemed necessary to undergo a rite of passage, to travel through the scorched earth of counter-cinema' (1989, ix).

With regards to problem (1), Mandy Merck created a list of several key theoretical reactions to 'Visual Pleasure' a decade after its publication – by David Rodowick, John Ellis, Janet Walker, Steve Neale, Ian Green, and Mulvey's later essays (Merck 1987, 4–5; the list could be extended several-fold). Her reference to Rodowick is his key essay from 1982, 'The Difficulty of Difference', revised and expanded as the first chapter of his book with the same title (1991). To evaluate the well-formedness of 'Visual Pleasure', we can turn to Rodowick's close reading, which identifies several blind spots:

(1) If active male voyeurism is aligned with sadism, then passive female narcissism should be aligned with masochism. But Mulvey does not introduce the concept of masochism into her argument since, Rodowick argues, she does not want to align it with femaleness (1991, 11, 16).[10]
(2) One would expect voyeurism to be paired with exhibitionism, but Mulvey pairs voyeurism with fetishism. For Freud, fetishism is not passive, and so it fits uneasily into the passive side of Mulvey's binary oppositions.
(3) The male on screen is only considered as a relay of the masculine look; he is not treated as an erotic object (1991, 11).
(4) Mulvey only theorized a masculine subject position; women's (heterosexual and homosexual) viewing positions were not theorized, for women were only discussed as objects of the masculine gaze.
(5) Rodowick also finds problematic Mulvey's alignment of maleness with activity and scopophilia, and femaleness with passivity and narcissism. He argues that 'none of Freud's texts on sexual difference suggests an unequivocal distinctiveness between

maleness and femaleness' (1991, 10). And: 'In Freudian theory ... the relation of the body to the drives is not governed by such straightforward binary logic. Instead, Freud draws a complex picture of the relations that attach the aims of the drives to systems of representation' (15).

Rodowick summarizes his analysis of Mulvey's essay by restating his key points, that 'Mulvey draws upon Freud's schema only to substitute fetishism for exhibitionism, and to exclude masochism. And where the schema is marked by a logic of binary opposition, Freud characterizes the mutability of his pairs as "ambivalence"' (15).

These lacuna and conceptual problems in Mulvey's argument generated several productive research programmes. In terms of point (3), a series of essays were written in the 1980s on the eroticized male body (e.g. Dyer [1982], Neale [1983], Hansen [1986]). Point (4) generated a search for a specific female subject position (for example, Silverman [1980], Doane [1982], de Lauretis [1984], Modleski [1988], some of which did define the female subject position as masochistic, while Mulvey defined it as transvestite).[11] Rodowick calls this search for a female subject position unfortunate, since it assumes a binary oppositional model of sexual identity, an essentialist notion where each identity is fully formed and complete in itself. Here we return to the criticism of the images approach, which is premised on pre-existing referents fully formed, simply waiting to be represented. But now this criticism is levelled at textual theories of subjectivity for positing pre-existing, fully formed subject positions simply waiting to be occupied by spectators. This notion of a fully formed identity is simply an ideological effect. Cowie emphasizes how the text's illusory reality effect tries to produce the illusion of a unified subject effect: 'The issue is not ... to condemn realism as a system of deception, but to acknowledge its role in the construction of identity as unified, and to recognise our relation to realism as a relation of desire, a desire for that unified identity' (Cowie 1997, 5–6). Both Cowie and Rodowick employ Freud's theory of fantasy to argue that this process of constructing a unified gendered identity is never complete and fixed (just as Heath argued that the suturing process is interminable). And in response to point (5), Rodowick and Cowie, amongst others, argued that Freud's theory of fantasy is more appropriate for theorizing gendered spectatorship, because it represents the vicissitudes of spectatorship, thus avoiding the rigidity and essentialism of the static binary model of sexual identity (Rodowick 1991, Chapter 4; Cowie 1997, Chapter 4).

This ability to generate several new lines of research is a mark that a theory is well-formed. But one significant rebuttal of Mulvey's essay emerged from analytic philosophy. Noël Carroll attempts to reverse the innovations of Mulvey's essay (1996, 260–74). Along with other film theorists, he challenged the generality of her psychoanalytic perspective – however, not to modify it, but to reject it outright (in line with Popper's maximally severe falsificationist methodology). He points out the many instances where men are objects of an erotic gaze, and where women are active in Hollywood films. Unlike other film theorists, he then advocates returning to an images approach, but one bolstered by a cognitive theory of emotions. This amounts to studying the influence of film images on the way men and women spectators think. Carroll begins to tackle this issue via the application of Ronald de Sousa's notion of 'paradigm scenarios', in which we respond emotionally to present situations and objects on the basis of past associations and experiences: 'Recurring, negative images of women in film may warp the emotions of those who deploy them as paradigm scenarios in several different ways' (1996, 270). Carroll gives the example of the film *Fatal Attraction*: '*Fatal Attraction*, for example, provides a paradigm scenario for situations in which a married man is confronted by a woman who refuses to consider their affair as easily terminable as he does. … [S]tudying the image of the woman Alex [the ex-lover] that it portrays is relevant to feminists because it illuminates one pattern of emotional attention toward women that is available to men' (1996, 269). Carroll acknowledges that such an approach to film requires considerable development to become a viable theory.

At the end of his essay, Carroll challenges Mulvey's primary background assumption, that castration is the key to understanding patriarchal images of women:

> There is no problem of visual pleasure without the supposition of regularly recurring male castration anxiety with respect to visual emphasis on female form. So if, like me, you are skeptical about this supposition, then Mulvey has not solved the problem of visual pleasure, for there was no problem to solve in the first place, and, therefore, no pressure on rival theories to address the issue.
>
> (Carroll 1996, 272)

Carroll does not spell out his scepticism further, but presumably it is based on his common-sense intuition. From his perspective, all the paradoxes listed above would disappear, and his theory would take at face value films such as *The Revolt of Mamie Stover*, rather than perceive a conflict between its surface image of a strong woman and the purported underlying definition of her as a construct of patriarchy. This conflict between Mulvey and Carroll – or, more generally, psychoanalytic and cognitive-analytic theories – is based on their background assumptions, on the models of human actions they hold, and their propensity to rely either on surface common-sense intuitions, or on a decentred, split subjectivity, as the bedrock of (self) knowledge. There is no 'resolution' of these conflicting worldviews, unless one dies out (such as the belief the world is flat, or when chemistry replaced alchemy). But Carroll's critique does offer a counterpoint to the excesses of psychoanalytic theory, and plainly reveals that problems emerge from background assumptions, and that these assumptions need to be analysed in conjunction with the problematic state of affairs that they generate.

Notes

1 In a chapter called '"Images of Women" Criticism' (1985, 42–49), Tori Moi criticizes the book *Images of Women in Fiction: Feminist Perspectives* (Cornillon 1972) for privileging a reflectionist view of literature: 'Such a view resolutely refuses to consider textual production as a highly complex, "over-determined" process with many different and conflicting literary and non-literary determinants. … Instead, writing is seen as a more or less faithful reproduction of an external reality to which we all have equal and unbiased access' (Moi 1985, 45).

2 'Sexism in an image cannot be designated materially [or empirically] as a content in the way that denotative elements such as colours or objects in the image can be pointed to. Rather it is in the development of new or different definitions and understandings of what men and women are and in their roles in society which produces readings of images as sexist' (Cowie 1977, 19). Mulvey also makes this point in the quotation opening this chapter: it is only through psycho-analysis that 'A previously invisible world whose images, sensations and inklings had previously evaded one's grasp materialised with the language that could name its objects, like the appear-ance of invisible ink in front of a flame'.

3 Annette Kuhn (1982, Chapter 4) offers an account of this distinction between the American sociological images approach and the British feminists. She also points out that, in 1976, the American feminist journal *Camera Obscura* began publication, based on the theories of Marxism, semiotics, and psychoanalysis.

4 Alison Butler remarks: 'A minor literature is the literature of a minority or marginalized group, written, not in a minor language, but in a major one, just as Kafka, a Czech Jew, wrote in German' (Butler 2002, 19). She then quotes Meagan Morris: 'A minor literature is not "mar-ginal," it is what a minority constructs *in a major language*' (Morris, in Butler, 20).

5 All further quotations from Mulvey's essay will be cited in the text with page numbers in parentheses.

6 This reaction against cinéphilia and auteurism began in the new, radicalized *Cahiers du Cinéma* in 1969. The editors took a key auteur, John Ford, as their object of Marxist and psychoanalytic analysis (editors of *Cahiers du Cinéma*, 1972). A few years later (in fact, in 1975, the same year as Mulvey's essay), Christian Metz expressed the film theorist's ambivalent relation to his/her beloved object of study when he wrote:

> To be a theoretician of the cinema, one should ideally no longer love the cinema and yet still love it: have loved it a lot and only to have detached oneself from it by taking it up again from the other end, taking it as the target for the very same scopic drive which had made one love it. Have broken with it, as certain relationships are broken, not in order to move on to something else, but in order to return to it at the next bend in the spiral. ... Not have forgotten what the cinéphile one used to be was like, in all the details of his affective inflections, in the three dimensions of his living being, and yet no longer be invaded by him: not have lost sight of him, but be keeping an eye on him. Finally, be him and not be him, since all in all these are the two conditions in which one can speak of him.
>
> (Metz 1975, 26)

7 Cowie points out the contradiction between voyeurism and fetishism: 'Fetishism and voyeurism appear here as alternative and incompatible strategies [in the male psyche's defence against cas-tration], since the voyeur is seeking to see again the woman's castration, while the fetishist is piling up an elaborate display which disavows that very knowledge' (Cowie 1997, 170).

8 Later, Mulvey adds 'curiosity' to this list: 'Like voyeurism, curiosity is active and thus, in Freud's terms, masculine, but it can confuse the binary male/female, active/passive opposition that I associate with visual pleasure' (1989, x). Mulvey was tempted to think of curiosity as feminine and the opposite of the masculine fetish. But in her book *Fetishism and Curiosity*, she notes that 'rather than seeing fetishism and curiosity as irreconcilably polarized, I tried to find a more dialectical relation between them' (Mulvey 1996, xi).

9 Yet, the examples are highly selective – only two Sternberg films and three Hitchcock films, which were chosen because they fit the theory. But Mulvey is explaining abstract theoretical terms via concrete filmic examples, which not only clarifies the concepts, but also says something sig-nificant about the films themselves.

10 However, Mulvey does use the term 'masochism' (and aligns it with passive female narcissism) when analysing *Vertigo*: '[Scottie] reconstructs Judy as Madeleine, forces her to conform in every

detail to the actual physical appearance of his fetish. Her exhibitionism, her masochism, make her an ideal passive counterpart to Scottie's active sadistic voyeurism' (16).

11 In her essay 'Afterthoughts on "Visual Pleasure and Narrative Cinema" Inspired by King Vidor's *Duel in the Sun* (1946)', originally published in 1981 (reprinted in Mulvey 1989, 29–38), Mulvey returned to her 'visual pleasure' argument and to Freud's theory of sexuality. Freud suggests that both sexes share a pre-Oedipal masculine phase, and that the development of a normative heterosexual femininity involves the repression of the residual masculine tendencies in female sexuality. This masculine side of femininity does not, however, disappear completely. For example, Mulvey argues that when female spectators watch male-oriented films, they can either identify with the masculine heterosexual desire, or refuse to do so. If they do take up this identification, they temporarily remember and 'rediscover that lost aspect of [their] sexual identity' (31). Mulvey therefore argues that Freud's work seems to support a 'trans-sex identification' (33) for heterosexual women, in which their identity is not fixed and static, but oscillates between femininity and their residual pre-Oedipal masculinity. This creates an unstable, restless identity: 'the female spectator's fantasy of masculinisation [is] at cross-purposes with itself, restless in its transvestite clothes' (37).

Chris Straayer points out that 'care should be taken that the theorized transvestite or bisexual viewer does not inadvertently suppress the homosexual viewer' (Straayer 1994, 346). She argues that 'Women's desire for women deconstructs male/female sexual dichotomies, sex/gender conflation, and the universality of the oedipal narrative. Acknowledgement of the female-initiated active sexuality and sexualized activity of lesbians has the potential to reopen a space in which straight women as well as lesbians can exercise self-determined pleasure' (343).

EARLY CINEMA SPECTATORSHIP

Tom Gunning's 'The Cinema of Attraction(s): Early Film, Its Spectator, and the Avant-Garde'

> I proposed the cinema of attractions as a tool for critical analysis of early films and as a means of describing the differences between various periods of film history. Its value lies ultimately in how it opens up films and generates discussion, in a historically specific and analytically detailed manner, of the nature of film spectatorship.
>
> (Gunning 2006, 38)

Problem-situation

In this chapter I aim to rationally reconstruct the conceptual structure of, and the assumptions underlying, Tom Gunning's essay 'The Cinema of Attractions'. Although a contribution to film history, Gunning's essay is amenable to this type of analysis because it is theoretically informed, and clearly constitutes problem-driven research that attempts to understand and explain – rather than simply describe – a temporal sequence of historical events pertaining to early cinema. To contextualize Gunning's essay, I shall briefly review a number of essays he wrote prior to 'The Cinema of Attractions'.

From non-continuity to attractions

After watching over 500 fiction films from the 1900–1906 period at the Brighton Symposium in 1978, Gunning initially systematized his experiences under the cinematic concept of 'non-continuity' (1982). A non-continuous cinema 'maintains the separateness of its component parts, instead of absorbing them into an illusion of a continuous narrative flow' (1982, 220). Each shot is a complete unit in itself, and no attempt is made to integrate it into other shots to create a synthetic unity from the individual shots. Gunning lists seven characteristics of the non-continuity style (some of which reappear in his definition of the attraction),[1] and relates it to the popular arts of the time (comic strips, magic lanterns, and vaudeville). The term 'non-continuity' is a forerunner to 'attraction', and Gunning probably abandoned the first in favour of the second because 'non-continuity' is a negative characterization of early cinema (it presupposes

136

narrative coherence to be the prescriptive norm from which early cinema deviates), whereas 'attraction' is a positive designation of early cinema's qualities (it is judged in its own terms as a distinct aesthetic system).[2] In 1978 we therefore witness Gunning formulating the concept of attraction under a different name, and comparing it to the popular arts. He makes no attempt at this stage to link early cinema to the avant-garde.

In 1984 Gunning expanded his study of non-continuity by identifying it as a 'genre' of early cinema and by sketching out three other 'genres': single-shot films (which are complete in themselves); cinema of continuity (in which fragmented shots are linked together by a continuity of action from shot to shot); and cinema of discontinuity (exemplified by the use of parallel editing, which specifies the spatial and temporal relations between shots) (1984). Gunning presents these genres as a straightforward historical progression, from single shots to non-continuity, continuity and finally discontinuity. His systematization of his own data therefore remains basic. However, I think his precise delineation of the four genres can be symbolized in a more rigorous fashion – in terms of A. J. Greimas's semiotic square (1983). The four corners – and the three relations established between them (opposite, contrary, and imply) – represent the necessary logical possibilities and intelligibility of phenomena (see Figure 7.1).

The semiotic square consists of 'a correlation between two pairs of opposed terms' (Culler 1975, 92). S1 and S2 are the first two opposed terms, while S2 and S1 are the second two opposed terms. When linked together, the two oppositions form additional relations – of implication and contradiction. S1 becomes the unmarked positive of the four terms. As well as being the opposite of S2, it is the contrary of S1, while S2 is implied by S1. Each term can be described in the same way – according to the term it opposes, contradicts, and implies.

Gunning's four genres fit into this model because all three relations rigorously hold up between them (see Figure 7.2).

The single shot is the unmarked positive term (S1) because it is the most basic unit (for it preserves spatial-temporal unity). The single shot therefore implies the concept of continuity, which can be slotted into the S2 position (this link of implication is signified by the dotted line). The single shot is the opposite of non-continuity

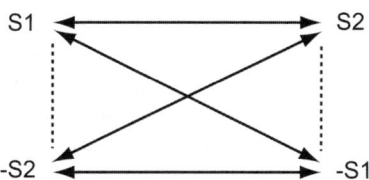

Figure 7.1 Greimas's semiotic square

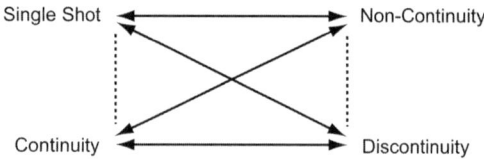

Figure 7.2 Tom Gunning's 'genres' of early cinema organized into a semiotic square

(which therefore occupies the S2 position), because non-continuity creates a noticeable disruption in spatial-temporal unity. The single shot is the contrary of discontinuity, which also disrupts spatial-temporal unity by cutting between two spaces (as in parallel editing). But rather than creating a noticeable disruption, discontinuity can be used to create suspense. Similarly, we can start with any other term in the square and define its three relations. For example, discontinuity is the opposite of continuity; it is the contrary of the single shot; and it implies non-continuity, and so on.

At the very beginning and ending of his essay, Gunning mentions that his research into early cinema links up to his interest in avant-garde film-making. But he does not explore this link in the essay. Instead, he refers the reader to his earlier paper written in 1979 – 'An Unseen Energy Swallows Space' (in Fell 1983). In this 1979 essay Gunning cautiously explores historical and conceptual links between early cinema and the avant-garde. He begins by noting that the impetus for the comparison comes from the American avant-garde film-makers themselves, some of whom (Ken Jacobs, Ernie Gehr, Hollis Frampton) directly use early cinema techniques in their films. He also adds a personal note by saying that it is by watching avant-garde films that he came to appreciate early cinema as a distinct aesthetic practice. He then presents, via three case studies, reasons for accepting the links between early cinema and the avant-garde. His reasons are: both create a contradictory space via multiple superimpositions (Méliès on the one hand, Deren and Brakhage on the other); both involve an acknowledgement of the spectator via the look at the camera; and both are known to explore space via the panoramic shot.

Gunning begins to generalize by referring to the way both types of cinema construct space and address the spectator in a manner different to classical film-making. He initially introduced the concept of attraction into this discussion in collaboration with André Gaudreault, in their joint 1985 conference paper 'Le cinéma des premiers temps: un défi à l'histoire du cinéma?' Developing the concept of attraction from Eisenstein, the authors distinguish monstrative attractions (1895–1908) from the system of narrative integration (1909–14). Gunning subsequently refined the concept of the attraction in his famous paper 'The Cinema of Attraction' published in 1986.

Analysing the problematic state of affairs

Identifying what is problematic

Under this first heading we need to understand the problematic state of affairs Gunning addresses in 'The Cinema of Attractions' (1986/1990).[3] We shall investigate what is problematic; isolate each component of the problematic state of affairs; determine how they are interrelated; and identify background assumptions.

From all the multitude of problematic aspects pertaining to early cinema, Gunning extracts one in order to simplify and delimit his research. In addressing this primary problematic state of affairs, he inevitably feels the need to address secondary ones. He formulates his primary problematic at the end of his essay's opening paragraph:

> Its [early cinema's] inspiration for the avant-garde of the early decades of this [the twentieth] century needs to be re-explored.
>
> (1986, 64/1990, 56) [problematic 1]

Gunning uses the concept of the attraction to explore the relation between early cinema and the avant-garde. As we shall see, the concept of the attraction has conceptual, psychological, and explanatory import. In regard to explanation, Gunning attempts to demonstrate the generalizable nature of the concept of the attraction: that is, it does not only apply to a few scattered examples, but is a general characteristic of early cinema and the avant-garde. It therefore has predictive capacity and can be tested and justified.[4] One of the key issues in evaluating the well-formedness and significance of the concept of the attraction is whether Gunning has overextended its range of applicability.

A secondary problematic state of affairs Gunning addresses involves periodization. He notices

> the strangely heterogeneous relation that film before 1906 (or so) bears to films that follow.
>
> (64/56) [problematic 2]

He thereby identifies 1906 as a crucial date in film's historical development. By calling this relation '*strangely* heterogeneous', he clearly identifies it as a problematic state of affairs that needs to be addressed and solved.

This heterogeneity also exposes another (secondary) problematic that he addresses:

> The history of early cinema, like the history of cinema generally, has been written and theorized under the hegemony of narrative films.
>
> (64/56) [problematic 3]

The problematic Gunning addresses here is therefore the *hegemony* of film history, which relates all films positively or negatively to the monolith of narrative, as opposed to the *heterogeneity* of the actual relation between the films.

Now that we have identified what is problematic for Gunning and isolated each one (problematic 1, 2, and 3), we can begin to see how they are interrelated. Gunning uses the primary problematic (the link between early cinema and the avant-garde) to address and solve problematics 2 and 3 (periodization and heterogeneity/hegemony). The as-yet unstated concept of the 'attraction' is the gel that binds together and solves these problematics.

Gunning isolates and lists the primary components of problematic 1 in the essay's subtitle: 'Early Film, Its Spectator, and the Avant-Garde'. These terms, simply orga-nized as a list,[5] are brought together under the umbrella of the essay's title: 'The Cinema of Attraction(s)'. He does not discuss his four primary components – early film, its spectator, the avant-garde, and attractions – all at once. Instead, he begins with early cinema, before offering his initial definition of the cinema of attractions – a cinema of display, or exhibitionism, which naturally leads to a characterization of the spectator address implied by exhibitionism (an acknowledged spectator, in opposition to the unseen voyeur), before returning to the term 'attractions' (which he and Gaudreault first used in their joint paper in 1985) and fleshing out its definition: the term derives from Eisenstein (and his avant-garde theatre and film practices), who in turn borrows it from the circus and the fairground – especially the fairground attraction and its sensual and psychological impact. Gunning ends by mentioning the cinema of 'narrative integration' (a term he and Gaudreault first used in their 1985 paper), which does not simply replace the cinema of attractions, but absorbs it, as can be seen in some mainstream genres such as musicals, as well as contemporary blockbusters. Rather than set up a relation of opposition between early and narrative cinema, Gunning establishes a relation of inclusion (before 1906 early cinema existed by itself; there-after it becomes a subset of narrative cinema).

Background assumptions

Determining how the primary components simply listed in the subtitle are conceptually and historically related is one of the principal aims of the essay – especially the relation between early cinema and its 'inspiration' for avant-garde film movements (French Impressionism, Surrealism, German Expressionist, Soviet montage school, the American avant-garde). We will examine the interrelation between these components to reveal Gunning's background assumptions. Gunning's use of the verb 'inspire' is relevant here: it literally means to breathe air into something. More generally, it means a procedure of internalizing (air) to give something life, or to animate it. By using 'inspire' to relate early cinema to the avant-garde, Gunning is implying that the avant-garde internalized early cinema, which in turn animated the avant-garde.

This latter assumption can be located in Gunning's opening lines, where he quotes Fernand Léger praising the *montage court* in the first three sections of Abel Gance's *La Roue* (1922), a renowned avant-garde film from the French Impressionist movement. Gunning begins from Léger's background assumptions concerning the uniqueness of cinema in general, based on his reaction to an individual film. Léger's praise is governed by the specificity thesis, in which he locates film's specificity in its unique ability to harness the act of pure vision, of 'making images seen'.

Noël Carroll identifies the specificity thesis as a prescriptive rather than descriptive theory with two components: 'One component is the idea that there is something that each medium does best. The other is that each of the arts should do what differentiates it from the other arts' (1988a, 83). Theorists and critics who uphold the specificity thesis therefore encourage film-makers to identify and then exploit film's essential defining qualities. The specificity thesis, therefore, is not only prescriptive, but also essentialist. Leger praises *La Roue* because it exploits what he considers to be the specific qualities of film.

Aware of the pitfalls of the specificity thesis, Gunning chooses his words carefully to align himself with Léger. Gunning writes: 'I want to *use* it [the specificity thesis] …' (64/56; emphasis added). He therefore suggests he will employ the specificity thesis merely in an instrumentalist fashion; he will observe its habitual way of thinking without fully committing himself to it as a means to explore his problematic states of affairs. Gunning therefore 'uses' the specificity thesis (at a distance) when he writes immediately before formulating problematic number 1: 'It is precisely this harnessing of visibility, this act of showing and exhibition which I feel cinema before 1906 displays most intensely' (63–64/56). Cinema's specificity, according to Gunning, lies in its 'act of showing and exhibition', and early cinema and the avant-garde exploit this specificity.

Gunning's use of the word 'inspire' also identifies two of his background assumptions: that early cinema did not simply die out after 1906, but became integrated into both narrative film and the avant-garde, and breathed life into them. This in turn leads to another background assumption: that cinema was born out of a modernist aesthetic and mode of experience (an assumption he downplays in correspondence with David Bordwell, as we shall see below).

In summary, although Gunning delimits his argument to cinema before 1906, he implies that showing and exhibition are film's specific qualities, and that early cinema is special because it exploits this specific quality of film in an unadulterated form – these specific qualities become the dominant trait in most films prior to 1906. Films after 1906 become enslaved to narrative, although they occasionally acknowledge their specificity in musicals, prolonged action sequences, or other moments of spectacle, such as the fetishization of women (not developed by Gunning, but key to Mulvey's analysis of Sternberg's films, as we saw in the previous chapter).

Describing the problematic state of affairs

Collecting data

Gunning collects a total of nine primary film examples (all are analysed only briefly): *La Roue* (Gance, 1922), *Voyage dans la lune* (Méliès, 1902), *The Bride Retires* (France, 1902), *The Gay Shoe Clerk* (Porter, 1903), *Photographing a Female Crook* (Biograph, 1904), *Hooligan in Jail* (Biograph, 1903), *Personal* (Biograph, 1904), *How a French*

Nobleman Got a Wife Through the New York Herald Personal Columns (Edison, 1904), and *Ben Hur* (1924). He also mentions the names of other film-makers: Lumière, G. A. Smith, Griffith, Eisenstein, Keaton, and Jack Smith, plus a few films in passing (without discussing them): *The Baby's Breakfast* (1895), *The Black Diamond Express* (1896), and *Un chien andalou* (1929).

Systematizing data (classifying, correlating, ordering, measuring)

One of the key innovative (and contentious) aspects of Gunning's essay is the way he uses classification to organize his data. His conceptual distinction between attraction/narrative enables him to rewrite the history of early cinema, by positing a break in its periodization (occurring around 1906), rather than its continuous linear teleological development towards narrative. This break defines early (pre-1906) cinema positively, by identifying it as a distinct unified practice with its own rules and conventions, rather than (as in the standard – continuous and linear – film history) negatively, as merely an imperfect narrative cinema.

Yet, while standard film history is predominately written under the aegis of narrative, it does, of course, posit a heterogeneous, discontinuous history – usually summed up as the opposition Lumière versus Méliès (in which Lumière films are defined negatively, as non-narrative, rather than positively). What Gunning actually does is not replace a hegemonic film history with a heterogeneous one; instead, he replaces one heterogeneous history (albeit defined as narrative/non-narrative) with another more authentic heterogeneous history, in which the heterogeneity is located elsewhere. His heterogeneous history radically posits a homogeneous relation between Lumière and Méliès while locating heterogeneity between the cinema of attractions (before 1906) and cinema of narrative integration (after 1906). He unites Lumière and Méliès under the banner of the attraction:

> Whatever differences one might find between Lumière and Méliès, they should not represent the opposition between narrative and non-narrative film-making, at least as it is understood today. Rather, one can unite them in a conception that sees cinema less as a way of telling stories than a way of presenting a series of views to an audience.
>
> (64/57)

Both Lumière and Méliès addressed spectators in the same way by presenting them with attractions. Gunning revises standard film history (which frames Méliès as a proto-narrative film-maker), by arguing that, for Méliès, narrative is only a pretext for stringing together a series of attractions: 'the trick film ... is itself a series of displays, of magical attractions, rather than a primitive sketch of narrative continuity' (65/57–58).[6] Gunning even quotes Méliès making a statement to this effect (64/57).

Constructing problems

It is in constructing problems that the concept of 'the attraction' comes into play. The attraction is primarily a cinematic concept, concerning the general nature of film. Gunning's focus therefore falls on the cinematic, although he also uses phenomenological and meta-theoretical concepts. Because he is not analysing individual films per se, the filmic plays a negligible role in the essay.

Phenomenological concepts

Gunning challenges the intuitions of standard film historians and those who accept their histories as empirically sound. He reinterprets the same data used by traditional film historians and puts them under a different classification.

Cinematic concepts

We have already seen that Gunning inherits Léger's background assumptions concerning the nature of film in general (based on Léger's reaction to an individual film, Gance's *La Roue*): Léger locates film's specificity in its 'act of showing and exhibition'. Following Léger, Gunning implies that showing and exhibition are film's specific qualities, and that early cinema exploits this specific quality of film. Gunning labels this quality an 'attraction', a cinematic concept that aims to deproblematize the primary problematic he addresses in his essay – early cinema's inspiration for the avant-garde – for the concept of attraction names the common feature they share.

But the concept of the attraction is not sufficient in itself to link early cinema to the avant-garde. To make the link viable, Gunning introduces a concept familiar to the modern or 'contemporary film theory' of the 1970s: the abstract concept of the subject (or spectator) position. As we saw in Chapter 5, the contemporary film theorists defined the classical narrative film as a realist discourse that attempts to construct an illusory, coherent subject position – a voyeuristic position where meaning is realized. They then defined avant-garde and modernist film as a discourse that deconstructs meaning, narrative, and the illusory, coherent subject position through reflexive practices that foreground film's materiality.

It is the spectator's role in the equation that really holds the key to the relationship between early cinema and the avant-garde. More specifically, Gunning introduces the concept of the deconstructed 'spectator position' to link early cinema and the avant-garde. In the cinema of attractions, the spectator is not positioned as a voyeur absorbed into and spying on a self-enclosed narrative world; instead, the cinema of attractions is exhibitionist, knowingly/reflexively addressing the spectator and providing him or her with a series of views.

Gunning then acknowledges the origin of the term, in Eisenstein's theatrical and filmic work, which fleshes out the desired impact of attractions on the audience:

> In his search for the 'unit of impression' of theatrical art, the foundation of
> an analysis which would undermine realistic representational theater,

Eisenstein hit upon the term 'attraction'. An attraction aggressively subjected the spectator to 'sensual or psychological impact' [Eisenstein]. According to Eisenstein, theater should consist of a montage of such attractions, creating a relation to the spectator entirely different from the absorption in 'illusory imitativeness'.

(66/59)

Eisenstein is precise about the spectator effect an attraction should create: an attraction employs shock as an aesthetic and political strategy, an assault on the senses that also changes the audience's political consciousness. In fact, his theory is premised on the attraction's impact: adhering to a basic tenet of Constructivist art,[7] he argues that one cannot separate out attraction and its impact on the spectator. This in turn became the principle behind his montage theory, in which the juxtaposition of two attractions creates a third meaning, which is not contained in the attractions themselves but is actively constructed by the spectator (who is nonetheless strongly guided by the film).

The origin of the term 'attraction' does not end with Eisenstein. Gunning reminds us that Eisenstein in turn borrows it from the circus – from fairground attraction, the mass form of entertainment that delivers a sensual and psychological impact (66/59). And it is, finally, in this impact created by a mass art form that Gunning presents arguments that address his main problematic – the relationship between early cinema (the cinema of attractions) and the avant-garde. If early cinema can be defined as a cinema of attractions, then it is precisely this 'exhibitionist confrontation rather than diegetic absorption' offered by both early cinema and the avant-garde that links the two together: 'I believe that it was precisely the exhibitionist quality of turn of the century popular art that made it attractive to the avant-garde' (66/59). An attraction is non-illusionistic, non-deceptive, and non-voyeuristic.[8] Instead, it declares its intentions; it is exhibitionistic and aims to astonish rather than deceive.

Less dramatically, the concept of attraction also aims to solve Gunning's second and third problematics, of periodization and hegemony, because it is the demise of the attraction and the rise of narrative that creates 'the strangely heterogeneous relation that film before 1906 (or so) bears to films that follow' (64/56).

In the same way, the concept of the attraction aims to unite Lumière and Méliès (and, more generally, the oppositions between formalism/realism, and documentary/fiction), thereby overturning their opposition as posited in standard histories and theories of film.

We have already seen that, for Gunning, early cinema did not simply die out after 1906, but became integrated into both narrative film and the avant-garde, and breathed life into them. This is one of his general background assumptions concerning the nature of film.

Meta-theoretical concepts

Gunning makes four meta-theoretical statements (reflecting on the aims and nature of theoretical inquiry):

(1) The history of cinema has been written under the hegemony of narrative (64/56).

(2) By studying early cinema in the context of the archive and academy, we risk missing its vital relation to vaudeville, its original context of reception (66/59–60).

(3) In positing a periodization that includes the cinema of attractions and cinema of narrative integration, Gunning points out that 'it would be too easy to see this as a Cain and Abel story, with narrative strangling the nascent possibilities of a young iconoclastic form of entertainment' (68/60).

(4) In a similar vein, he urges the reader not to conceive the cinema of attractions as a truly oppositional (avant-garde) programme. 'This view', he writes, 'is too sentimental and too ahistorical' (70/61).

The first two statements point to the problems of assuming that cinema was born into a narrative tradition, and that studying the films in isolation from their original context of reception downplays their function as an attraction. (Charles Musser criticizes Gunning for not taking this far enough – he accuses him of only developing a textual analysis of the films shown in vaudeville, which downplays the lecturer's role of narrativizing the images on screen. See Musser 1994.) The third statement avoids the simple logical inversion of the relationship between attraction and narrative; instead Gunning implies the relationship between them is more complex than a binary logic of opposition allows. The fourth statement similarly downplays the temptation to politicize early cinema as a negative, critical practice.

Evaluating data and problems

Genuineness, correctness, and comprehensiveness

Gunning's essay is data-driven, based on the viewing of over 500 films of the early period, nine of which are mentioned in the essay. The work of Bordwell, Staiger, and Thompson (1985) and Barry Salt (2009) presents a similar comprehensive base on which to construct film history. Yet, despite this empirical focus, the inferences and generalizations Gunning makes are contentious and open to dispute. I pointed out above that one of the key issues in evaluating the concept of attraction is whether Gunning overextends its applicability. All research that goes beyond mere description of data necessarily makes generalizations and relies on implicit assumptions, but such generalizations and assumptions need to be critically evaluated. We shall explore this issue via problematic 1.

Problematic 1

Has Gunning clearly formulated and successfully solved his first problematic (re-exploring the relationship between early cinema and the avant-garde by means of the concept of the attraction)? And is it based on correct assumptions? Can early cinema (Lumière and Méliès), the avant-gardes (French Impressionism, German Expressionism, Soviet montage, Surrealism, the American avant-garde), as well as vaudeville, circuses and fairgrounds, and contemporary Hollywood blockbusters, really be discussed under the same concept? Is not the concept of the attraction being stretched too far? This problematic raises two issues:

145

(1) the uneasy relation between pre-classical and post-classical narrative cinema;
(2) the thorny cultural generalization that early cinema and the avant-garde 'expressed' the visual experience of modernity.

I shall address (1) below. In relation to (2), I shall defer to David Bordwell's commentary on several of Gunning's essays. Bordwell first summarizes how Gunning presents a cultural explanation of the cinema of attractions, and then expresses his concerns:

> Tom Gunning suggests that many tactics of the 'cinema of attractions' reflect culturally determined modes of experience at the turn of the century. He adduces examples of an 'aesthetics of astonishment' – locomotives hurtling to the viewer, early audiences' wonder at magical transformations, the charm of the very illusion of motion. The attraction, Gunning claims, at once epitomizes the fragmentation of modern experience and responds to alienation under capitalism. It reflects the atomized environment of urban experience and the new culture of consumption; like an advertisement, the movie's isolated gag or trick tries to grab attention.
>
> (Bordwell 1997, 144)

> The more exactly Gunning ties modernity to this phase of stylistic history, though, the more problematic the case seems to become.
>
> (Ibid.)

Bordwell then criticizes Gunning's claims that not all early films express modernity, for the concept of attraction loses its explanatory power and becomes merely contingent. Bordwell's critique implies that Gunning artificially inflated the importance of attractions in early cinema as a way to justify his primary research problematic – his investigation of the influence of early cinema on the avant-garde. Other theoretically informed film historians then presented counter-evidence (especially Charles Musser on Porter [1994] and Alison McMahan on Alice Guy Blaché [2002]), which diminishes and compromises the concept's predictive power.

In a long endnote (1997, note 100, 301–2), Bordwell also responds to Gunning's claim that he does not see attractions as a causal consequence of modernity; instead, he simply identifies a rich 'congruence' (Gunning's word) between modernity and early cinema. Gunning is again choosing his words carefully, because 'congruence' simply suggests 'similarity', or 'analogy', between early films and modernity, rather than causality. Gunning is trying to avoid theorizing early films as a mere effect of a more general cause (modernity) while still attempting to articulate the relationship between early films and their cultural-historical context.

In relation to issue (1), Gunning argues that 'recent spectacle cinema has reaffirmed its roots in stimulus and carnival rides, in what might be called the Spielberg-Lucas-Coppola cinema of [special] effects' (70/61) – or 'tamed attractions', as he writes in the next sentence.[9] The attractions are tamed because they have lost their political shock value, leaving only an aesthetic shock. If the attraction loses its political shock value, can it still be considered an attraction? The link between attraction and political shock value remains indeterminate in Gunning's essay. We do not discover if the political shock value is a necessary condition for the definition of an attraction. Moreover, can we really claim that special effects in contemporary cinema are non-illusionistic, that they are not co-opted into the ideology of realism and credibility?

Well-formedness and significance

Problematics 2 and 3

In his second and third problematic states of affairs, Gunning examines the same data already classified by other film historians, and offers a different classification. The second and third problematics are conceptual, not empirical, involving the reclassification of familiar data. These problematics, while grounded in empirical data (over 500 films), are nonetheless conceptual, because the data (the films) equally support both Gunning's claims and the contrary claims of both standard film historians and Gunning's critics. Gunning is therefore using theory (theoretical concepts) to revise film history.

To give just one concrete example: the close-up in *The Gay Shoe Clerk* (Porter, 1903). For standard film historians, the close-up signifies Porter's proto-narrative tendencies. Gunning puts this data (the close-up) under a different classification and argues that it is an attraction because its function is to display a woman's ankle. In his turn, Gunning has been criticized for misclassifying the data. According to Charles Musser, for example, Gunning mislabels the close-up in *The Gay Shoe Clerk* wholly as an attraction. Musser argues that the close-up is an attraction integrated into 'a quite complex narrative unfolding' because it maintains the illusion of the fourth wall, and sets up different spaces of awareness between the lovers and the chaperone (1994, 210). While clearly formulated, Gunning's second and third problematics are not based on uncontested assumptions, and are therefore not clearly solvable, because the theory is underdetermined by the data.

In sum, Gunning's concept of the cinema of attractions is formulated in tentative language ('inspire', 'congruence'), is based on indeterminate assumptions (especially the indeterminacy of the link between early cinema and modernity and the link between an attraction and political shock value), and is therefore not solved in a clear-cut manner. Nonetheless it is generally recognized as an original idea that had a significant impact on the reconceptualization and reperiodization of early cinema. This is evident from *The Cinema of Attractions Reloaded* (Strauven 2006), a 450-page volume offering a comprehensive overview of the origins of the concept of the 'attraction' and its extension and application to both early and post-classical cinema.

Notes

1 These seven characteristics are: (a) the actor's engagement with the audience; (b) ellipsis in the two-shot film; (c) repeated action edits; (d) the anthology format; (e) abrupt transitions from documentary to staged shots; (f) tableaux format; (g) the introductory shot. See Gunning 1982, 222–28.

2 In a paper published in French in 1980 and translated into English in 1982, André Gaudreault, who also began developing a theory of early film form and later became Gunning's collaborator in formulating the cinema of attractions, cautioned against the negativity of the concept of non-continuity: '... our purpose is not to contrast what is narrative and what is not, but rather to compare two narrative forms which do not deny one another, even though the later one became institutionalized at some point' (Gaudreault 1982, 202). Although he goes on to quote Gunning's concept of 'non-continuity' to characterize the earlier mode of film-making, he is clearly unhappy with the concept. He also argues that narrativity exists in some form since film's inception.

3 I shall reference the original essay (Gunning 1986) and its reprint (Gunning 1990). The reprint adds the 's' to the word 'attraction' and also adds two summary paragraphs in the middle of the essay (final paragraph on p. 58; top paragraph on p. 59).

4 More accurately, the theory can be tested via 'post-dictions', which are 'predictions about phenomena, events, states of affairs, and so on in a past reality' (Botha 1981, 45). To state that Gunning's theory has a predictive/post-dictive capacity means that, in discovering pre-1906 films after formulating his theory of attractions, Gunning and other scholars should be able to predict that these films will be dominated by the aesthetics of attractions rather than narrative. This empirical dimension of Gunning's theory has been tested and contested by a number of film scholars, as we shall see below.

5 The list is the most unstructured way to organize information. Other, more structured patterns include: topical nets, hierarchies, matrixes, linear strings, falling dominoes, and branching trees. See Chambliss and Calfee 1998, 32–37 for definitions of these terms.

6 André Gaudreault (1987) calls this the laws of 'trickality'. This essay was first published in French in 1984.

7 Standish Lawder points out that Constructivist art 'was not developed as an aesthetic experiment, but sprang from [the artists'] passionate desire to incite the spectator to action' (1975, 65).

8 Gunning presents attractions as non-illusionist, non-deceptive, and non-voyeuristic; a technique aimed to astonish rather than deceive. Yet the magic trick aims to deceive, and does not involve the spectator in its achievement, according to Eisenstein: 'In so far as the trick is absolute and complete within itself, it means the direct opposite of the attraction, which is based exclusively on something relative, the reactions of the audience' (Eisenstein 1988, 88). The precise relationship between the trick film and the cinema of attractions therefore requires further exploration. Whereas Eisenstein opposes the trick to the attraction, Gunning conflates them.

9 Linda Williams also emphasizes the differences between early and post-classical cinema of attractions:

> The point of invoking the term 'attractions' ... is not to argue that contemporary post-modern American cinema has reverted to the *same* attractions of early cinema. While there is certainly an affinity between the two, this new regime entails entirely different spectatorial disciplines and engages viewers in entirely different social experiences.
>
> (2000, 356)

8

ANOTHER LACAN

Slavoj Žižek's 'The Universal: Suture Revisited'

There is a notion which played a crucial role in the heyday of Theory, the notion which, perhaps, condenses everything Theory was about in cinema studies, and is, consequently, the main target of the Post-Theoreticist criticism – the notion of *suture*, which concerns precisely the gap between the Universal and the Particular: it is this gap that is ultimately 'sutured'.

(Žižek 2001, 31)

Suture is usually conceived of as the mode in which the exterior is inscribed in the interior, thus 'suturing' the field, producing the effect of self-enclosure with no need for an exterior, effacing the traces of its own production.

(Žižek 2001, 55)

Problem-situation

Slavoj Žižek opens his book *The Fright of Real Tears: Krzysztof Kieślowski Between Theory and Post-Theory* (2001)[1] by identifying two problematic issues: the first is an 'external' critique of contemporary film theory – or simply Theory – from what he calls the perspective of post-theory (the cognitivism and historicism found in David Bordwell and Noël Carroll [eds.] 1996). The second issue is the internal difference between Theorists who simply 'engage' with the psychoanalysis of Jacques Lacan and those few who fully endorse his theory.

The internal difference is straightforward to address. While numerous film scholars 'engage' with Lacan, Žižek notes that 'except for Joan Copjec, myself and some of my Slovene colleagues, I know of no cinema theorist who effectively accepts Lacan as his or her ultimate background' (2).[2] Žižek uses the post-theory critique as an opportunity to internally demarcate 'Theory proper' from its 'jargonistic imitation' (5). Žižek argues that 'the reading of Lacan operative in the 70s and 80s was a reductive one – there is "another Lacan" reference to whom can contribute to the revitalisation of the cinema theory (and of critical thought in general) today' (7). This 'other Lacan' is promoted by the New Lacanians, who

> emphasize Lacan's late notions of drive, *jouissance*, and the real at the expense of his early concepts of desire, the imaginary, and the symbolic;

most are more interested in cultural studies and elements of popular culture than in literature [or film] alone; most construe the universe as ironic, tragic, or perversely paradoxical (so that everything contains its opposite); and because most color culture and its artifacts in dark tones, they are fascinated by film noir and related forms and themes.

(Mellard 1998, 395)

For the New Lacanians (not only Žižek, but also Joan Copjec, Juliet Flower MacCannell, and others), the terms 'patriarchy', 'modernism', and 'monopoly capitalism' are no longer adequate in naming the way contemporary Western societies are organized. The New Lacanians replace these terms with 'post-patriarchal', 'post-Oedipal', 'postmodern', and 'global capitalism'. In their reading of Lacan, the New Lacanians shift emphasis away from the imaginary-symbolic towards the imaginary-real, with an emphasis on *jouissance* rather than Oedipal desire regulated by the symbolic/the Other. They stress the fictional status of the symbolic/the Other and the constitutive role of fantasy in social organization. Fantasy is not formulated in opposition to social reality, but is enabling, for it structures the social reality itself. This is why Žižek does not identify contemporary Western societies as post-ideological (for that notion is premised on Marx's problematic formulation of ideology as false consciousness; see Chapter 5).[3]

Žižek's second problematic issue, the external critique of Theory by post-theory, is a meta-theoretical dispute, involving a fundamental opposition in the ontological status each confers upon theory and knowledge. Following Peter Dews, Rares Piloiu traces this opposition to Schelling and Fichte: 'If Fichte postulated the existence of a transcendental subject (somehow prefacing Husserl's transcendentalism) as the cornerstone of processes of reflection and understanding ..., Schelling would instead prefer the suspension of any positive determination of understanding or subjectivity' (2002, para. 30). Piloiu places the positive philosophy of science (particularly Karl Popper) on the side of Fichte, while Nietzsche, Bergson, Derrida (and other post-structuralists such as Ernesto Laclau and Chantel Mouffe) appear on the negative, 'irrational' side with Schelling. Within film theory, we can place the Theorists 'on the side of' Schelling, while the post-theorists are 'on the side of' Fichte. More generally, Žižek's Theory is not only founded on the German idealism of Schelling, but also on Kant and Hegel, on Marxism, as well as on Lacanian psychoanalysis.

Žižek characterizes post-theory as a theory premised on the gradual accumulation of knowledge. It is a 'modest, mid-level empirically verifiable research programme' (14) that insists on 'gradual generalisations based on careful empirical research' (16). Post-theory is grounded in an Aristotelian world of stable (full, self-determining, rational) discrete, separate entities. Such a conception 'is always a knowledge of something objectively present and describable in positive terms' (Piloiu 2002, para. 28).

Post-theory is opposed to Theory's negative philosophy. Theory does not focus on an aggregate of objects with certain attributes objectively present and describable in positive terms, but on negativity – on alienation, antagonism, contradiction, dislocation, division, failure, gaps, instability, and paradox. Negativity is articulated through the logic of the Hegelian dialectic, premised on ceaseless contradiction between always emerging opposing ideas. Hegel's dialectic is a dynamic model of transformation that proceeds from an idea (e.g. the individual) to its negation (the universal). Crucially, the negation does not simply extinguish the initial idea; instead, the negation absorbs or 'sublates' it.[4] This can be expressed in a proposition, such as 'the individual is universal'. This proposition is contradictory, and so must itself be negated, in a ceaseless activity of sublation and negation that takes the contradictory ideas beyond themselves to higher levels of thought. For Žižek, all theory and its 'objects' (subjectivity, the Other, and so on) are founded on the dialectic. They are not stable, fixed entities, but are in constant transformation, for they contain their own negation within themselves. This negativity triggers the necessity for fantasy, ideology, suture, and the universal, which attempt to repress this negativity and create the impression of smoothness, totality, fullness, stability, and self-enclosure. But these attempts necessarily fail; it is impossible to achieve fullness within a system that contains within itself its own negation. In terms of Kurt Gödel's incompleteness theorems, a system cannot be consistent and complete. Not all statements within a system can be proved within its boundaries; one always has to look outside the system. What this means in Žižek's terms is that negativity exists at the core of subjectivity and the Other (just as at the core of the number system is the concept of zero, or the absence of number). The task of fantasy, ideology, suture, and the universal is to attempt to *repress* this inherent negativity or incompleteness within the system, for subjectivity and the Other will work only when this negativity is concealed. It is from this position of dialectics and negativity that Žižek develops his critique of post-theory. More specifically, Žižek counters post-theory by employing Hegel's concept of the Concrete Universal, Laclau and Mouffe's radicalization of hegemony, and by using these concepts to reformulate suture theory on a more general level.

Suture is a theory of representation – the representation of subjectivity in language (or, more generally, the symbolic order). We have already seen in Chapter 5 that the subject is represented in language in the form of a signifier: 'A given signifier (a pronoun, a personal name) grants the subject access to the symbolic order, but alienates it not only from its own needs but from its drives. That signifier stands in for the absent subject (i.e. absent in being) whose lack it can never stop signifying' (Silverman 1983, 200). The 'I' is an abstract universal signifier that stands in for the subject in language. But this signifier's reference is not fixed, or full of meaning. The 'I' only fleetingly signifies the subject at the moment of speaking; at all other moments it remains empty. To that extent, the 'I' in language is equivalent to the 0 (zero) in the number system.[5] The subject is therefore represented in language at a price – it is split in two, between the 'speaking subject' and the 'subject represented in language'; and it is represented in language by an empty signifier, which it only fills temporarily. This temporary filling-in signifies the suturing of the split subject. In Lacanian terms, this moment of suture is a nodal point (*point de capiton*) that temporarily fixes meaning. It would be misleading to suggest that there is a 'whole' subject pre-existing language, which is subsequently split. The subject only comes into being through its representation within various internal and external languages; it is constituted in and by this split. In general terms, therefore, suture names the relation between the permanently split subject and its split representation in language; it names the temporary patching up of an essential lack. It is a positive process in the sense that the negative, alienated split subject is temporarily healed, which creates the impression that the subject is whole and coherent.

Suture in the cinema similarly creates a temporary impression of coherence and unity in the subject. The spectator is represented in filmic discourse via an abstract universal subject position, an empty position formally inscribed in the film[6] that each spectator comes to occupy. When a spectator does successfully occupy this subject position, he or she is sutured into the film, creating an impression of coherence. But this impression is regularly shattered:

> When the viewer discovers the frame—the first step in reading the film—the triumph of his former possession of the image fades out. The viewer discovers that the camera is hiding things, and therefore distrusts it and the frame itself which he now understands to be arbitrary. He wonders why the frame is what it is. This radically transforms his mode of participation—the unreal space between characters and/or objects is no longer perceived as pleasurable. It is now the space which separates the camera from the characters. The latter have lost their quality of presence. The spectator discovers that his possession of space was only partial, illusory. He feels dispossessed of what he is prevented from seeing. He discovers that he is only authorized to see what happens to be in the axis of the gaze of another spectator, who is ghostly or absent [the Absent One].
>
> (Daniel Dayan, quoted in Silverman 1983, 203)

When the spectator perceives the frame, he or she experiences the emptiness of the formal subject position and his or her split from it. At that moment, the spectator is no longer sutured into the film. The film then works (typically via a new shot) to re-suture the spectator back into the subject position by trying to eliminate what Oudart calls the Absent One, the gap that opens up between the spectator and the image.

Suture became a privileged example in the post-theory critique – it represents or stands in for Lacanian psychoanalysis and its influence on film theory. In part one of *The Fright of Real Tears* ('The Universal: Suture Revisited', 13–68), analysed below, Žižek extends and develops the concept of suture. Žižek's problem-situation is therefore conceptual, and involves criticizing known 'solutions' (the post-theory critique of Theory) from a new theoretical perspective (New Lacanianism). The result is not a return to the old theory of suture, but its dialectical transformation into a new concept called 'interface'.

The final part of the problem-situation involves placing suture in a larger cultural context. Žižek regards post-theory's criticism as part of a wider critique of Theory and cultural studies: 'the antagonism between Theory and Post-Theory is a particular case of the global battle for intellectual hegemony and visibility between the exponents of post-modern/deconstructionist cultural studies and, on the other hand, cognitivists and popularisers of hard sciences' (2). The background assumptions here concern the value and (in)effectiveness of Theory as a form of radical, transformative politics, and what Žižek regards as post-theory's profound political resignation (13).

Analysing the problematic state of affairs

Identifying what is problematic

Three problematic states of affairs drive 'The Universal: Suture Revisited':

(1) a *meta-theoretical problematic* that involves the post-theory critique of Lacanian psychoanalysis;
(2) a *conceptual problematic* to reformulate suture by placing it into a much broader – New Lacanian – context (which includes Lacan's concept of the Symbolic Gaze, political concepts such as hegemony, and philosophical concepts such as the Universal, Particular, and Individual); and
(3) an *empirical problematic* to carry out an analysis of the suturing process in new forms of problematic data – i.e. problematic examples unrecognized by traditional theories of suture. Žižek's theoretical reformulation of suture has given rise to new cases that need to be analysed and solved.

Problematic (1) has already been addressed in the problem-situation section above. We shall address (2) and (3) in the following pages.

Background assumptions

Many of the background assumptions behind Žižek's theory of suture have already been highlighted in the problem-situation section: that subjectivity is constituted on negativity and lack, and that Žižek formulates the concept, not from a standard reading of Lacan (focused around the imaginary, the look, identification, the image, representation, desire, the symbolic, Oedipus complex, and sexual identity), but from the New Lacanian perspective (which emphasizes drive, *jouissance*, the Real, the post-Oedipal/post-patriarchal).

In addition, Žižek's key contribution to the suture debate involves reconceptualizing it in terms of the Concrete Universal and hegemony. The main logical move in the essay is to conceptually link up suture with hegemony, the universal, the particular, and the singular. Žižek derives the concept of the Universal from Hegel and Ernesto Laclau, in which it can only be understood in relation to the particular: 'the fundamental lesson of dialectics is that universality as such emerges, is articulated "for itself," only within a set of particular conditions' (8). He develops this point in *The Ticklish Subject* (first published just before his chapters on suture) by bringing in the concept of the singular:

> We should therefore consider three, not just two, levels: the empty *Universal* …, the *particular* content which hegemonizes the empty Universal …, and the

individual, the symptomatic excess which undermines this hegemonic content. ... One can see immediately in what sense the individual is the dialectical unity of Universal and Particular: the individual (as symptomatic excess) bears witness to the gap between the Universal and Particular.

(2008, 212)

The 'concrete universal' combines 'universal abstract truths' with 'particular (empirical, historical) facts'. For Žižek, the universal is an empty category, but is filled in with particular facts. At first, there appears to be symmetry between the two terms: the particular is an instance of the universal; the universal is manifest in the particular (where it acquires a concrete existence). The universal and particular seem to constitute a reciprocal, self-enclosed system. But Žižek's main point is that the particular can never adequately manifest the universal; the particular struggles with and displaces the universal (26). Laclau emphasizes that the link between universal and particular is contingent, that other facts can and do fill in the universal at different times.[7] The universal is not, therefore, a transcendental, static category which is filled in by particular substances; instead, we *begin* with various concrete instances, which at various times can become universal. However, there is always a remainder between the universal and the particular (the individual, or symptom, discussed below).

Laclau and Mouffe (2001) develop a post-structural reading of hegemony. They oppose deterministic, essentialist, and totalizing theories of society (which conceive the social as stable and closed), and replace them with a social model based on contingency, indeterminacy, and plurality. Hegemony is a temporary moment of stability created between diverse contingent groups within an otherwise unstable society. By means of consent, the diverse groups temporarily adopt the ideology of the ruling group as the universal norm (so it is via hegemony that the universal is filled in with a particular substance). Consensus is therefore created by welding together the diverse groups into the ideology of the dominant group. Laclau and Mouffe's rereading of hegemony stresses that hegemony is always temporary, and continually open to revision.

Žižek builds upon this reworking of hegemony. He argues from a New Lacanian perspective that hegemony is premised on a twofold distinction between internal differences within the Symbolic, and an external difference – the difference between the Symbolic and that which exists outside it – the Lacanian Real. But, the key to Laclau and Mouffe's reformulation of hegemony, Žižek argues, is that *the external difference is represented internally*: the 'external', the Lacanian Real, is *in* the Symbolic. As such, the Real constitutes the blind spot in the Symbolic. It is the Real that blocks any notion that the Symbolic is self-sufficient and fully enclosed within itself. More generally, it is because the Real is in the Symbolic that the Symbolic necessarily fails.[8]

In Žižek's formulation, both the concrete universal and the concept of hegemony follow the logic of suture. Because the concrete can never adequately actualize the universal, and because the Real is internal to the Symbolic, a permanent gap, or split, opens up, which can only be sutured temporarily. In terms of hegemony:

154

We can see clearly now the homology between suture in cinema and the logic of hegemony: in both cases, external difference is mapped onto the inside.

(32–33)

'suture' means that *external* difference is always an *internal* one, that the external limitation of a field of phenomena always reflects itself within this field, as its inherent impossibility to fully become itself.

(57)

This mapping of the external in the internal is what suture and hegemony share: both attempt to 'tame' the threatening exterior (the Real, the Absent One), or bridge the gap between them, by representing them internally. This logic of mapping also applies to the concrete universal: the particular is mapped onto the universal:

suture ... concerns precisely the gap between the Universal and the Particular: it is this gap that is ultimately 'sutured'.

(31)

But, in all three cases, the mapping process is never fully completed.

Describing the problematic state of affairs

Collecting data

Above I listed the three problematic states of affairs that Žižek addresses in 'The Universal: Suture Revisited'. The third is empirical, involving new problematic data. Žižek typically develops an argument by briefly introducing theoretical concepts, and then working through them with examples from popular culture (the problematic data). Žižek boldly claims that the examples are subordinate to the concepts, for he discusses Kieslowski (and others) 'in order to accomplish the *work* of Theory' (9). The debates generated by Žižek's stance will be taken up in the 'evaluating data and problems' section below.

In 'The Universal: Suture Revisited', the problematic data are collected from a variety of films and are limited to examples in which the suturing process clearly breaks down:

(1) *Impossible subjectivity*, which subverts the standard, straightforward recodification of an objective shot as subjective, as in the murder of Arbogast, as he falls down the stairs in the Bates house in *Psycho* (1960) (35–36); or the birds' apparent point of view of the burning of the petrol station in *The Birds* (1963) (36). In these examples, the subjectivity intervening to fill in the Absent One (the gap between the spectator and image), is not that of a character in the diegesis, and therefore the suture does not take place.

(2) The *sudden intrusion of a violent event* (which Žižek interprets as the Real) into the exchange of subject and objective shots, as in the moment in *The Birds*

when Melanie in the row boat on Bodega bay is suddenly struck on the head by a seagull (38).

(3) The *unexpected objectivization of a subjective shot*, as when a character enters their own point-of-view shot (Žižek mentions examples from Kieslowski's *Blind Chance* [1981] and Antonioni's *Cronaca di un amore* [1950]; 38–39).

(4) *Interface*, a concept Žižek invents to name the new problematic data he examines, which consists of the *combination of the subjective and objective in the same shot*, which thereby takes on a spectral/fantasmatic dimension (an imaginary scenario which stages an impossible scene).

Interface, as manifest in this combined subjective-objective shot, is the key concept in Žižek's reworking of suture, and he illustrates it with seven films – Kieslowski's *Decalogue* 6 (1989), *Double Life of Veronique* (1991), and the *Three Colours* trilogy (1993–94), Syberberg's *Parsifal* (1983), Welles's *Citizen Kane* (1941), and Lynch's *Lost Highway* (1997). However, his main example derives from Veit Harlan's *Opfergang* (1944) (42–49, discussed below). The range of problematic data is therefore broad and eclectic, with one example (*Opfergang*) analysed in detail.

Systematizing data *(*classifying, correlating, ordering, measuring*)*

Žižek classifies his film examples according to whether they successfully or unsuccessfully follow the logic of suture. As with Oudart (1969; 1977/78) in his analysis of Bresson's *The Trial of Joan of Arc* (1962), Žižek focuses on those moments where the suture process breaks down, which he classifies into the several groups listed above: impossible subjectivity, the sudden intrusion of a violent event, the unexpected objectivization of a subjective shot, and interface.

Although interface is the fourth type of failed suture, it also stands in for all four, as the name the process of failed suture in general. 'Interface' designates the moment that suture does not quite work, when the smooth transition from subjective to objective, or vice versa, is interrupted or exposed. (In this sense, interface is a reflexive or meta-form of suture.) All examples of failed suture are correlated together under the same class, labelled interface. They appear to constitute an unordered class. Measuring and symbolizing the examples are not significant aspects of 'The Universal: Suture Revisited'.

Constructing problems

Phenomenological concepts

Žižek follows Daniel Dayan's description of suture (mentioned above), which involves three perceptual stages: (1) pleasure and immersion in looking at the visual field (fullness); (2) awareness of the frame and Absent One (a gap, or absence); followed by (3) a shot that answers this sense of gap the spectator feels.[9] Suture theorists therefore construct their main concept from the spectator's immediate experiences (but, like other Theorists, suture theorists then offer an underlying explanation of that experience).[10] Žižek interprets Dayan's explanation of this experience as one that begins with a shot appearing to be objective (stage 1), but is then subjectivized (stage 2), so the subjectivity is displaced onto a character in the diegesis (stage 3). For Žižek, following William Rothman (1975), the relationship between subjectivity and objectivity should be reversed: 'the ultimate threat is not that of an objective shot which will not be "subjectivised," allocated to some protagonist within the space of diegetic fiction, but that of a *point-of-view shot* which will not be clearly allocated as the point of view of some protagonist, and which will thus evoke the spectre of a free-floating Gaze without a determinate subject to whom it belongs' (33). Such a free-floating 'gaze' would be the visual equivalent of what Michel Chion calls the acousmatic voice (34).

Filmic concepts

Deep focus

Žižek criticizes Bordwell's use of the concepts of the universal and particular when discussing deep focus throughout cinema history: 'it is misleading to conceive of these concrete figurations of depth of field as subspecies of the universal genus' (18). The meaning of these concrete figurations is not simply their manifestation of the universal, but also a matter of 'the "mediated" totality of each historical epoch of cinematic style, the way depth of field is located in the articulated whole of stylistic procedures' (18). In other words, Žižek argues that deep focus needs to be studied in relation to all the other filmic techniques available at a particular time, as well as the uses of the 'same' technique in different cultures.

Cross-cutting

Žižek makes a rather vague reference (20) to cross-cutting in the two versions of Edwin S. Porter's *Life of An American Fireman* (1903) without naming the film.[11] But his main examples derive from D. W. Griffith, especially his anchoring of cross-cutting in the last-minute rescue, just one of many forms that cross-cutting has taken in the history of film. Žižek conceptualizes cross-cutting as an iterable sign, and subsumes it under the universal/particular opposition: 'A dialectical history of cross-cutting, presenting this notion in its "concrete universality," would consist precisely in the deployment of the successive forms of particular fantasmatic scenarios which hegemonised this universal procedure' (21–22). This he opposes to Bordwell's post-theoretical, gradual, mid-level historical generalizations. Žižek argues that generalizations do not capture the universal, for each particular manifestation of the universal is a failed manifestation. Instead, we need to examine the *exceptions* (see below, in 'cinematic concepts').

In theorizing suture, Žižek inevitably discusses *shot/reverse shot* extensively, although he makes a clear distinction (as does Heath [1981a, 76–112]) between suture as a general concept that denotes the relation of a subject to all forms of discourse (including the cinema), and suture as actualized or manifested in cinema through a variety of techniques, including shot/reverse shot. Suture is therefore a cinematic (rather than filmic) concept.

Cinematic concepts

Žižek privileges two main concepts we can subsume under the cinematic: Suture as Interface, and Gaze. In addition, central to both is the concept of the symptom (the individual, or the exception).

Gaze

Lacan introduced the split subject into the realm of vision by distinguishing the transparent look (which is Imaginary) from the opaque Gaze (which is opaque because it is deflected through the Symbolic). Unlike the Imaginary look, which signifies the subject's (temporary) feeling of mastery and omniscience via vision (exemplified in the mirror phase), the Symbolic Gaze belongs to the Other, not to the subject. The Gaze is on the side of the object, and controls the subject. Contemporary film theory (see especially Heath, Mulvey, and the standard theory of suture developed by Oudart and Dayan) was dominated by the transparent Imaginary look. Along with Žižek, only a few film scholars (Copjec, McGowan) have explored in any detail the Symbolic theory of the opaque Gaze.

Suture as Interface

In reinstating the concept of suture, Žižek privileges one configuration, which he calls interface. Žižek has previously used the term outside the discussion of suture. In general terms, interface means 'a screen, a frame, through which we communicate with the "suprasensible" virtual universe to be found nowhere in reality' (1999, 98). Interface therefore consists of a fantasmatic or spectral dimension. Žižek's main aim is to theorize suture in terms of the Symbolic Gaze, rather than the Imaginary look. In standard suture, 'the exterior is inscribed in the interior, thus "suturing" the field, producing the effect of self-enclosure with no need for an exterior, effacing the traces of its own production' (55). In cinematic terms, what Oudart calls the Absent One is transferred from the level of enunciation to the diegesis. This is not confined to any particular *filmic* figure, such as shot/reverse shot, or a point-of-view (subjective/objective) sequence of shots, but is a general condition of *cinematic* discourse (as well as other forms of discourse). In philosophical terms, suture designates the temporary filling in of the gap between the universal and particular.

How does interface differ from standard suture? The term 'interface' literally means 'a surface lying between two portions of matter or space, and forming their common boundary' (OED). In chemistry, for example, interface names a common boundary between two substances (air/liquid, liquid/solid, and so on). In cinematic terms, Žižek implies that two different substances come into contact, although the contact is not seamless, is not completely sealed at the boundary. The interface 'operates at a more radical level than the standard suture procedure: it takes place when suturing no longer works – at this point, the interface-screen field enters as the direct stand-in for the "absent one"' (52). In the interface, the exchange between the two 'substances' – the universal and particular, the inside and outside, the subjective and objective shots – fails to suture; the gap between them is not filled in. The interface is a form of artificial suturing, in which the normally invisible boundary becomes visible; the visible interface-screen functions as a fantasmatic supplement between inside and outside, subjective and objective, universal and particular.

Despite the well-known problems involved in discussing the cinematic concept of suture on the filmic level (reducing it to shot/reverse shot, or even to shots), Žižek discusses interface primarily in filmic terms (in terms of individual filmic examples). On this level, interface is actualized as a shot that contains its own counter-shot – the two levels of suture are represented in the same frame:

> [I]nterface could appear as a simple condensation of shot and reverse-shot within the same shot; but it is not only that, since it adds to the included reverse-shot a *spectral* dimension, evoking the idea that there is no cosmos, that our universe is not in itself fully ontologically constituted, and that, in order to maintain an appearance of consistency, an interface-artificial moment must suture-stitch it (a kind of stage-prop that fills in the gap, like the printed background that closes off reality).
>
> (52–53)

Žižek develops what he means by the added spectral dimension: 'when the gap can no longer be filled in by an additional signifier, it is filled in by a spectral *object*, in a shot which, in the guise of the spectral screen, includes its own counter-shot. In other words, when, in the exchange of shots and counter-shots, a shot occurs to which there is no counter-shot, the only way to fill this gap is by producing a shot which contains its own counter-shot' (54).

Žižek's main example is what he calls a 'double interface' in *Opfergang* (Veit Harlan, 1944). In the final moments of the film, Albrecht and his mistress Aels are lying in separate beds – Albrecht in hospital recovering from typhus, and Aels at home dying. Yet, they 'meet' in a fantasmatic space in which they say goodbye to each other. Žižek calls this the 'supremely condensed "suturing" shot/counter shot' (43):

> on the right side of the screen, we get the close-up of the dying Aels, and, on the left side, the American shot of Albrecht, these two appearances communicating. ... Albrecht tells Aels the big secret that he really loves [his wife] Octavia and that he is here to bid her farewell; after a mysterious exchange about what is real and what a mere phantasmagoric appearance (a kind of reflexive comment on what we see), Aels wishes him the best of luck in his marriage; then, Albrecht's image disappears, so that we see just a slightly blurred image of her as an island of light on the right side of the screen, surrounded by blue darkness. This image gets gradually more and more blurred – she dies.
>
> (43)

Žižek tries to determine whose fantasy this image belongs to. As Aels's fantasy, the image represents the real Aels and her fantasy image of Albrecht. But Žižek argues that this shot of Aels and Albrecht can be codified at a higher level as Albrecht's fantasy. His fantasy therefore absorbs and mediates Aels plus Aels's fantasy of him. He fantasizes about Aels forgiving him, in order to rescue his marriage: 'The two fantasies are thus interwoven in a kind of spatial warp, and this impossible fantasy of the double sacrifice provides the only consequent solution to the male problem of being divided between a loving wife and a loving mistress – it provides a formula for getting out of the deadlock without betraying anyone' (48). Žižek concludes that 'Shot and counter-shot are here not only combined within the same shot – it is *one and the same* image which is *at the same time* the shot (of the hallucinating Aels) and the counter-shot (what appears as a counter-shot to Albrecht in his hospital bed)' (49). In other moments of interface, the spectral fantasy is introduced into everyday reality. In *Opfergang* the spectral fantasy takes over completely, embedding one fantasy into another.

As a spectral screen, the interface is a visible flat surface area between the two levels of suture: the universal, the outside, the Absent One, the subject of enunciation on one side, and the particular, the subject in the utterance (the diegesis) on the other side. As a visible surface, the interface cannot efface traces of the outside; it remains visible. The interface is therefore a material manifestation of the opaque Symbolic Gaze. The opacity produces a supplement, an excess, what Žižek calls the symptom, or the exception.

Symptom (the exception, individual)

In suture, the exterior (otherness, the Real) is internalized. But the process is never entirely successful; there is always an excess, something left over that 'sticks out'. In philosophical terms, the symptom is the failure of the particular to completely stand in for the universal. In Lacanian terms, the symptom is a surplus value: the *objet petit a*.

The interior, the exterior, the symptom, or the subjective, objective, the *objet petit a*: each element has several names, but their structure remains the same – the symptom exists between the other two terms, holding them together while blocking a complete assimilation of the exterior into the interior, the objective into the subjective: '*objets petit a* are neither subjective nor objective, but the short circuit of the two dimensions: the subjective stain/stand in that sustains the order of objectivity, and the objective "bone in the throat" that sustains subjectivity' (65). If one tries to remove the 'bone in the throat', the mediator, then the fantasy of a stable subjectivity and objectivity collapses.

Meta-theoretical concepts

'The Universal: Suture Revisited' was initially motivated by a meta-theoretical dispute between Theory and post-theory, characterized in the 'problem-situation' section of this chapter as an opposition between an empirical, positive theory of knowledge versus a negative theory. For Laclau and Mouffe, conflict between different theoretical paradigms can be located on the ontological level:

160

[T]he strictly ontological question asks how entities have to be, so that the objectivity of a particular field is possible. There is a process of mutual feedback between the incorporation of new fields of objects and the general ontological categories governing, at a certain time, what is thinkable within the general field of objectivity. The ontology implicit in Freudianism, for instance, is different and incompatible with a biologist paradigm.

(Laclau and Mouffe 2001, x)

Each film theory paradigm has distinct ontological categories that are not necessarily recognized by other paradigms: certain objects within one paradigm are not thinkable in a different paradigm. The Theorists and post-theorists clearly have radically different ontologies, which are spelled out in their background assumptions. Throughout his work, Žižek attempts to break this impasse between different paradigms via the concept of the universal – in its non-transcendental, concrete, contingent formulation. Yet a common inter-theoretical meeting ground still eludes the Theorists and post-theorists.

The concept of suture demonstrates what happens when one theoretical paradigm appropriates a theory from another paradigm. Suture is based on Frege's theory of numbers, a theory often regarded to be the origin of analytic philosophy. Appropriated within the negative continental tradition, what appeared to Frege to be a consistent, self-enclosed theory becomes a theory based on negativity – a negativity Frege attempted to conceal via the numeral 0. Continental theorists interpreted this number as a paradox, and described its concealment via the suture process. Similarly, Godel's incompleteness theorems, developed in the analytic tradition, strengthen Žižek's reading of subjectivity, the Other, and so on as necessarily incomplete objects. Yet we cannot take for granted the apparent identity or similarity of concepts across paradigms. Are the two theorists from significantly different paradigms talking about the same thing? Do the analytic and continental philosophers mean the same thing when they talk about zero, or incompleteness? One way out of this deadlock is to adopt Wittgenstein's philosophy developed in his *Philosophical Investigations*, to describe diverse *uses* of specific terms in different language-games (outlined in the following chapter).

Evaluating data and problems

Genuineness, correctness, and comprehensiveness

The main problem that plagued the standard theory of suture was the lack of correspondence between this abstract concept and its concrete embodiment in particular films. To make the concept 'stick', it was invariably discussed in relation to the 'obvious' example of shot/reverse shot. Suture became synonymous with this privileged example – the particular concrete example became a false universal, which is one reason for its downfall. Žižek's attempt to overcome this impasse by expanding the concept and applying it to new examples has generated controversy – especially around the words 'apply' and 'example' in problematic (3) – to analyse suture in new forms of problematic data.

Žižek's examples present several distinct moments when suture fails: impossible subjectivity, the sudden intrusion of a violent event, the unexpected objectivization of a subjective shot, and interface. (It is important to note that each example is accurately described and analysed, meeting the criterion of correctness.[12]) Žižek illustrates his main concept, interface, with seven examples across several decades and different national cinemas. Although only one example, *Opfergang*, is analysed in detail – mainly because it offers an extreme, reflexive illustration of the theory of interface[13] – within the logic of Žižek's argument, this one example is important because it represent the exceptional instance that embodies the universal.

Outside of Žižek's logic, and within a more conventional film studies perspective, it could be said that the selection of examples is eclectic, and the analyses themselves are brief. To that extent, the 'Suture Revisited' section of *The Fright of Real Tears* does not meet the criterion of comprehensiveness, because the sample is not representative, and most examples are introduced and dropped quickly once a theoretical point has been made. But Žižek is quite clear that this is a deliberate policy – he uses the examples for his main purpose, in order to theorize. He argues against the 'representative sample' as a valid criterion for gaining knowledge: 'such careful empirical generalisation never brings us to a true universality. Why not? Because all particular examples of a certain universality do not entertain the same relationship towards their universality: each of them struggles with this universality, displaces it in a specific way, and the great art of dialectical analysis consists in being able to pick out the exceptional singular case which allows us to formulate the universality "as such"' (26). In terms of Žižek's negative philosophy, an example cannot fully illustrate or embody the concept applied to it – there cannot be a full relation between them. The example must, therefore, necessarily fail – unless it is elevated to the level of the exception. The key to understanding Žižek's use of examples is the significance of the exception within his negative theory, the paradoxical element that *constitutes and subverts* at the same time. There is no place for paradox and the inconsistencies of the unconscious within positivist philosophy, whose early phrase, dominated by logicism (and, indeed, by Carnap's form of rational reconstruction) attempted to eliminate inconsistencies and paradoxes via logic. This partly explains the devastating impact of Gödel's incompleteness theorems on logicism.

Whether the data in 'The Universal: Suture Revisited' is genuine depends again on one's ontological perspective: suture emerged out of the philosophy of negativity and only makes sense, is only genuine, within that perspective. On top of the accurate descriptions and analyses of film examples is overlaid the themes from Žižek's negative philosophy. For instance, in *The Birds* the seagull attack on Melanie in the boat is an instance of the Lacanian Real (38). This is a genuine, self-evident issue only for those who fully endorse Lacanian theory. John Orr emphasizes this point in his review of *The Fright of Real Tears*. Speaking of the Symbolic theory of the Gaze, he writes: 'In Žižek's neo-Lacanian formulation the Gaze is pure off-the-wall metaphysic, something returned by the eyeless object, anthropomorphic, bounced back by any Thing devoid of the power of sight: hence its *perverse attraction for Theorists of a certain persuasion*' (2003; emphasis added).

Žižek's discussion in 'The Universal: Suture Revisited' of other filmic techniques – cross-cutting and deep focus – is also sketchy. In response to Žižek's comment that Bordwell conceptualizes 'concrete figurations of depth of field as subspecies of the universal genus', Bordwell responds that he in fact reverses this proposition, focusing instead on the different forms of deep focus throughout film history (2005a, 298 n.59). Bordwell does not use the term 'universal genus'; instead, he talks about contingent universals when theorizing film style: 'They are contingent because they did not, for any metaphysical reasons, have to be the way they are; and they are universal insofar as we can find them to be widely present in human societies' (1996b, 91).

Is there any conceptual overlap between Bordwell's contingent universals and Žižek's concrete universal? Whereas Žižek would describe the wide presence of some artistic conventions in terms of hegemony, Bordwell refers to a continuum ranging from sensory triggers that automatically stimulate spectators at one end to culturally specific skills at the other end (1996b, 93–96). But both agree that 'cross-cultural' and 'universal' are not transcendental categories given in advance, but are social.

Well-formedness

I now turn to the evaluation of problematic (2), Žižek's expansion of the concept of suture from a new Lacanian perspective. 'The Universal: Suture Revisited' successfully addresses its second problematic by presenting an expanded theory of suture, one explicitly premised on the logic of the Hegelian dialectic, hegemony, and the concrete universal. Using this expanded theory, Žižek incorporates new filmic phenomena, overcoming the limitations of the narrowly applied standard theory. He successfully analyses this problematic data from a New Lacanian perspective. In that regard, 'The Universal: Suture Revisited' is not an isolated piece of research – either in film theory or in terms of Žižek's other work, for it is written from the same perspective and articulates the same agenda, but within the narrower domain of film theory.

One potential problem with Žižek's broader agenda is his reliance on Laclau's hegemonic universal. The problem is that the universal is filled in with a *purely contingent* content, implying that the content does not manifest the universal but merely substitutes for it; and one type of content is as good as any other, for none can adequately stand in for the universal. Yet, for Žižek, it is again the exception that short-circuits the contingent content of the particular and becomes the universal.

Žižek's politics of the universal is founded on the philosophy of negativity. This is an original and significant framework (in Casetti's terms, a useful methodological theory) from which to theorize cinema, although it remains under-developed in 'The Universal: Suture Revisited' and in *The Fright of Real Tears* generally. (Žižek's passing remarks on deep focus and cross-cutting were provisional and severely underdeveloped, making them ripe for critique from the post-theory perspective.) But, like other original research it can lead to the formation of new research programmes; it opens up a new and different perspective on film – clearly not a complete, totalizing perspective, but an intervention. For example, McGowan defends Žižek's method of analysing film examples by suggesting that he consistently writes about the way 'films organize and deploy the spectator's enjoyment. ... Žižek has consistently foregrounded the question of enjoyment and the way in which texts structure it' (2007b, 5). Žižek makes enjoyment (*jouissance*) a concept key to theorizing film spectatorship, since it is central to explaining cinema's appeal. Fabio Vighi also argues for the significance of *jouissance* in Žižek's film theory and analysis, but places its emphasis in the film itself, not the film-spectator relationship: 'before it can be used to describe the complex interrelation between film and audience, enjoyment ought to be seen as a self-reflexive cinematic category insofar as it is embedded in film and determines its conditions of possibility' (2009, 4). And Robert Bird justifies Žižek's downplaying of film aesthetics by arguing that he is developing a theory of film ethics, based on the dialectics between aesthetic distanciation and ideological/religious engagement, a dialectical tension Žižek discovers in Kieslowski (Bird 2004).

Significance

Many reviewers of *The Fright of Real Tears* celebrate Žižek's bravura performance, of bringing high Theory, European culture, and American popular culture together, while denouncing his lack of a specific film studies perspective (see reviews by Orr, and Sheila Skaff and Chris Luebbe, already cited, amongst several others). Bordwell calls it a book of 'impressionistic criticism', 'a fairly conventional book of free-associative film interpretation' (2005b). These criticisms are levelled at the bulk of the book devoted to Kieslowski, not rationally reconstructed here, although McGowan and Bird do suggest that there is more to the book than mere impressionistic criticism.

In terms of Botha's criteria for significance, the section of the book devoted to suture encounters a danger in the formulation of the standard theory, of being reduced to a particular instance: shot/reverse shot for the standard theory, a single shot combining the subjective and objective for Žižek's concept of suture as interface. Nonetheless, the broadly conceptualized notion of suture as interface is sufficiently different to the standard theory; it thereby transforms our pre-existing ideas, and is sufficiently distinct from the standard conception.

Notes

1 My rational reconstruction of *The Fright of Real Tears* is confined to the first section entitled 'The Universal: Suture Revisited' (13–68). This section contains three chapters: 'Universality and its Exception' (13–30); 'Back to the Suture' (31–54); and 'The Short-Circuit' (55–68). Most of my focus will fall on 'Back to the Suture'. All quotations from these chapters will be cited in the text with page numbers in parentheses.

2 Žižek wrote this in 2001. Since then, we can add several names to the list, including Todd McGowan (2007a) and Fabio Vighi (2009).

3 'If our concept of ideology remains the classic one in which the illusion is located in knowledge, then today's society must appear post-ideological: the prevailing ideology is that of cynicism; people no longer believe in ideological truth; they do not take ideological propositions seriously. The fundamental level of ideology, however, is not of an illusion masking the real state of things but that of an (unconscious) fantasy structuring our social reality itself. And at this level, we are of course far from being post-ideological society' (Žižek 1989, 33). The claim that we can step

outside of ideology is the ultimate ideological gesture, for it assumes the direct perception of reality free from all distortion.

4 In absorbing the initial idea, the negation preserves and mediates some aspects of it. In other words, the idea is preserved in and mediated through its negation.

5 In his discussion of suture, Jacques-Alain Miller (1977/78) refers to zero as the empty signifier: unlike other numbers, it does not represent anything. It exists outside the number system, but is internally represented in that system by the empty signifier '0'. Zero therefore has a contradictory status: unlike other numbers, it represents nothing; but like other numbers it is represented by a signifier. Its nothingness is sutured over by being conferred the status of a number.

6 That is, formally inscribed in the film 'on screen' and 'in frame', to use Heath's terms from Chapter 5.

7 R. Moolenaar adds some detail to Žižek's use of the universal: 'The key component of the leftist position Žižek wants to elaborate is an equation of the assertion of Universalism with a *militant, divisive position of one engaged in a struggle*. So "true" universalists are not those who preach global tolerance of differences and all-encompassing unity, but those who engage in a passionate fight for the assertion of the truth they are committed to: a truth that demands for a radical subjective stance and, precisely as such, is addressed to all and everybody' (2004, 287). In several of his books Žižek refers to the Third Estate in the French Revolution (those not belonging to the clergy or nobility), proclaiming themselves to be The Nation as such, as true universalists.

8 Žižek clarifies the logic of the internal/external division in his response to standard glosses of the relationship between the Symbolic and the Real: 'the determination of the Real as that which resists symbolization is itself a symbolic determination, that is, the very gesture of excluding something from the Symbolic, of positing it as beyond the prohibitive Limit (the Sacred, Untouchable), is a symbolic gesture (a gesture of symbolic exclusion *par excellence*). ... In contrast to this, however, one should insist on how the Lacanian Real is strictly *internal* to the Symbolic: it is nothing but its inherent limitation, the impossibility of the Symbolic fully to "become itself"' (in Butler, Laclau, and Žižek 2000, 120; ellipsis in the original).

9 Edward Branigan identifies what he takes to be the nine successive stages of suture, each stage representing the spectator's changing awareness – his/her alternating attention between absorption in the imaginary and awareness of the symbolic. Branigan confines his exhaustive description to Oudart's analysis of one shot in *The General* (Keaton, 1926). After presenting these nine successive stages (2006, 135–36), Branigan redescribes them entirely in terms of framing: the spectator's awareness moves from the non-framed, to the unframed, framed, deframed, and then the reframed (in the subsequent shot) (2006, 136).

10 Žižek points out that the post-theorists rely on an unproblematic, common-sense notion of the spectator, for which there is not need for underlying concepts of absence, gaps, the gaze, and so on (34).

11 The 1903 version of the film was apparently re-edited in the 1930s to delete the overlap of time between the two scenes (interior/exterior) in the earlier version, thereby making it conform to the classical use of cross-cutting. This is an instance of what I referred to in the introduction to this book as 'present-mindedness', of imposing present values onto the past. For a detailed analysis of the two versions of the film, see André Gaudreault (1990).

12 Sheila Skaff and Chris Luebbe argue in their review of *The Fright of Real Tears* that, as the book progresses, the theorizing becomes more prominent and the examples are analysed in a more cavalier manner, with less accuracy and detail: '[Žižek] makes mistakes when summarizing films. He leaves gaps in his arguments when the films' plots contradict his ideas'. For example, he 'attempts to analyze *Decalogue: One* in detail, but unfortunately he makes basic mistakes regarding the action of the film that render his reading untrustworthy'. '*The Fright of Real Tears* stubbornly dissatisfies by trying to act as a lone trail-blazer on a busy superhighway. There simply is much better, more pertinent, more intelligent scholarship available. Other scholars have taken better care to recall correctly the plots of Kieslowski's films and to consider in depth the religious and social circumstances behind their production' (2003).

13 *Opfergang* is also an extreme example because it was an official film made by the Nazi party, a detail Žižek only comments on in passing.

THE DEATH OF THE CAMERA

Edward Branigan's 'What Is a Camera?'

Film theory needs to be rethought. It must seek a new relationship to its own language. I will pursue this goal by examining the many tangled, abstract languages that have been crafted by film theorists.

(Branigan 2006, xiii)

I believe that a productive approach to the nature of the 'camera' would be to examine the sorts of pictorial metaphors we routinely entertain thinking about it. What are the implicit scenarios that make different cameras become present to our mental imagery? ... In deciding which scenario might be appropriate for a given occasion, the claims of film history and criticism will be relevant.

(Ibid., 126)

Problem-situation

Entrenched in its own concepts, a school of thought fails to perceive the alterity of other schools of thought. Schools become locked into their own self-imposed conceptual boundaries, and talk past, rather than with, one another. Humanities scholars have recently perceived the need to move away from this impasse. Some embrace the ethical philosophy of Emmanuel Levinas, while others look to Wittgenstein's later philosophy for a solution. Rather than step inside one school or way of thinking and privilege its system of concepts, Wittgenstein describes how each way of thinking uses particular words and concepts in specific contexts. This way, one identifies the source of conflict between schools – conceptual or linguistic confusions over how each uses the 'same' words. In his earlier philosophy (the *Tractatus Logico-Philosophicus* [1922]), Wittgenstein examined, from the singular perspective of logic, the correspondence of words to facts, and formulated their truth conditions. But in his later work (*Philosophical Investigations* [1953]), he shifted emphasis towards the role words play in particular schools of thinking – which he variously called 'contexts', 'language-games', 'grammars', 'environments', or 'forms of life', and which Edward Branigan calls 'scenarios' in the second quotation above. For Wittgenstein, the way words are used determines their truth value. Truth is not, therefore, absolute or innate, fixed and predetermined by logic, but relative to language-games, and no overarching concept can rule over all

166

possible uses of a word: 'A language-game specifies what can be meaningfully said about an object (and its range of movements) and hence determines what kind of object something is – its nature or essence' (Branigan 2006, 6). Several language-games may use the same word, but with different (incompatible, contradictory, or overlapping) meanings and truth values. Several distinct meanings of the same term therefore exist, and confusion or conflict between different language-games results from their different use of the same terms. Wittgenstein's solution to resolving conflicts involved developing a philosophy to describe precisely the diverse uses of specific terms in different language-games. The strength of his philosophy lies in its ability to foreground the basis of a conflict by identifying the different actualizations of a concept in specific contexts.

Markus Rheindorf spells out the four stages of what a Wittgensteinian analysis involves (the following is my paraphrase of Rheindorf 2005, paragraphs 38–41):

> The first step of any grammatical examination always consists of deliberately allowing for the multiplicity of meanings of a given term, accepting even the most irritating and seemingly sloppy usage.
>
> The second step is to pose and answer, as comprehensibly as possible, the question of how to describe the actual context of situation in which the term in question is used.
>
> The third and perhaps most significant step in Wittgenstein's method is the finding of 'interconnecting links', so that the cases included in the study of the usage of a given term are not left in isolation. These links will, one can safely assume, not always align with accepted categories, but instead reveal 'family resemblances', subtle transitions and tensions in places where one did not expect to find them.
>
> The fourth and final step of Wittgenstein's procedure consists of a hypo-thetical testing of cases. This step makes transparent the criteria by which the term is used and which define the conceptual frame of possible uses of the term. (This is where Wittgenstein's method becomes normative.)

Wittgenstein's method overlaps to some extent with P. W. Bridgman's operationalism. In Chapter 2 we encountered operationalism when analysing Barry Salt's statistical style analysis. In that chapter, the term referred to the public, repeatable procedures Salt followed to measure and systematize his data. Operationalism makes explicit definitions, assumptions, and especially procedures that usually remain implicit and vague. In this chapter, we encounter a different aspect of operationalism, an aspect that overlaps with Wittgenstein – the way different procedures and background assumptions lead to the generation of multiple concepts. Carnap summarizes Bridgman's position:

> Bridgman preferred to say that there is not just one concept of intensity of electric current, but a dozen concepts. Each procedure by which a magnitude can be measured provides an operational definition for that magnitude. Since there are different procedures for measuring current, there are different

concepts. For the sake of convenience, the physicist speaks of just one concept of current. Strictly speaking, Bridgman believed, he should recognize many different concepts, each defined by a different operational procedure of measurement.

(Carnap 1995, 235)

Similarly, in his move away from logical positivism's principle of verifiability and reductionism, Wittgenstein develops an account of language in use, where meaning varies from one manifestation to the next in different environments. Both Wittgenstein and Bridgman offer performative definitions of concepts (although neither employs the term). They move away from concepts pre-existing in some abstract, transcendental realm; instead, concepts seem to be constituted in the public acts of use, or measurement. Meaning in both cases is understood in terms of contingent variations. Of course, we need to ask: can the meaning of a concept be reduced to the way it is used in a particular instance? In the same way, can it be reduced to the procedures by which it is measured? Carnap provides one answer: 'Bridgman could speak of having operational definitions for his theoretical terms only because he was not speaking of a general concept. He was speaking of partial concepts, each defined by a different empirical procedure' (1995, 236). The key, then, to Bridgman's operationalism is that the dozen concepts of electrical current are only partial concepts that have (to use Wittgenstein's term) a family resemblance. If the dozen definitions of current were presented as full, general concepts, then Bridgman would be open to the charge of relativism.

In *Projecting a Camera* (2006), where his chapter 'What Is a Camera?' appears (65–96),[1] Branigan uses Wittgenstein's method in *Philosophical Investigations* to describe the multiple, contradictory, literal, and metaphorical meanings of fundamental concepts as they are used to talk about films – terms such as 'movement', 'point of view', 'camera', 'causality', and 'frame'.[2] He combines this with the cognitive theory of George Lakoff and Mark Johnson, who are well known for their analysis of metaphors in everyday discourse (especially *Metaphors We Live By* [1980]). Branigan problematizes these seemingly obvious, everyday intuitive concepts, and offers a systematic account of their multiple conflicting uses. He identifies and precisely describes: eleven theories of point of view (Chapter 2); thirteen types of movement (Chapter 2); eight distinct meanings of camera (Chapter 3); fifteen different definitions of frame (Chapter 4); and fifteen misleading causal formulas about film (Chapter 5). In Chapter 1, 'The Life of a Camera', Branigan introduces two types of analysis: reduction and connection, and favours the latter. He follows P. F. Strawson's formulation of the distinction between reduction and connection (Strawson 1992). In a reductive analysis (including a rational reconstruction), objects (and concepts) are dismantled to reveal their ultimate constituents. Such analyses are hierarchical, based on levels of analysis, and move vertically (either down, from large to small units; or up, from small to large). Reductive analysis is premised on the surface/depth model, and aims to identify the ultimate system of codes underlying the surface text.

Connective analysis, associated with Wittgenstein's later theory (and, to some extent, Bridgman's operationalism), studies the links or relations between concepts in particular situations and contexts. Connective analysis is non-hierarchical, for it moves horizontally. It therefore rejects the surface/depth model, and replaces it with the notion of multiple connections on the surface. It rejects the author as a guarantor of meaning, replacing this figure with an impersonal, indefinite text (not linked to a definite author), constructed from public language (rather than an author's private utterance); or, more specifically, several public languages (language-games).

Before rationally reconstructing how Branigan uses connective analysis in 'What Is a Camera?', we need to note in passing that reductive analysis is more complex than Branigan characterizes it. It is a form of mereology, the theory that studies the logical relations between parts and the whole, and the relations between the parts within the whole. Lubomír Doležel identifies two types of mereology – anatomy and morphology, both of which posit that a whole is made up of parts. But '[w]hereas anatomy is satisfied with separating and identifying the parts, morphology informs us that the diverse parts make up a higher-order, structured whole. Morphology is a theory of the formation of complex structures from individual parts' (1990, 56). Branigan focuses exclusively on anatomy when talking about reductive analysis, no doubt because it dominated the classical semiotics of Barthes and film theory since the 1960s, especially the film semiotics of Christian Metz (and, more generally, the numerous textual analyses of film developed by Raymond Bellour [2000], amongst many others).

While the shift from reduction to connection is clearly grounded in Wittgenstein's later philosophy, Branigan also identifies it in Barthes's 'The Death of the Author' (1977). For Barthes in this early post-structuralist essay, meaning is not fixed, predetermined, and guaranteed by 'the author' (or by society, history, the psyche, liberty, or a system of codes), whose singular meaning the reader tries to determine. Instead, meaning is dispersed across the surface of the text. Indeed, the idea of an author fixing a text's meaning is simply one conception of the text within a particular language-game.

Branigan points out that the camera has traditionally been theorized in the same way as the author – as a single, monolithic entity guaranteeing meaning. Branigan performs, analogous to Barthes's death of the author, the 'death of the (singular, monolithic) camera', which leads to its re-emergence in *Projecting a Camera* as an impersonal and indefinite entity: that is, leads to the identification of the many shifting, overlapping, contradictory *conceptions* of the camera that exist in public discourses about the cinema: 'I believe that the word "camera" is a radial concept that extends far beyond the properties of a (definite) physical apparatus able to record the real world and having a weight and serial number' (148). Every conception of a camera emerges out of a different language-game, each of which specifies how one identifies and talks about a camera. Branigan therefore notes that 'camera' has a radial meaning, for it has been discussed and conceptualized in different language-games, creating ambiguous (that is, polysemic) conceptions of the camera.

Analysing the problematic state of affairs

Identifying what is problematic

The chapter's title – 'What Is a Camera?' – is formulated as a question that states the chapter's problematic state of affairs. Yet the question does not appear to identify anything problematic (we all know what a camera is); neither does its form (seeking a camera's essence) fit into Wittgenstein's later philosophy, Branigan's stated framework. Branigan is well aware of these issues. He notes, firstly, that film scholars should examine their intuitively obvious beliefs, even though they may appear self-evident and certain. Secondly, he realizes the question he asks is ontological (like Bazin's famous question 'What is cinema?' [1967; 1971]), but unlike Bazin he does not seek an ontological answer. Although the question seeks the intrinsic properties of a camera, its material and shape, Branigan instead seeks to describe language-games, how we speak about cameras in different contexts.

Branigan transforms the ontological question 'What is a camera?' into the following series of interrelated language-game questions:

> Here are the questions I wish to address in this chapter: How do we discuss a 'camera'? In what contexts? What does 'camera' mean as a term used by critics? How has the idea of a 'camera' become meaningful to us within a cinematic institution? What do we do with the word 'camera' when it functions in a description?
>
> (68)

The terminology indicates the components of the problematic state of affairs: these questions emphasize 'discussion', 'context', 'use of terms', the 'idea' of a camera within 'institutions', the 'word' camera and how it 'functions'. Branigan is interested in describing the word 'camera' in its many uses; he therefore refers (as Bridgman does, in relation to electrical current) to many types of camera. Another component of the problematic state of affairs is that these multiple cameras may be contradictory, which creates confusion when different critics use these incompatible meanings: 'one critic's camera is not necessarily that of another critic' (71). Like Wittgenstein (and Bridgman), Branigan describes the contingent, variable conditions that create these differences in meaning.

Background assumptions

Branigan's main background assumption is Wittgenstein's concept of 'language-game', which he uses to rethink the entire activity of theorizing about the cinema. Branigan narrows down this huge task by analysing 'the complicated sets of meanings devised for the word "camera"' (xiv). He emphasizes that the cameras he discusses are fictitious or hypothetical, generated by spectators to think, talk about, and generally make sense of a film. In 'What Is a Camera?' Branigan devises a typology of eight conceptions of a camera – the way cameras are created – through eight discourses about film.[3]

Describing the problematic state of affairs

Collecting data

Because 'What Is a Camera?' is meta-theoretical, Branigan collects his data from film scholarship, rather than films. His main source of information is the work of film scholars who represent the different language-games and institutions from which the different meanings of the word 'camera' derive. These scholars include: Rudolf Arnheim, Jean-Louis Baudry, André Bazin, Noël Burch, Raymond Durgnat, Christian Metz, Laura Mulvey, Kristin Thompson, and Paul Willemen.

Systematizing data (classifying, correlating, ordering, measuring)

Systematic description represents Branigan's major task in this chapter. He describes a class of eight conceptions of camera, each of which he identifies according to the way their interpretive communities define them. The criteria for definition include: meaning (presence and absence); mental processes; and narrativity. He also identifies a representative film theorist who holds each meaning of a camera, and the representative film-makers who, these theorists argue, manifest each meaning of a camera.

The eight conceptions of camera are not ordered as a simple list. Instead, Branigan establishes a typology of camera types, held together by logical relations:

Camera 1

The first camera in Branigan's typology is used to name the origin of the sensory stimuli spectators perceive while watching a film. The camera is the unifying principle that links sensations present on the screen to the absent represented objects. 'A focus on sensory processes', Branigan writes, 'forms the basis of an *illusion* theory of meaning' (74). A film's narrative aims to perpetuate this perceptual illusion manifest in each image. Jean-Louis Baudry is a representative of this definition of a camera, and the attempt to create illusion is manifest in the work of the large majority of film-makers.

Camera 2

The second camera simply consists of sensory material that is experienced in its own right. This conception focuses on the camera's (and narrative's) ability to defamiliarize – to make present to our senses entities that traditionally remain unnoticed, thereby rendering the spectator's everyday perceptions of reality unfamiliar (rather than attempting to replicate them, as in camera 1; in logical terms, camera 2 is the contrary of camera 1). Noël Burch's early work (*Theory of Film Practice* [1973]) typifies this approach. Burch inventories the possible forms and sensations the camera produces. This type of camera is manifest in avant-garde films that refuse the dominant ideological practice of illusionism.

Camera 3

Branigan calls this the orthodox view, in which the camera is conceived as a tool for creating photographic images that are causally linked to their referents via the physics of light. The resulting image is conceived as a fingerprint of the absent reality. Camera

171

3 is therefore similar to 1, except that the illusion is not simply perceptual, but ontological. Bazin is representative of this position. His conception of the camera is manifest, of course, in all photographic films, although some directors exploit it (beginning with the Lumière brothers). Bazin's psychological description of the photographic process constitutes camera 4.

Camera 4

Whereas the photographic image's link to reality defines camera 3, the spectator's viewing of the resulting image defines camera 4. The camera, present before a scene, acts in the place of an absent spectator. Bazin describes the spectator's viewing situation in terms of the camera's imitation of human perception. He privileges directors and movements that emphasize this imitative process via deep focus and a lateral depth of field (Renoir, Welles, neorealism). For Bazin, realism is generated from a combination of cameras 3 and 4. These two cameras therefore logically complement one another.

Camera 5

The fifth camera in Branigan's typology discloses human consciousness. The camera makes present on screen what is typically hidden – the residue of a character's or the film-maker's state of mind. The spectator's activity involves attempting to reconstruct the perceptions of a character or the thoughts of the director (the latter is designated the film's ultimate source of meaning). This type of camera is therefore informed by expressionism and auteurism. Andrew Sarris (1968) wrote a history of narrative film based on this type of camera, which privileged a select pantheon of film directors who triumphed in expressing themselves within the dominant narrative cinema.

Camera 6

This camera is based on a communication model of film. Communication replaces expression and the single author is replaced by a series of implied authors, narrators, characters, and observers. Communication is premised on the transmission of a literal meaning, aided by the camera (and narrative): 'The camera provides the physical and psychological *channel* by which we enter and remain in communication' (82). In Roman Jakobson's terms (1960), the camera provides a phatic link between sender and receiver of messages. Branigan cites Seymour Chatman's *Story and Discourse* (1978) as a representative text. Branigan mentions the reflexivity of European art cinema (which places emphasis upon the channel of communication) as typical films that manifest this type of camera. Logically, camera 5 (expression) is a subset of 6 (communication).

Camera 7

Unconscious desire replaces the conscious transmission of information in this camera. Meaning is premised on psychoanalytic theory, which explains the tension between present, manifest signs and the absent, unconscious processes that govern them. Both the camera and narrative in this language-game play a central role in visualizing on screen the unconscious desires and fantasies. Laura Mulvey's 'Visual Pleasure and Narrative Cinema' (1975), which explains how dominant cinema articulates the patriarchal unconscious, is the canonical text based on this type of camera. Just as camera 5 becomes a subset of 6, both 5 and 6 become a subset of 7.

Camera 8

This final camera names 'part of a mental procedure employed by a spectator to solve interpretive problems' (90). The word 'camera' is a semantic label applied to the cognitive procedures spectators activate when watching a film in order to make sense of certain stimuli on screen: 'the term "camera" becomes a reading hypothesis or heuristic aimed at comprehending fictional space and time' (88). The camera-as-semantic-label or reading-hypothesis is Branigan's own formulation, and supplements his theory of the levels and agents of narration in *Narrative Comprehension and Film* (1992).

Another way to describe these eight cameras would be to follow Bridgman's operationalism and outline the different procedures that need to be used to identify the different cameras, which would involve making explicit exactly what we are measuring when we identify each camera. What unique procedure, for example, is used to empirically identify camera 5, which expresses human consciousness? Expression – a pressing outward of what is concealed within – can be measured. Branigan makes an empirical statement in defining camera 5: 'What is present on the screen for our inspection is ... the residue of some other person's consciousness' (80). In terms of character consciousness, this residue present on the screen consists of shots containing signs that signify distorted states of consciousness such as dizziness (out-of-focus shots, erratic movement of the camera). Such shots can be readily identified and their distortion measured, and physically compared to less or undistorted shots. The expression of more neutral states of mind, such as perception, is harder to identify and measure. Their measurement would need to be indirect, by specifying the relation of these shots to more abstract concepts such as narrative trajectory and cause-and-effect narrative logic.

Symbolizing the results

Towards the end of 'What Is a Camera?' (95) Branigan summarizes his eight types of camera in a table (see Figure 9.1).

Constructing problems

Phenomenological concepts

The phenomenological level is Branigan's starting point. He rigorously represents the place the concept of a 'camera' occupies in various discourses (theories) of film, the institutions and contexts that generate this concept, in order to account for the

173

Major Conceptions of the Camera	Theory of Narrative Meaning: How Are Present Entities Related to Absent Entities?	Example of One Favored Camera Technique	One Major Value of Narrativity for Society	One Major Principle for the Writing of a History of Narrative
1. Camera as Origin of a Sensory Display (A Machine)	Illusion (e.g., of depth)	Kinetic Depth	Hallucinatory Involvement	Edison, Griffith (vs. Lumière, Méliès)
2. Camera as Sensory (or Material) Form	Defamiliarization	Unmotivated Camera	Art as Social and Political Tool	Pressure from an Avant-garde
3. Camera as Recorder of the Profilmic (An Act of Pointing)	Casual: the Physics of Light Rays / Bazinian Theory	Deep Focus (Objective Camera)	Reproduction of Visible, Unobtrusive Reality	Lumière (vs. Méliès)
4. Camera as Agent for a Postfilmic Viewing Situation	Perceiver Sees A as He or She Would See B (subjunctive conditional)	Lateral Depth of Field	Reproduction of Human Perception at Work	Renoir, Welles; Neorealism
5. Camera as Expressive of Bodily and Mental States	Intention	Subjective Camera	Celebration of the Individual and the Inner World	The Auteur
6. Camera as Channel for Communication	Casual: Signal Transmission	Personification of the Camera (= narrator's presence objectified)	Information (and information about information = reflexivity)	Art Cinema
7. Camera as Phantasy	Unconscious Mechanisms	Visualization of Dream-Thought ("representability")	Visual Pleasure and the Dynamic of the Repressed	Classical Cinema
8. Camera as Semantic Label or Reading Hypothesis	Symbol	?	The World as Narrative Text	Types of Reference: Filmic and Nonfilmic Codes; Reading Procedures

Figure 9.1 Edward Branigan's table of eight conceptions of the camera

thoughts, feelings, and beliefs we have when watching and writing about a film. He problematizes intuitions we take for granted (such as what a camera is) by showing how they only make sense within a limited, bounded language-game, and that numerous language-games exist for talking about and analysing film. Branigan describes the ways various games compete with one another in describing films.

Filmic and cinematic concepts

Branigan argues that language determines our understanding of individual films, of 'the cinema', and other fundamental concepts (such as 'movement', 'point of view', 'camera', 'frame', and 'causality'). He therefore discusses film and the cinema indirectly, through an analysis of the various discourses that surround them. Although he primarily describes these discourses, he also begins to evaluate them. For example, he rules out the discourse that asks ontological questions about the nature of the cinema or a camera because these questions are metaphysical: they attempt to provide a final answer about what the cinema or a camera is by defining necessary and sufficient conditions. Through his Wittgensteinian framework, Branigan argues that filmic and cinematic concepts are not metaphysical, and are not free from ambiguity and contradiction. The theorist, he insists, should focus on the way different institutional languages about film create ambiguity and contradiction.

Meta-theoretical concepts

Branigan takes a meta-theoretical approach to solving the problematic state of affairs identified in the previous sections. The 'What is a camera?' problem does not receive an ontological answer; instead, Branigan takes a 'step back' and examines eight theoretical answers. *Projecting a Camera* does not operate on the level of individual films, or of 'the cinema' in general, but works on the level of the language film theorists employ to talk about individual films, the cinema, cameras, and so on.

For Rudolf Botha, meta-theory represents 'difficulties encountered by the [theorist] in connection to the nature, aspects and conduct of his inquiry as an intellectual enterprise' (1981, 57). As the first quotation opening this chapter indicates, Branigan's ultimate aim is to analyse the language of film theory in order to rethink the entire enterprise of theorizing the cinema. Meta-theory focuses attention on the accuracy and correctness of theories. Branigan rejects all theories based on objectivism, in which the film itself is the sole determinant of its own singular meaning. In place of this rigid semantics, Branigan draws upon Wittgenstein to develop a method that 'offers neither discovery nor proof but is merely a tool of convenience in generating a plausible interpretation within a relevant context. In such an approach, the camera also becomes a tool of convenience' (89).

Evaluating data and problems

Genuineness, correctness, and comprehensiveness

Branigan's source of information regarding types of camera derives from a genuine but privileged mode of writing, canonical film theories, all of which he describes in meticulous detail. Other examples are mentioned throughout the book, making his study of the concept 'camera' comprehensive. But examples can be extended indefinitely – either by examining other film theories of the past, or by waiting to analyse future theories, or by changing to another source of information, such as popular reviews or everyday talk about films (perhaps via eavesdropping when leaving the cinema). Information-gathering involves a long-term process of identifying and collecting new instances of the concept 'camera' (or any other concept). The community of users of this concept will continue to grow indefinitely. This is another consequence of a connective analysis – the surface connections are not self-enclosed and finite, but open-ended and potentially infinite.

Well-formedness and significance

On the surface, the 'What is a camera?' question does not seem to identify anything problematic, and therefore seems ill-formed and insignificant. However, the seeming obviousness of the word 'camera' does not imply we understand what it actually means. Its meaning is not self-evident. Branigan's meta-theoretical framework asks the question 'What is a camera?' in a philosophically interesting way, one which demonstrates, through detailed investigation of several language-games in film theory, that our common-sense understanding is flawed or unclear. Once we have grasped this dimension of Branigan's book, the well-formedness and significance of its problems become apparent. I stated at the beginning of this chapter the intellectual impasse that exists in humanities scholarship. The 'What Is a Camera?' chapter (and *Projecting a Camera* in general) explicitly addresses this impasse as manifest in film theory. It also locates the source of the impasse – the language of film theory; presents a rigorous and sophisticated analysis of that language; and, in doing so, offers a coherent solution to the impasse, in the form of a Wittgensteinian perspective on numerous schools of film theory. Branigan therefore demonstrates in Chapter 3 that the problems he addresses are clearly formulated, and he solves them through his analysis of eight types of camera. The chapter is also significant for defamiliarizing the most fundamental concepts of film theory. It renders the camera completely strange by describing its multiple, contradictory, literal and metaphorical meanings, and by rethinking it as a semantic label (camera 8), all of which adds greatly to our existing knowledge of film.

Nonetheless, a few fundamental tensions concerning background assumptions exist. Some readers may detect a tension between my rational reconstruction and Branigan's method, for I am using an internal, logic-based method of analysis to examine an external, socio-historical approach to film theory. (A tension also exists between Branigan's connective method and my reductionist analysis.) As I read Chapter 3, I wondered if Branigan's approach works 'all the way down', or whether a pre-existing immutable core of meaning (subsequently inflected by different contexts) continues to exist. Branigan forcefully argues that there is no pre-existing, context-free camera waiting to be taken up in different language-games, or that each conception of a camera is only a partial concept; instead, each concept of the camera is invented within each game to serve a particular function. It is this assumption behind the concept of language-game that leaves Wittgenstein and Branigan open to the charge of relativism.

The problem is that each language-game possesses it own criteria of rationality. The meanings of the concepts within each game are determined by the presuppositions and rules of that game. Relativists argue it is therefore inappropriate to critique a language-game with external criteria, for each game is self-affirming and as arbitrary as the next. This makes comparison of and judgements between games impossible, and suggests that games other than our own are cognitively inaccessible to us. At best, one can only point out the irreducible differences between games. There is no basis for rational discussion between communities; there is only persuasion – linguistic or military.

But we need to be aware that several types of relativism exist, and Wittgenstein only commits himself to the mildest version. Paul O'Grady (2004) points out that relativism is not a monolithic position. He goes on to identify several types: logical relativism (which argues that classical Aristotelian logic is only one of many); alethic (truth is relative to a language-game, and no contradictions exist between each game's conception of truth); ontological (the nature of reality is conceptualized differently by the language and presuppositions of each language-game; reality is relative to language and presuppositions); epistemological (knowledge of the world is relative to each language-game); and rational (standards of rationality are relative to each language-game) (O'Grady 2004, 323–25). O'Grady argues that Wittgenstein clearly advocates only one type – ontological relativism, which is in turn constrained by what he calls Wittgenstein's naturalism. Wittgenstein, according to O'Grady, argues that we are all

> ... constrained by the cognitive limitations of human beings relating to their environment. Humans are constituted in a certain way. We are animals, with physical inclinations, dispositions, limitations, desires, goals, projects, tasks. To achieve the latter successfully means limiting the range of concepts used and truths believed. ... The crucial point for Wittgenstein is that primitive, pre-conceptual shared actions lie at the bottom of all efforts at reasoning and understanding.
>
> (2004, 332–33)

Wittgenstein allows for ontological diversity constrained by anthropological mini-mums, and rejects the radical logical, alethic, epistemological, and rational versions of relativism.

Where does 'What Is a Camera?' stand in regard to relativism? On the one hand, it uses a strong version of Wittgenstein's ontological relativism, in the form of the language-game. It is therefore open to the problems listed above concerning the relativism of language-games. On the other, it begins to overcome this radical form of relativism through a series of what Branigan calls 'intermediate' or 'middle-level' approaches to theory (which are analogous to Wittgenstein's naturalism). He mentions: the bodily motivated conventions of Lakoff and Johnson; ecological approaches to film (e.g. Torben Grodal); the mild realism of Daniel Dennett; and David Bordwell's moderate con-structivism (147). These approaches are weaved into the complex prose of 'What Is a

177

Camera?' and remain tentative and subordinate to the detailed and sustained analyses of film concepts.

Projecting a Camera is not the type of book you can read in a weekend and then put aside. It offers a daunting challenge to our everyday, intuitive understanding of film and theoretical concepts. Like Deleuze's two cinema books (1986, 1989), it may take the discipline several years to come to terms with Branigan's innovative perspective, to implement his original insights, and rethink film studies along the lines he proposes. At a time when most film theory consists merely of a set of conventions for interpreting individual films, Branigan focuses our attention back to film theory – to the fragmentary, figurative, and social practices that constitute the activity we commonly call 'theorizing the cinema'.

Notes

1 Quotations from 'What Is a Camera?', Chapter 3 of *Projecting a Camera*, will be cited in the text with page numbers in parentheses. An earlier version of Branigan's chapter was published under the same title in Mellencamp and Rosen (1984, 87–107).

2 We already encountered this type of description in Chapter 5, in Heath's delineation of eight different conceptions of 'frame' as used in theoretical discussions of film.

3 As well as the eight theoretical conceptions of the camera described in Chapter 3, the index lists 32 general conceptions of the camera. In total, the index for the word 'camera' and all its variations runs into six pages, and offers a detailed conceptual map of the nuances behind this term.

CONCLUSION

Teaching theory

Film Theory: Rational Reconstructions has attempted to reveal the underlying questions, problems, and assumptions that shape film theory arguments; it critically engages with and interrogates the claims of film theory. To the extent that it has been successful, this book can assist humanities scholars and students seeking guidance on research design – on how to formulate viable research questions and dissertation topics. The difference between a novice and a professional researcher is that the novice sees research too much as an exercise in information gathering. Too many graduate students in the humanities simply gather information and summarize it when writing. Turning them into professional researchers involves identifying problematic states of affairs, and formulating them into problems to guide research. One pedagogical consequence of this book is to refocus humanities scholars away from simple information gathering towards problem-driven research.

In their discussion of intellectual virtues, R. C. Roberts and W. J. Wood locate the issue more specifically in the practice of reading, of turning students into careful, critical readers. Commenting on Locke's *Of the Conduct of the Understanding*, they argue that excellent reading

> is digestion, critical assessment, and systematic assimilation of what is read to a coherent view of things. ... knowledge is not just a collection of facts; [the good reader] critically insists on good reasons for affirming what he affirms and denying what he denies. He does not just seek support for his prejudices but is open to learning, willing to take a critical look at his own preexisting views. Insofar as tutoring can teach these things in the course of a curriculum of reading, it is not just skill purveyance, but an education, a nurturing in the intellectual virtues.
>
> (2007, 123)

Roberts and Wood list these overlapping intellectual virtues: charity (reading a text with respect); open-mindedness (reserving judgement on difficult passages); patience and perseverance (rereading difficult passages on the assumption that the text does make sense at some level); humility (reading all the text carefully, rather than skipping, skimming, or speed reading); and self-control (setting aside negative reactions a

179

difficult text may evoke, in an effort to understand) (2007, 122). In each chapter of this book I have tried to read the texts under discussion in terms of a few of these virtues. This involves evaluating theories according to their own criteria, that is, within the context of their 'inputs', or the ideas from which they originated. And because I choose canonical essays and books to analyse – those that have been successful with film scholars over the years – the theories usually come out with positive evaluations (although Metz's early film semiotics does not stand up too strongly in terms of well-formedness of research questions). But outside the internal criteria of each theory, we encounter clashes and conflicts, where fields of research are turned into battlefields. Scholars have a tendency to overemphasize the differences between their own work and previous research, and to downplay the strengths of previous research, in an attempt to appear novel and innovative.

Is there a diagnosis for these conflicts? One reason is the inadequate formulation of a theory – or, more likely, the inadequate importation of a theory into film studies (for example, Metz's importation of structural linguistics). But even here, I would encourage students and researchers to focus primarily on the positive results that have been achieved, and recommend taking the research further (Metz was too tentative in his early research, whereas Michel Colin, Dominique Chateau, Roger Odin, and Francesco Casetti were less doubtful, more definite of the value of linguistics in the study of film). Ideally, the film scholar needs to become a linguist before studying film from a linguistic perspective, or a psychoanalyst, cognitive scientist, analytic philosopher. ... This is equally true if one plans to criticize a theory. As Nietzsche argued, the atheist must become a priest before he or she can attack religion. (In regards to the conflict in Chapter 8, for example, Žižek needs to become more of a post-theorist before criticizing them.) Before subjecting a theory to negative criticism, we need to question our own prejudices, and revise them if necessary: a never-ending task.

We discovered another reason for conflicts in Chapter 8. Laclau and Mouffe locate conflict between different theoretical paradigms on the ontological level, in which certain objects within one paradigm are not conceivable in a different paradigm. Theorists from one paradigm (e.g. cognitive theory) simply do not recognize the objects of study of another paradigm (such as the cognitivist's stance towards the concept of the unconscious).

In teaching theory, the conflicts and differences between paradigms can be held in abeyance until students recognize and understand the agenda, problems, and assumptions internal to each theory. In Chapter 9, we saw Branigan employing Wittgenstein's *Philosophical Investigations* to describe the multiple meanings of concepts as they are used to talk and theorize about films. Rather than privilege one particular use over others, he presents a systematic account of a concept's multiple uses. This approach, learning about each theory from the inside (which, admittedly, can take years) follows one of the virtues listed above – charity, or more specifically, the 'principle of charity'. I have already quoted Donald Davidson's account of this principle in considering Carroll's critique of Heath in Chapter 5. But it is worth quoting again here: 'We make maximum sense of the words and thoughts of others when we interpret in a way that optimizes agreement. ... [W]e improve the clarity and bite of declaration of difference, whether scheme or shared opinion, by enlarging the basis of shared language or shared opinion' (Davidson 1973–74, 19). When encountering an unfamiliar or alien argument (one that conflicts with our own background knowledge and assumptions), we can (1) simply reject it; (2) try to adopt, even if temporarily, the argument's assumptions as a way of optimizing agreement, insights, and understanding; or (3) transform the argument through dialectics (Žižek's preference, which assumes one has successfully mastered option (2)). Throughout this book I have managed to avoid the first option and have tried to practice the second. It is an option that can be intellectually rewarding, if carried out with enough diligence.

BIBLIOGRAPHY

Abramson, Ronald. 1976. 'Structure and Meaning in the Cinema'. In *Movies and Methods*, edited by Bill Nichols, 558–68. Berkeley: University of California Press.

Althusser, Louis. 1971. *Lenin and Philosophy and Other Essays*. Translated by Ben Brewster. New York: Monthly Review Press.

Andrew, Dudley. 1976. *The Major Film Theories*. New York: Oxford University Press.

——1984. *Concepts in Film Theory*. New York: Oxford University Press.

——1993. 'The Unauthorized Auteur Today'. In *Film Theory Goes to the Movies*, edited by Jim Collins, Hilary Radner, and Ava Preacher Collins, 77–85. New York: Routledge.

——2009. 'The Core and the Flow of Film Studies'. *Critical Inquiry* 35 (4): 879–917.

Anon. 1975. Advert in *Film and History* 5 (3): 19.

Apel, Karl-Otto. 1976. 'The Transcendental Conception of Language-Communication and the Idea of First Philosophy'. In *History of Linguistic Thought and Contemporary Linguistics*, edited by Herman Parret, 32–61. Berlin: Walter de Gruyter.

Arnheim, Rudolf. 1957. *Film as Art*. Berkeley: University of California Press.

Baker, G. P., and P. M. S. Hacker. 2004. *Wittgenstein: Understanding and Meaning: Volume 1 of an Analytical Commentary on the Philosophical Investigations, Part II: Exegesis §§1–184*, 2nd Edition. Oxford: Wiley-Blackwell.

Balzer, Wolfgang, and Heide Göttner. 1983. 'A Theory of Literature Logically Reconstructed – Reconsideration of the Example: Roman Jakobson'. *Poetics* 12: 489–510.

Barthes, Roland. 1967. *Writing Degree Zero* and *Elements of Semiology*. Translated by Annette Lavers and Colin Smith. London: Jonathan Cape.

——1974. *S/Z*. Translated by Michael Howard. New York: Hill and Wang.

——1977. 'The Death of the Author'. In *Image, Music, Text*, 142–48. Translated by Stephen Heath. London: Fontana.

Bazin, André. 1967. *What Is Cinema?* Volume 1. Translated by Hugh Gray. Berkeley: University of California Press.

——1971. *What Is Cinema?* Volume 2. Translated by Hugh Gray. Berkeley: University of California Press.

Baudry, Jean-Louis. 1976. 'The Apparatus'. *Camera Obscura* 1: 104–26.

Bellour, Raymond. 2000. *The Analysis of Film*, edited by Constance Penley. Bloomington: Indiana University Press.

Bettetini, Gianfranco. 1973. *The Language and Technique of the Film*. Translated by David Osmond-Smith. The Hague: Mouton.

Benamou, Michael. 1977. Foreword to *Cine-Tracts* 1 (2): 2.

Benveniste, Emile. 1971. *Problems in General Linguistics*. Translated by Mary Elizabeth Meek. Coral Gables: University of Miami Press.

Bird, Robert. 2004. 'The Suspended Aesthetic: Slavoj Žižek on Eastern European Film'. *Studies in East European Thought* 56 (4): 357–82.

Blanco, Ignacio Matte. 1998. *The Unconscious as Infinite Sets: An Essay in Bi-logic*. London: Karnac books.

Bolas, Terry. 2009. *Screen Education: From Film Appreciation to Media Studies*. Bristol: Intellect.

Bordwell, David. 1985. *Narration in the Fiction Film*. Madison: University of Wisconsin Press.

——1989. *Making Meaning: Inference and Rhetoric in the Interpretation of Cinema*. Cambridge, MA: Harvard University Press.

——1996a. 'Contemporary Film Studies and the Vicissitudes of Grand Theory'. In *Post-Theory: Reconstructing Film Studies*, edited by David Bordwell and Noël Carroll, 3–36. Madison: The University of Wisconsin Press.

——1996b. 'Convention, Construction, and Cinematic Vision'. In *Post-Theory: Reconstructing Film Studies*, edited by David Bordwell and Noël Carroll, 87–107. Madison: University of Wisconsin Press.

——1997. *On the History of Film Style*. Cambridge, MA: Harvard University Press.

——2005a. *Figures Traced in Light: On Cinematic Staging*. Berkeley: University of California Press.

——2005b. 'Slavoj Žižek: Say Anything': http://www.davidbordwell.net/essays/zizek.php

Bordwell, David, Janet Staiger, and Kristin Thompson. 1985. *The Classical Hollywood Cinema: Film Style and Mode of Production to 1960*. London: Routledge.

Bordwell, David, and Noël Carroll, eds. 1996. *Post-Theory: Reconstructing Film Studies*. Madison: University of Wisconsin Press.

Botha, Rudolf P. 1981. *The Conduct of Linguistic Inquiry: A Systematic Introduction to the Methodology of Generative Grammar*. The Hague: Mouton.

Branigan, Edward. 1992. *Narrative Comprehension and Film*. New York and London: Routledge.

——2006. *Projecting a Camera: Language Games in Film Theory*. New York: Routledge.

Bridgman, P. W. 1927. *The Logic of Modern Physics*. New York: Macmillan.

Brooks, Peter. 1995. *The Melodramatic Imagination: Balzac, Henry James, Melodrama, and the Mode of Excess*. Second edition. New Haven: Yale University Press.

Buckland, Warren. 1989. 'Critique of Poor Reason'. *Screen* 30 (4): 80–103.

——2000. *The Cognitive Semiotics of Film*. Cambridge: Cambridge University Press.

Bühler, Karl. 1990. *Theory of Language: The Representational Function of Language*. Translated by Donald Fraser Goodwin. Amsterdam: John Benjamins Publishing Company.

Bunge, Mario. 1973. *Method, Model and Matter*. Boston: D. Reidel Publishing Company.

——1998. *Philosophy of Science: From Problem to Theory*. Revised edition. New Brunswick, NJ: Transaction Publishers.

Burch, Noël. 1973. *Theory of Film Practice*. Translated by Helen R. Lane. New York: Praeger.

Butler, Alison. 2002. *Women's Cinema: The Contested Screen*. London: Wallflower.

Butler, Judith, Ernesto Laclau, and Slavoj Žižek. 2000. *Contingency, Hegemony, Universality: Contemporary Dialogues on the Left*. London: Verso.

Callenbach, Ernest. 1985. '[Review of] *Film Style and Technology: History and Analysis*'. *Film Quarterly* 38 (4): 45–50.

——2008. 'Da Capo'. *Film Quarterly* 62 (1): 58–65.

Carnap, Rudolf. 1995. *An Introduction to the Philosophy of Science*, edited by Martin Gardner. New York: Dover.

——2003. *The Logical Structure of the World*. Translated by Rolf A. George. Chicago: Open Court.

Carroll, Noël. 1982. 'Address to the Heathen'. *October* 23: 89–163.

——1988a. *Philosophical Problems of Classical Film Theory*. Princeton: Princeton University Press.

——1988b. *Mystifying Movies: Fad and Fallacies in Contemporary Film Theory*. New York: Columbia University Press.

——1996. *Theorizing the Moving Image*. Cambridge: Cambridge University Press.

Carus, A. W. 2007. *Carnap and Twentieth Century Thought: Explication as Enlightenment*. Cambridge: Cambridge University Press.

Casetti, Francesco. 1998. *Inside the Gaze: The Fiction Film and Its Spectator*. Translated by Nell Andrew with Charles O'Brien. Bloomington: Indiana University Press.

——1999. *Theories of Cinema, 1945–1995*. Translated by Francesca Chiostri and Elizabeth Gard Bartolini-Salimbeni, with Thomas Kelso. Revised and updated. Austin: University of Texas Press.

Cassar, Ignaz. 2008. 'Envisioning Inversion'. *Parallax* 14 (2): 1–6.

Caughie, John. 1981. 'Auteur-Structuralism'. In *Theories of Authorship: A Reader*, edited by John Caughie, 123–30. London: BFI.

Cavell, Stanley. 1971. (Enlarged edition, 1979). *The World Viewed: Reflections on the Ontology of Film*. Cambridge, MA: Harvard University Press.

Chambliss, Marilyn J., and Robert Calfee. 1998. *Textbooks for Learning: Nurturing Children's Minds*. Oxford: Blackwell Publishers.

Chateau, Dominique. 1987. *Le cinéma comme langage*. Brussels: AISS – Publications de la Sorbonne.

Chatman, Seymour. 1978. *Story and Discourse: Narrative Structure in Fiction and Film*. Ithaca and London: Cornell University Press.

Colin, Michel. 1985. *Langue, film, discours: Prolégomènes a une sémologie générative du film*. Paris: Klincksieck.

——1995. 'The *Grande Syntagmatique* Revisited'. In *The Film Spectator: From Sign to Mind*, edited by Warren Buckland, 45–86. Amsterdam: Amsterdam University Press.

Comolli, Jean-Louis, and Jean Narboni. 1990. 'Cinema/Ideology/Criticism'. In *Cahiers du Cinéma 1969–1972: The Politics of Representation*, edited by Nick Browne, 58–67. Cambridge, MA: Harvard University Press.

Cook, Pam. 1991. 'Melodrama and the Women's Picture'. In *Imitations of Life: A Reader on Film and Television Melodrama*, edited by Marcia Landy, 248–62. Detroit: Wayne State University Press.

——1999. 'Structuralism and Auteur Study'. In *The Cinema Book*, 2nd edition, edited by Pam Cook, 282–99. London: British Film Institute.

Cook, Pam, and Claire Johnston. 1974. 'The Place of Women in the Cinema of Raoul Walsh'. In *Raoul Walsh*, edited by Phil Hardy, 93–109. Edinburgh: Edinburgh Film Festival.

Copjec, Joan. 1982. 'The Anxiety of the Influencing Machine'. *October* 23: 43–59.

Cornillon, Susan, ed. 1972. *Images of Women in Fiction*. Bowling Green, Ohio: Bowling Green State University Popular Press.

Coward, Rosalind, and John Ellis. 1977. *Language and Materialism: Developments in Semiology and the Theory of the Subject*. London: Routledge and Kegan Paul.

Cowie, Elizabeth. 1977. 'Women, Representation and the Image'. *Screen Education* 23: 15–23.

——1997. *Representing the Woman: Cinema and Psychoanalysis*. Basingstoke: Macmillan Press.

Cubitt, Sean. 2004. *The Cinema Effect*. Cambridge, MA: MIT Press.

Culler, Jonathan. 1975. *Structuralist Poetics: Structuralism, Linguistics, and the Study of Literature*. London: Routledge and Kegan Paul.

Currie, Gregory. 1995. *Image and Mind: Film, Philosophy, and Cognitive Science*. Cambridge: Cambridge University Press.

Daddesio, Thomas. 1995. *On Minds and Symbols: The Relevance of Cognitive Science for Semiotics*. Berlin: Mouton de Gruyter.

Davia, Greg. 1998. 'Thoughts on a Possible Rational Reconstruction of the Method of "Rational Reconstruction"'. http://www.bu.edu/wcp/Papers/Scie/ScieDavi.htm

Davidson, Donald. 1973–74. 'On the Very Idea of a Conceptual Scheme'. *Proceedings and Addresses of the American Philosophical Association* 47: 5–20.

Delanda, Manuel. 2002. *Intensive Science and Virtual Philosophy*. New York: Continuum.

De Lauretis, Teresa. 1984. *Alice Doesn't: Feminism, Semiotics, Cinema*. Bloomington: Indiana University Press.

Deleuze, Gilles. 1986. *Cinema 1: The Movement-Image*. Translated by Hugh Tomlinson and Barbara Habberjam. London: Athlone Press.

——1989. *Cinema 2: The Time-Image*. Translated by Hugh Tomlinson and Robert Galeta. London: Athlone Press.

Derrida, Jacques. 1978. *Writing and Difference*. Translated by Alan Bass. London and New York: Routledge.

Doane, Mary Ann. 1982. 'Film and the Masquerade: Theorising the Female Spectator'. *Screen* 23 (3–4): 74–88.

——1987. *The Desire to Desire. The Woman's Film of the 1940s*. Basingstoke: Macmillan.

Doležel, Lubomír. 1990. *Occidental Poetics: Tradition and Progress*. Lincoln: University of Nebraska Press.

Dumont, Jean-Paul, and Jean Monod. 1970. *Le foetus astral. Essai d'analyse structurale d'un mythe cinématographique*. Paris: Christian Burgeois Editeur.

Durgnat, Raymond. 1982. 'From Signs to Meaning in the Cinema'. *Film Reader* 5: 300–323.

Dyer, Richard. 1982. 'Don't Look Now: The Male Pin-Up'. *Screen* 23 (3–4): 61–73.

Eckert, Charles. 1973. 'The English Cine-Structuralists'. *Film Comment* 9 (3): 46–51.

Eco, Umberto. 1976a. 'Articulations of the Cinematic Code'. In *Movies and Methods*, edited by Bill Nichols, 590–607. Berkeley: University of California Press.

——1976b. *A Theory of Semiotics*. Bloomington: Indiana University Press.

Editors of *Cahiers du Cinéma*. 1972. 'John Ford's *Young Mr. Lincoln*'. *Screen* 13 (3): 5–44.

Eisenstein, Sergei. 1988. 'Montage of Attractions'. In *The Film Factory: Russian and Soviet Cinema in Documents 1896–1939*, edited by Richard Taylor and Ian Christie, 87–89. Cambridge, MA: Harvard University Press.

Elsaesser, Thomas. 1971. 'A Comparative Study of Imagery in Thomas Carlyle's and Jules Michelet's Histories of the French Revolution'. Unpublished PhD thesis in Comparative Literature, University of Sussex.

——1972. 'Tales of Sound and Fury: Observations on the Family Melodrama'. *Monogram* 4: 4–15. Republished in *Home is Where the Heart Is: Studies in Melodrama and the Woman's Film*, edited by Christine Gledhill, 43–69. London: British Film Institute, 1987.

——2006. 'Discipline Through Diegesis: The Rube Film Between "Attractions" and "Narrative Integration."' In *The Cinema of Attractions Reloaded*, edited by Wanda Strauven, 205–23. Amsterdam: Amsterdam University Press.

——2012. *The Persistence of Hollywood*. New York: Routledge.

Foster, Don. 2001. *Author Unknown: On the Trail of Anonymous*. London: Macmillan.

Foucault, Michel. 1981. 'What is an Author?' [extract]. In *Theories of Authorship: A Reader*, edited by John Caughie, 282–91. London: British Film Institute.

Gaudreault, André. 1982. 'Temporality and Narrativity in Early Cinema (1895–1908)'. *Cinema 1900–1906: An Analytical Study*, compiled by Roger Holman, 201–18. Brussels: FIAF.

——1987. 'Theatricality, Narrativity, and Trickality: Reevaluating the Cinema of Georges Méliès'. *Journal of Popular Film and Television* 15 (3): 111–19.

——1990. 'Detours in Film Narrative: The Development of Cross-Cutting'. In *Early Cinema: Space, Frame, Narrative*, edited by Thomas Elsaesser, 133–50. London: British Film Institute.

Genette, Gérard. 1997. *Palimpsests: Literature in the Second Degree*. Translated by Channa Newman and Claude Doubinsky. Lincoln: University of Nebraska Press.

Gledhill, Christine, ed. 1987. *Home is Where the Heart Is: Studies in Melodrama and the Woman's Film*. London: British Film Institute.

Gordon, John. 1987. *Finnegans Wake: A Plot Summary*. New York: Syracuse University Press.

Greimas, A. J. 1983. *Structural Semantics: An Attempt at a Method*. Translated by Daniele McDowell, Ronald Schleifer, and Alan Velie. Lincoln: University of Nebraska Press.

Gunning, Tom. 1982. 'The Non-Continuous Style of Early Film (1900–906)'. In *Cinema 1900–1906: An Analytical Study*, compiled by Roger Holman, 219–30. Brussels: FIAF.

——1983. 'An Unseen Energy Swallows Space: The Space in Early Film and Its Relation to American Avant-Garde Film'. In *Film Before Griffith*, edited by John Fell, 355–66. Berkeley: University of California Press.

——1984. 'Non-Continuity, Continuity, Discontinuity: A Theory of Genres in Early Films'. *Iris* 2 (1): 101–12.

——1986. 'The Cinema of Attraction: Early Cinema, Its Spectator, and the Avant-Garde'. *Wide Angle* 8 (3/4): 63–70.

——1990. 'The Cinema of Attractions: Early Cinema, Its Spectator, and the Avant-Garde'. In *Early Cinema: Space, Frame, Narrative*, edited by Thomas Elsaesser, 56–62. London: British Film Institute.

——2006. 'Attractions: How They Came into the World'. In *The Cinema of Attractions Reloaded*, edited by Wanda Strauven, 31–39. Amsterdam: Amsterdam University Press.

Hansen, Miriam. 1986. 'Pleasure, Ambivalence, Identification: Valentino and Female Spectatorship'. *Cinema Journal* 25 (4): 6–32.

Harris, Roy. 1987. *Reading Saussure*. London: Duckworth.

Hart, Clive. 1974. *A Concordance to Finnegans Wake*. New York: Paul P. Apel.

Haskell, Molly. 1974. *From Reverence to Rape: The Treatment of Women in the Movies*. New York: Holt, Rinehart and Winston.

Heath, Stephen. 1972a. *The Nouveau Roman: A Study in the Practice of Writing*. London: Elek.

——1972b. 'Ambiviolences: Notes pour la lecture de Joyce'. *Tel Quel* 50: 22–43 and 51: 64–76.

——1973. 'Trames de lecture (A propos de la dernière section de *Finnegans Wake*)'. *Tel Quel* 54: 4–15.

——1974. 'Lessons from Brecht'. *Screen* 15 (2): 103–28.

——1975/6. 'From Brecht to Film'. *Screen* 16 (4): 34–44.

——1976. 'On Screen, In Frame: Film and Ideology'. *Quarterly Review of Film Studies* 1 (3): 251–65.

——1981a. *Questions of Cinema*. London: Macmillan.

——1981b. 'The Work of Christian Metz'. *Cinema and Semiotics: Screen Reader 2*, edited by Mick Eaton and Steve Neale, 138–61. London: Society for Education in Film and Television.

——1983. 'Le père noël'. *October* 26: 63–115.

——1984. 'Ambiviolences: Notes for Reading Joyce'. In *Post-Structuralist Joyce: Essays from the French*, edited by Derek Attridge and Daniel Ferrer, 31–68. Cambridge: Cambridge University Press.

Henderson, Brian. 1973. 'Critique of Cine-Structuralism (Part 1)'. *Film Quarterly* 27 (1): 25–34.

Hirst, Paul. 1979. *On Law and Ideology*. London: Macmillan.

Holsinger, Bruce. 2005. *The Premodern Condition: Medievalism and the Making of Theory*. Chicago: University of Chicago Press.

Jakobson, Roman. 1960. 'Closing Statement: Linguistics and Poetics'. In *Style in Language*, edited by Thomas Sebeok, 350–77. Cambridge, MA: MIT Press.

Jakobson, Roman, and Morris Halle. 1956. *Fundamentals of Language*. The Hague: Mouton.

Jameson, Fredric. 1981. *The Political Unconscious: Narrative as a Socially Symbolic Act*. Ithaca: Cornell University Press.

Johnston, Claire. 1973. 'Women's Cinema as Counter-Cinema'. In *Notes on Women's Cinema*, edited by Claire Johnston, 24–31. London: Society for Education in Film and Television.

Johnston, Claire, 1975. 'Feminist Politics and Film History'. *Screen* 16 (3): 115–24.

Kauppi, Niilo. 1993. *The Making of an Avant-Garde: Tel Quel*. Berlin: Mouton de Gruyter.

Kinder, Marsha, and Beverle Houston. 1980. *Self and Cinema: A Transformalist Perspective*. Pleasantville, NY: Redgrave Pub. Co.

Kitses, Jim. 1969. *Horizons West; Anthony Mann, Budd Boetticher, Sam Peckinpah: Studies of Authorship within the Western*. London: Thames and Hudson/British Film Institute.

Kjørup, Søren. 1978. 'Iconic Codes and Pictorial Speech Acts'. In *Danish Semiotics*, edited by Jørgen Dines Johansen and Morten Nøjgaard, 101–22. Copenhagen: Munksgaard.

Kofman, Sarah. 1998. *Camera Obscura: Of Ideology*. Translated by Will Straw. London: Athone.

Kristeva, Julia. 1998. 'The Subject in Process'. Translated by Patrick ffrench. *The Tel Quel Reader*, edited by Patrick ffrench and Roland-François Lack, 133–78. London: Routledge.

Kubler, George. 1962. *The Shape of Time*. New Haven, CT: Yale University Press.

Kuhn, Annette. 1982. *Women's Pictures: Feminism and Cinema*. London: Routledge and Kegan Paul.

Lacan, Jacques. 1977. *Ecrits: A Selection*. Translated by Alan Sheridan. London: Tavistock.

Laclau, Ernesto, and Chantal Mouffe. 2001. *Hegemony and Socialist Strategy: Towards a Radical Democratic Politics*. Second edition. London: Verso.

Lakoff, George. 1987. *Women, Fire, and Dangerous Things: What Categories Reveal About the Mind*. Chicago: University of Chicago Press.

Lakoff, George, and Mark Johnson. 1980. *Metaphors We Live By*. Chicago: University of Chicago Press.

Larrain, Jorge. 1979. *The Concept of Ideology*. London: Hutchinson.

——1983. *Marxism and Ideology*. London: Macmillan.

Laudan, Larry. 1977. *Progress and its Problems: Towards a Theory of Scientific Growth*. Berkeley: University of California Press.

Lawder, Standish D. 1975. 'Eisenstein and Constructivism (*Strike, Potemkin*)'. In *The Essential Cinema*, edited by P. Adams Sitney, 58–87. New York: Anthology Film Archives and New York University Press.

Leach, Edmund. 1970. *Lévi-Strauss*. London: Fontana.

Lévi-Strauss, Claude. 1963. *Structural Anthropology*. Translated by Claire Jacobson and Brooke Grundfest Schoepf. New York: Basic Books.

——1970. *The Raw and the Cooked. Introduction to a Science of Mythology: 1*. Translated by John and Doreen Weightman. London: Jonathan Cape.

MacCabe, Colin, ed. 1981. *The Talking Cure: Psychoanalysis and Language*. London: Macmillan.

McHugh, Roland. 1980. *Annotations to Finnegans Wake*. Baltimore: The Johns Hopkins University Press.

McGowan, Todd. 2007a. *The Real Gaze: Film Theory After Lacan*. Albany: State University of New York Press.

McGowan, Todd, 2007b. 'Introduction: Enjoying the Cinema'. *International Journal of Žižek Studies* 1 (3): 1–13: http://zizekstudies.org/index.php/ijzs/article/view/57/119

McMahan, Alison. 2002. *Alice Guy Blaché: Lost Visionary of the Cinema*. New York: Continuum.

Mansfeld, Jaap. 1994. *Prolegomena: Questions to be Settled Before the Study of an Author, or a Text*. Leiden: E. J. Brill.

Martinet, André. 1964. *Elements of General Linguistics*. Translated by Elisabeth Palmer. London: Faber and Faber.

Marx, Karl, and Frederick Engels. 1970. *The German Ideology*, edited by C. J. Arthur. London: Lawrence and Wishart.

Mellard, James M. 1998. 'Lacan and the New Lacanians: Josephine Hart's *Damage*, Lacanian Tragedy, and the Ethics of *Jouissance*'. *PMLA* 113: 395–407.

Mellen, Joan. 1973. *Women and Their Sexuality in the New Film*. New York: Dell Publishing.

187

Mellencamp, Patricia, and Philip Rosen, eds. 1984. *Cinema Histories, Cinema Practices*. Los Angeles: University Publications of America.

Merck, Mandy. 1987. 'Introduction – Difference and its Discontents'. *Screen* 28 (1): 2–9.

——2007. 'Mulvey's Manifesto'. *Camera Obscura* 66: 1–23.

Metz, Christian. 1974a. *Film Language: A Semiotics of the Cinema*. Translated by Michael Taylor. New York: Oxford University Press.

——1974b. *Language and Cinema*. Translated by Donna Jean Umiker-Sebeok. The Hague: Mouton.

——1975. 'The Imaginary Signifier'. *Screen* 16 (2): 14–76.

——1976. 'On the Notion of Cinematographic Language'. In *Movies and Methods*, edited by Bill Nichols, 582–89. Berkeley: University of California Press.

——1991. *L'Énonciation impersonnelle ou le site du film*. Paris: Méridiens Klincksieck.

Miller, Jacques-Alain. 1977/78. 'Suture (Elements of the Logic of the Signifier)'. *Screen*, 18 (4): 24–34.

Mitchell, Juliet. 1974. *Psychoanalysis and Feminism*. Harmondsworth: Penguin.

Modleski, Tania. 1988. *The Women Who Knew Too Much: Hitchcock and Feminist Theory*. New York: Routledge.

Moi, Tori. 1985. *Sexual/Textual Politics: Feminist Literary Theory*. London: Routledge.

Moolenaar, R. 2004. 'Slavoj Žižek and the *Real* Subject of Politics'. *Studies in East European Thought* 56 (4): 259–97.

Muller, John P., and William J. Richardson. 1982. *Lacan and Language: A Reader's Guide to Ecrits*. Madison: International Universities Press, Inc.

Mulvey, Laura. 1975. 'Visual Pleasure and Narrative Cinema'. *Screen* 16 (3): 6–18.

——1989. *Visual and Other Pleasures*. Basingstoke: Macmillan.

——1996. *Fetishism and Curiosity*. London: British Film Institute.

Musser, Charles. 1994. 'Rethinking Early Cinema: Cinema of Attractions and Narrativity'. *The Yale Journal of Criticism* 7 (2): 203–32.

Neale, Steve. 1983. 'Masculinity as Spectacle'. *Screen* 24 (6): 2–16.

Nichols, Bill. 1976a. 'Structuralism-Semiology'. In *Movies and Methods*, edited by Bill Nichols, 461–68. Berkeley: University of California Press.

——1976b. 'Style, Grammar, and the Movies'. In *Movies and Methods*, edited by Bill Nichols, 607–28. Berkeley: University of California Press.

——1985. '[Introduction to] Statistical Style Analysis of Motion Pictures'. In *Movies and Methods*, Volume 2, edited by Bill Nichols, 691–92. Berkeley: University of California Press.

Nowell-Smith, Geoffrey. 1967. *Visconti*. London: Secker and Warburg/British Film Institute.

——1970. 'Cinema and Structuralism'. *20th Century Studies* 3: 131–39.

——1973. 'I Was a Star-Struck Structuralist'. *Screen* 14 (3): 92–99.

O'Grady, Paul. 2004. 'Wittgenstein and Relativism'. *International Journal of Philosophical Studies* 12 (3): 315–37.

Odin, Roger. 1988. 'Du spectateur fictionalisant au nouveau spectateur: Approche sémio-pragmatique'. *Iris* 8: 121–39.

——1995a. 'For a Semio-Pragmatics of Film'. In *The Film Spectator: From Sign to Mind*, edited by Warren Buckland, 213–26. Amsterdam: Amsterdam University Press.

——1995b. 'A Semio-Pragmatic Approach to the Documentary Film'. In *The Film Spectator: From Sign to Mind*, edited by Warren Buckland, 227–35. Amsterdam: Amsterdam University Press.

Orr, John. 2003. 'Right Direction, Wrong Turning: On Žižek's _The Fright of Real Tears_' *Film-Philosophy*: http://film-philosophy.com/index.php/f-p/article/view/751/663

Oudart, Jean-Pierre. 1969. 'La Suture', *Cahiers du Cinema* 211: 36–39, and 212: 50–55.

——1977/78. 'Cinema and Suture', *Screen* 18 (4): 35–47.

Piloiu, Rares. 2002. 'Hegemony: Methods and Hypotheses, A Historical-Comparative Perspective'. *Reconstruction* 2 (2): http://reconstruction.eserver.org/022/hegemony.htm

Polan, Dana. 1981. 'Formalism and its Discontents'. *Jump Cut* 26: 63–66. Published online: http://www.ejumpcut.org/archive/onlinessays/JC26folder/DistantObserver.html

———1985. 'A Critique of Cinematic Reason: Stephen Heath and the Theoretical Study of Film'. *boundary 2* 13 (2/3): 157–71.

Quine, W. V. O. 1961. *From a Logical Point of View.* Cambridge, MA: Harvard University Press.

Ray, Robert B. 2008. *The ABCs of Classical Hollywood.* Oxford: Oxford University Press.

Rheindorf, Markus. 2005. 'Notes on Wittgenstein's Method, the Practice of Cultural History, and Early Film Theory'. *Reconstruction* 5 (2): http://reconstruction.eserver.org/052/rheindorf.shtml

Roberts, Robert C., and W. Jay Wood. 2007. *Intellectual Virtues: An Essay in Regulative Epistemology.* Oxford: Clarendon Press.

Rodowick, D. N. 1982. 'The Difficulty of Difference'. *Wide Angle* 5 (1): 4–15.

———1988. *The Crisis of Political Modernism: Criticism and Ideology in Contemporary Film Theory.* Urbana: University of Illinois Press.

———1991. *The Difficulty of Difference: Psychoanalysis, Sexual Difference, and Film Theory.* New York: Routledge.

Rohdie, Sam. 1969. '[Review of] Signs and Meaning in the Cinema'. *New Left Review* 55: 66–70.

———1976. 'Totems and Movies'. In *Movies and Methods*, edited by Bill Nichols, 469–81. Berkeley: University of California Press.

Rosen, Marjorie. 1974. *Popcorn Venus: Women, Movies, and the American Dream.* New York: Avon.

Rothman, William. 1975. 'Against "The System of the Suture."' *Film Quarterly* 29 (1): 45–50.

Rothman, William, and Marian Keane. 2000. *Reading Cavell's The World Viewed: A Philosophical Perspective on Film.* Detroit: Wayne State University Press.

Russell, Lee. 1964. 'Howard Hawks'. *New Left Review* 24: 82–85.

———1965. 'John Ford'. *New Left Review* 29: 69–73.

Salt, Barry. 1974. 'Statistical Style Analysis of Motion Pictures'. *Film Quarterly* 28 (1): 13–22.

———2006. *Moving into Pictures: More on Film History, Style, and Analysis.* London: Starword.

———2009. *Film Style and Technology: History and Analysis*, third edition. London: Starword.

Sarris, Andrew. 1962. 'Notes on the Auteur Theory in 1962'. *Film Culture* 27: 1–8.

———1968. *The American Cinema: Directors and Directions 1929–1968.* New York: Dutton.

Saussure, Ferdinand de. 1983. *Course in General Linguistics.* Translated by Roy Harris. London: Duckworth.

Searle, John. 1979. *Expression and Meaning: Studies in the Theory of Speech Acts.* Cambridge: Cambridge University Press.

Shaviro, Steven. 1993. *The Cinematic Body.* Minneapolis: University of Minnesota Press.

Silverman, Kaja. 1980. 'Masochism and Subjectivity'. *Framework* 12: 2–9.

———1983. *The Subject of Semiotics.* New York: Oxford University Press.

Skaff, Sheila, and Chris Luebbe. 2003. 'When an Exception is just an Exception: Slavoj Žižek's *The Fright of Real Tears: Krzysztof Kieslowski between Theory and Post-Theory*'. *Iowa Journal of Cultural Studies* 3: http://www.uiowa.edu/~ijcs/suburbia/skaff.htm

Sklar, Lawrence. 2000. *Theory and Truth: Philosophical Critique within Foundational Science.* Oxford: Oxford University Press.

Smith, Keith. 1998. *Lawyers, Legislators and Theorists: Developments in English Criminal Jurisprudence 1800–1957.* Oxford: Clarendon Press.

Smith, Murray. 1995. *Engaging Characters: Fiction, Emotion and the Cinema.* Oxford: Clarendon Press.

———1998. '[Review of] Gregory Currie, *Image and Mind*'. *British Journal of Aesthetics* 38 (3): 325–27.

Stam, Robert. 1989. *Subversive Pleasures: Bakhtin, Cultural Criticism, and Film.* Baltimore: Johns Hopkins University Press.

Stegmüller, Wolfgang, Wolfgang Balzer and Wolfgang Spohn, eds. 1982. *Philosophy of Economics.* Berlin: Springer Verlag.

Straayer, Chris. 1994. 'The Hypothetical Lesbian Heroine'. In *Multiple Voices in Feminist Film Criticism*, edited by Diane Carson and Linda Dittmar, 343–57. Minneapolis: University of Minnesota Press.

Strauven, Wanda, ed. 2006. *The Cinema of Attractions Reloaded*. Amsterdam: Amsterdam University Press.

Strawson, P. F. 1992. *Analysis and Metaphysics: An Introduction to Philosophy*. Oxford: Oxford University Press.

Tan, Ed S. 1996. *Emotion and the Structure of Narrative Film: Film as an Emotion Machine*. Translated by Barbara Fasting. Mahwah, New Jersey: Lawrence Erlbaum.

Tindall, William York. 1969. *A Reader's Guide to Finnegans Wake*. New York: Syracuse University Press.

Turvey, Malcolm. 2008. *Doubting Vision: Film and the Revelationist Tradition*. New York: Oxford University Press.

Vighi, Fabio. 2009. *Sexual Difference in European Cinema: The Curse of Enjoyment*. Basingstoke: Palgrave Macmillan.

Wilden, Anthony. 1968. *The Language of the Self: The Function of Language in Psychoanalysis*. Baltimore: Johns Hopkins University Press.

——1980. *System and Structure: Essays in Communication and Exchange*. Second edition. London: Tavistock.

Williams, Linda. 2000. 'Discipline and Fun: *Psycho* and Postmodern Cinema'. In *Reinventing Film Studies*, edited by Christine Gledhill and Linda Williams, 351–78. London: Arnold.

Wineburg, Sam. 2001. *Historical Thinking and Other Unnatural Acts*. Philadelphia: Temple University Press.

Wittgenstein, Ludwig. 1922. *Tractatus Logico-Philosophicus*. Translated by C. K. Ogden. London: Routledge & Kegan Paul.

——1953. *Philosophical Investigations*, edited by G. E. M. Anscombe and R. Rhees. Translated by G. E. M. Anscombe. Oxford: Blackwell.

Wollen, Peter. 1969. *Signs and Meaning in the Cinema*. London: Secker and Warburg/British Film Institute; 1970: Thames and Hudson/ British Film Institute; 1972: Secker and Warburg/British Film Institute; 1998: British Film Institute.

——1972. 'Godard and Counter Cinema: *Vent d'est*'. *Afterimage* 4: 6–17.

——2002. *Paris Hollywood: Writings on Film*. London: Verso.

Wood, Robin. 1965. *Hitchcock's Films*. London: Zwemmer.

——1968. *Howard Hawks*. London: Secker and Warburg/British Film Institute.

——1976. 'Hawks de-Wollenized'. In *Personal Views: Explorations in Film*, 193–206. London: Gordon Fraser.

Wong, Stanley. 2006. *Foundations of Paul Samuelson's Revealed Preference Theory: A Study in the Method of Rational Reconstruction*. Revised edition. London: Routledge.

Yoshimoto, Mitsuhiro. 1990. 'Myth of Demystification in Structural Film Criticism'. *Quarterly Review of Film and Video* 11 (4): 51–64.

Žižek, Slavoj. 1989. *The Sublime Object of Ideology*. London: Verso.

——1999. 'Cyberspace, or the Unbearable Closure of Being'. In *Endless Night: Cinema and Psychoanalysis, Parallel Histories*, edited by Janet Bergstrom, 96–125. Berkeley: University of California Press.

——2001. *The Fright of Real Tears: Krzysztof Kieślowski Between Theory and Post-Theory*. London: British Film Institute.

——2008. *The Ticklish Subject: The Absent Centre of Political Ontology*. New edition. London: Verso.

INDEX

191

Taylor & Francis

eBooks

FOR LIBRARIES

ORDER YOUR FREE 30 DAY INSTITUTIONAL TRIAL TODAY!

Over 23,000 eBook titles in the Humanities, Social Sciences, STM and Law from some of the world's leading imprints.

Choose from a range of subject packages or create your own!

Benefits for you

▶ Free MARC records

▶ COUNTER-compliant usage statistics

▶ Flexible purchase and pricing options

Benefits for your user

▶ Off-site, anytime access via Athens or referring URL

▶ Print or copy pages or chapters

▶ Full content search

▶ Bookmark, highlight and annotate text

▶ Access to thousands of pages of quality research at the click of a button

For more information, pricing enquiries or to order a free trial, contact your local online sales team.

UK and Rest of World: **online.sales@tandf.co.uk**

US, Canada and Latin America: **e-reference@taylorandfrancis.com**

www.ebooksubscriptions.com

ALPSP Award for BEST eBOOK PUBLISHER 2009 Finalist

Taylor & Francis **eBooks**
Taylor & Francis Group

A flexible and dynamic resource for teaching, learning and research.